The
Reference Shelf®

U.S. National Debate Topic: 2019-2020
Arms Sales

The Reference Shelf
Volume 91 • Number 3
H.W. Wilson
A Division of EBSCO Information Services, Inc.

Published by
GREY HOUSE PUBLISHING
Amenia, New York
2019

The Reference Shelf

The books in this series contain reprints of articles, excerpts from books, addresses on current issues, and studies of social trends in the United States and other countries. There are six separately bound numbers in each volume, all of which are usually published in the same calendar year. Numbers one through five are each devoted to a single subject, providing background information and discussion from various points of view and concluding with an index and comprehensive bibliography that lists books, pamphlets, and articles on the subject. The final number of each volume is a collection of recent speeches. Books in the series may be purchased individually or on subscription.

Publisher's Cataloging-In-Publication Data
(Prepared by The Donohue Group, Inc.)

Names: Grey House Publishing, Inc., compiler.

Title: U.S. national debate topic, 2019-2020. Arms sales / [compiled by Grey House Publishing].

Other Titles: US national debate topic, 2019-2020. Arms sales | United States national debate topic, 2019-2020. Arms sales | Arms sales | Reference shelf ; v. 91, no. 3.

Description: Amenia, New York : Grey House Publishing, 2019. | Includes bibliographical references and index.

Identifiers: ISBN 9781642652208 (v. 91, no. 3) | ISBN 9781642652178 (volume set)

Subjects: LCSH: Arms transfers--United States--History--21st century. | Military assistance, American--History--21st century. | United States--Foreign relations--History--21st century. | United States--Military policy--History--21st century. | Defense industries--History--21st century.

Classification: LCC HD9743.U6 U8 2019 | DDC 382.4562340973--dc23

Printed in Canada

Contents

3

Arms and Foreign Policy

4

The Wrong Hands: Arms Deals, War, and Terror

5

The Human Cost

Preface

The Arms Debate: American Security or International Turmoil

The United States is the world's most prolific producer and distributor of arms and military equipment. Having exploded into the arms trade business after World War II, the United States has since dominated an industry worth an estimated $100 billion each year and still growing. According to the Stockholm International Peace Research Institute (SIPRI), weapons sales between 2013 and 2017 were 10 percent higher than from 2008 to 2012. Much of this escalation can be attributed to the ongoing effort to combat radical militant organizations and the alleged need to provide weapons to war-torn regions to prevent instability. The United States accounts for 34 percent of all arms sales, an increase from 30 percent in 2012. Comparatively, the United States output of arms is 58 percent higher than that of the next most prolific arms dealer, Russia.[1]

America's role in arms trading is controversial. When the United States started dealing weapons during World War I, allied lobbyists and politicians created the perception that the arms trade benefitted the American middle and working classes. As America progressed as an arms dealer during World War II, it was argued that arms trading was a necessary feature of American foreign policy, enabling the United States to exert indirect influence over allies and even potential enemy states and providing leverage for essential economic and foreign policy initiatives. Nevertheless, America has had an active, growing anti-arms trading lobby since World War II which argues that America's involvement in the industry is immoral and creates more problems than it solves.[2]

Exploring the Industry

After World War I, Congress enacted the nation's first round of arms trade reforms, designed to give legislators oversight to prevent arms trades that could compromise national security or international relations. Subsequent reform efforts have likewise focused on attempting to strengthen legislative oversight. In 2019, the U.S. Department of State's Bureau of Political-Military Affairs (PM) is responsible for overseeing both government-to-government arms transfers and sales and commercial licensing of arms. The most recent legislative acts establishing policies for the industry are the Arms Export Control Act, the Conventional Arms Transfer Policy, and the Foreign Assistance Act of 1961.

Two types of arms deals: Foreign Military Sales (FMS) and Direct Commercial Sales (DCS).

Foreign Military Sales (FMS) are sales that take place between the United States and another government and thus are part of a diplomatic process that begins with a formal request from another nation. The sale may or may not be subject to congressional approval, depending on its size, and is otherwise managed by the Department of State (and so by the executive branch). Negotiating FMS agreements is a complicated process that might involve direct presidential negotiations as well as negotiations between State Department representatives and representatives of a foreign government. The United States sells both weapons that are manufactured within the United States and also weapons that have been acquired through other channels. As of 2019, FMS agreements result in the export of some $40 billion in defense equipment each year.

Direct Commercial Sales (DCS) represent the free market dimension of America's arms trade. DCS agreements take place between an American corporation and a foreign entity or government. These agreements are negotiated directly by corporate representatives and foreign representatives, and the U.S. government regulates the process through licensing. Companies wishing to deal weapons with foreign entities need to obtain an approved export license, which is potentially subject to congressional review, a process intended to ensure that DCS agreements do not pose a threat to American security or economic welfare. DCS agreements are, by far, the most significant aspect of U.S. weapons dealing activities, constituting $110 billion in sales annually.[3] Saudi Arabia is the leading recipient for American arms, purchasing nearly 18 percent of all arms sold by the United States, followed by the United Arab Emirates (UAE) with 7.4 percent, Australia (6.7 percent), Taiwan (5.7 percent), and Iraq (5.5 percent). Forty percent of American arms trades involve nations in the Middle East region.

Justifying the Arms Trade

Politicians often cite diplomatic or foreign policy goals when discussing arms trade agreements. Since World War II, arms trade agreements have been used to secure access to essential resources, especially petroleum resources, which explains much of the arms trade activity involving countries in the Middle East. Regions that suffer from instability are also characterized by a higher demand for weapons, a demand that might be met by competing nations like Russia or China if a vacuum in U.S. arms sales is created.

Though there is a perception that the arms trade is a major boon to the U.S. economy, research indicates that the economic benefits of arms trading, even in terms of denying economic advantages to competing nations, are relatively short-term and are limited in comparison to many other U.S. industries that come with lower levels of associated risk.[4] Arms manufacturers do provide employment and companies involved in the industry can serve as anchors for working-class communities centered around manufacturing, although the impact is limited compared to other kinds of manufacturing.

The Trump administration claims that arms sales enable the United States to:

> maintain a technological edge over potential adversaries, strengthen partnerships that preserve and extend our global influence; bolster our economy; spur research and development; enhance the ability of the defense industrial base to create jobs; increase our competitiveness in key markets; protect our ability to constrain global trade in arms that is destabilizing or that threatens our military, allies, or partners; and better equip our allies and partners to contribute to shared security objectives and to enhance global deterrence.[5]

A primary argument in favor of arms trading is an economic one. Another is that it enables the United States to avoid direct involvement in military activities (by strengthening partners and allies) and to exert influence over the foreign policies of recipient nations. The theory is that if the U.S. exports its own global policy outlook to other countries, allies like Saudi Arabia and the UAE will engage in activities that ultimately enhance global or U.S. security. Meeting foreign policy goals has been a primary justification for arms trading since World War II, when the United States exported billions in military equipment to allies in Europe in return for recipient nations' consideration U.S. interests in future economic and foreign policy decisions. Politicians and arms export supporters have continued to believe that the arms trade provides U.S. leverage and international influence. It is also often argued that arms exports can increase regional stability and this has been used as justification for arms dealing to Iraq, Syria, and Saudi Arabia, with the intention of strengthening allies and consolidating power.

Unintended Consequences

The Syrian radical group known as ISIS in the U.S. press, but more generally known as the Islamic State or "Daesh" in the rest of the world, emerged as one of the world's most influential radical Islamist organizations in 2014. The group has conducted hundreds of attacks in Syria, Iraq, Afghanistan, Pakistan, and elsewhere, and fueled the rise of splinter groups in Africa, the Middle East, and Europe. Research indicates that 90 percent of the weapons possessed by ISIS, weapons that enabled the group to conduct successful military invasions in Iraq and Syria, were weapons initially sold by the United States and European countries to allies like Saudi Arabia. Likewise, the organization Al-Qaeda, which was responsible for the September 11, 2001, terrorist attack on the United States, possesses an arsenal that includes thousands of small arms and heavy weapons sold through U.S. FMS and DCS agreements.[6]

There is no doubt that U.S. trade in weapons has resulted in small arms and other weapons falling into the hands of extremist militant groups. Research also indicates that the arms trade may not stabilize troubled regions, but may actually exacerbate political and military disputes, making it more likely that violent conflict will occur.[7] In some cases, such as Colombia and the Philippines, the American arms trade resulted in increased governmental power, yes, but also in the birth of more oppressive regimes. A 2017 study examining 189 countries between 1970 and

2009 found that the higher the degree of U.S. weapons and military training a country received correlated with a higher probability that the country would experience a military coup.[8]

Whether arms trades provide power to authoritarian governments, inadvertently increase the power of radical groups, or continue a cycle of violent conflict, there is little doubt that the trade in arms contributes to situations that threaten human welfare. Activists and social scientists, both in the United States and abroad, argue that the international arms trade does not benefit global society but, instead, fuels conflict and governmental abuse. Some seek to limit or at least reform the U.S. arms trade policy to better ensure that the United States does not engage in FMS or DCS when doing so carries a high risk of contributing to violent conflict.

Risk and Reward

In many ways, the U.S. arms trade business and foreign policy are permanently at odds. The arms trade flourishes when conflict occurs and yet politicians seek to use arms trades to limit conflict. Since World War II, the conventional wisdom has been that it is in America's best interest to dominate the global weapons trade and to utilize this power to secure American interests worldwide. Many U.S. corporate entities linked directly or indirectly to the arms trade profit from international turmoil and violence. At the same time, American politicians have a duty to protect the American people from harm and thus, address the international conflicts that pose a threat to Americans. It is unclear to what degree arms trading either secures America or exacerbates conflict and ultimately increases the risk to American safety and security.

While it is clear that the Trump administration plans on increasing arms trading, increasing public concern may pressure future leaders to reform the industry. The arms trade reflects some of the goals that Americans have identified as key goals for the nation's future, such as maintaining a robust economy and maintaining American influence abroad. But the arms trade also stands in opposition to other American values, such as promoting human rights and ending warfare. How this facet of American society evolves may come to reflect the degree to which the values of American society are changing and whether or not these changing values are more important to the American people than maintaining the advantages gained by adhering to the status quo of the preceding century.

Works Used:

Bowler, Tim. "Which Country Dominates the Global Arms Trade?" *BBC*. May 10, 2018. Retrieved from https://www.bbc.com/news/business-43873518.

Erickson, Jennifer. *Dangerous Trade: Arms Exports, Human Rights, and International Reputation*. New York: Columbia University Press, 2015.

Gold, David. "Costs of Arms Sales Undermine Economic Gains." *EPUSA*. 1998. Retrieved from http://www.epsusa.org/publications/newsletter/dec1998/gold.pdf.

Hartung, William D. "Arms Sales Decisions Shouldn't Be About Jobs." *Defense One*. Mar 26, 2018. Retrieved from https://www.defenseone.com/ideas/2018/03/arms-sales-decisions-shouldnt-be-about-jobs/146939/.

Joselow, Gabe. "ISIS Weapons Arsenal Included Some Purchased by U.S. Government." *NBC News*. Dec 14, 2017. Retrieved from https://www.nbcnews.com/news/world/isis-weapons-arsenal-included-some-purchased-u-s-government-n829201.

Savage, Jesse Dillon, and Jonathan D. Caverley. "When Human Capital Threatens the Capitol: Foreign Aid in the Form of Military Training and Coups." *Journal of Peace Research*. Jul 13, 2017. Retrieved from https://journals.sagepub.com/doi/abs/10.1177/0022343317713557.

Stohl, Rachel. "Trump Administration's New Weapons Export Policies Stress Benefit to U.S. Economy." *Just Security*. Apr 30, 2018. Retrieved from https://www.justsecurity.org/55496/trump-administrations-weapons-export-policies-stress-benefit-u-s-economy/.

Thrall, A. Trevor, and Caroline Dorminey. "Risky Business: The Role of Arms Sales in U.S. Foreign Policy." *Cato*. Cato Institute. Policy Analysis No. 836. Mar 13, 2018. Retrieved from https://www.cato.org/publications/policy-analysis/risky-business-role-arms-sales-us-foreign-policy.

"U.S. Arms Sales and Defense Trade." *U.S. Department of State*. Feb 4, 2019. Retrieved from https://www.state.gov/t/pm/rls/fs/2019/288737.htm.

Wezeman, Pieter D., Fleurant, Aude, Kuimova, Alexandra, Tian, Nan, and Siemon T. Wezeman. "Trends in International Arms Transfers, 2017." *SIPRI*. Stockholm International Peace Research Institute. March 2018. Retrieved from https://www.sipri.org/sites/default/files/2018-03/fssipri_at2017_0.pdf.

Notes

1. Bowler, "Which Country Dominates the Global Arms Trade?"
2. Wezemen et al., "Trends in International Arms Transfers, 2017."
3. "U.S. Arms Sales and Defense Trade," *U.S. Department of State*.
4. Thrall and Dorminey, "Risky Business: The Role of Arms Sales in U.S. Foreigh Policy."
5. Stohl, "Trump Administration's New Weapons Export Policies Stress Benefit to U.S. Economy."
6. Joselow, "ISIS Weapons Arsenal Included Some Purchased by U.S. Government."
7. Thrall and Dorminey, "Risky Business: The Role of Arms Sales in U.S. Foreign Policy."
8. Savage and Caverley, "When Human Capital Threatens the Capitol: Foreign Aid in the Form of Military Training and Coups."

1
History

Image from Marek Tuszyński's collection of WWII prints, via Wikimedia.

Willys jeep used by Polish First Army as part of the U.S. Lend-Lease program, Warsaw 1945.

Risk and Reward: The History of Arms Trading in the United States

Though historical records are sparse, arms and armaments have long been considered a valuable resource that has been exchanged between nations and societies, fueling the growth of both nations and corporations and transforming the economic and military balance of power around the world. Recent historical evidence has uncovered a previously unknown chapter in the history of American arms dealing, the role that foreign arms played in Colonial American history. In the book *Thundersticks*, historian David Silverman describes how Cuban and British arms dealers took advantage of the power struggles between Native American societies and the expanding American Colonies by selling weapons to both sides. The Seminole people of Florida went on to repel the U.S. Army in a series of three wars, between 1816 and 1858, and were the only Native American tribe that was never defeated and never surrendered (and the only tribe that never signed a formal peace treaty with the U.S. government), thanks in large part to European weapons.[1]

During the American Civil War, both the Union and the Confederacy depended on the international gun trade. In a *Military History* blog interview, historian Peter Tsouras explained that the Confederacy, when initially formed, possessed only a small fraction of the industrial capacity of the Union and so would not have been able to arm their military forces if not for the weapons trade:

> The output of British factories, mills, shipyards, and arsenals flooded through the Union blockade of Southern ports to provide the bulk of Confederate needs. Without the massive support, the Confederacy would surely have collapsed within 12 to 18 months. Given that the bloodiest years of the war were 1863-1865, it was British material support that allowed the vast majority of the blood-letting to occur.[2]

The Enfield rifle, one of the most common and effective weapons on both sides of the Civil War, was, in fact, a British import. Likewise, British companies sold ships, guns, merchant equipment, and food to both Confederate and Union fighters, profiting from this fractured era of American politics. This trade also forever altered the arms business in America, as seized or traded European weapons were imitated by American manufacturers and fueled the rise of domestic gun manufacturers.[3]

America Becomes an Arms Dealer

The United States came into its own as an arms supplier during World War I, a transformation made possible by the fact that the United States remained neutral in the war for the first three years. Selling material to both sides proved enormously profitable for American companies and from 1914, when the war started, to 1917, when the United States entered the war, American companies shipped more than $2 billion in supplies to Europe. In 1916 alone, U.S. companies sold more than $1 billion in arms to European forces. By 1920, the United States was responsible for more than half (52 percent) of the global arms trade. The evolution of the arms trade in the United States reflects a key characteristic of American conservativism: reluctance to regulate companies based on the belief that free-market forces will result in corporations serving public interests. In practice, this rarely occurs as companies tend to put maximizing profits before any other consideration. This was certainly the case during World War I, as the enormous profits reaped by weapons manufacturers resulted in a small number of companies accruing massive profit. The imbalance in profit was so great, in fact, that the federal government stepped in to establish a level of government oversight for companies supplying arms overseas.[4]

Much of Europe was devastated, both economically and physically, by the First World War, and many nations that purchased American weapons and supplies did so on credit and carried significant debt after the war. When World War II began in 1939, many of America's more fiscally-minded politicians were reluctant to allow American companies to deliver weapons or material to Europe. The 1934 Johnson Act reflected this sentiment, prohibiting the U.S. government from providing any credit to nations that had not repaid debts carried over from World War I. This became a contentious issue in Congress, and the 1939 Neutrality Act, formally declaring U.S. neutrality in the war, permitted the sale of weapons to belligerents only on a "cash and carry" basis. President Franklin D. Roosevelt, and other politicians wary of an Axis victory in the war, nonetheless searched for a way to provide aid to the UK, which could not provide cash payment for materials.

In 1940, the Roosevelt administration debuted a new arms trade policy, known as "Lend-Lease," in which the United States supplied the UK with weapons without requiring immediate payment. The Lend-Lease program also enabled recipients to repay the United States not by cash but by way of "consideration," meaning that the United States could influence the foreign policy of the UK and other recipients in return for forgiving debt. Through Lend-Lease programs, the United States distributed more than $50 billion in assistance to 30 countries and, through this debt of "consideration" became a leader in international politics, utilizing the debt of other nations to gain economic and military advantage on the global stage.[5]

The Modern Arms Race

Though the United States has been a major player in the international arms industry since World War I, the importance of arms deals to foreign policy and the U.S. economy did not begin to approach modern levels until the Cold War, the long period of economic and military instability that followed World War II as the United States, Russia, and China competed for global military dominance. Arms deals were a major part of how the United States influenced foreign policy abroad between the 1950s and the twenty-first century, fueled by intensive federal investment in arms research in an effort to maintain a perceived advantage over Russia and China.

During the Korean and Vietnam conflicts, arms "transfers" were used extensively to further perceived American interests in Asia, and America's arms trade policies since the Cold War have engendered mixed reactions within the region. During the early years of the Cold War, a majority of Americans had embraced the claim that it was important for America to contain communism, and yet American arms deals led to a number of controversial political situations. For one thing, dealing in arms essentially empowered the executive office to influence global military affairs in significant ways without legislative oversight. The problems with this system became clear during the Vietnam conflict when secret arms deals and Central Intelligence Agency (CIA) activities resulted in the executive branch fueling a war without congressional involvement. The result was the passage of the American Export Controls Act (AECA) in 1976, a new policy that gave the executive branch the power to negotiate and approve of arms deals, with oversight by the Departments of State and Defense, but that required congressional notification for sales over a certain value. It also required the White House to submit a political and military threat assessment to Congress for each proposed arms deal. Congress was further empowered to block arms deals within 30 days of notification.[6]

While well-intentioned, the AECA did little to limit presidential authority to conduct arms deals. Congress essentially abdicated legislative power to control finance when it came to arms dealing, in large part because there was little incentive for legislators to actively oppose arms dealing. Because each U.S. state has some direct investment in the nation's arms production industry, politicians on both sides of the aisle have routinely taken a generally pro-arms-trading stance. In many parts of the country, the defense industry is a dominant one, so many Americans have come to equate growth in arms production and sales as a key to prosperity. Since World War II, the defense and weapons manufacturing industry has grown into one of the most powerful lobbies in America. Politicians who oppose arms deals often face possible political, financial, and public reprisal.

Congressional reluctance to interfere with arms dealing has meant that, since the passage of the AECA, Congress has rarely used its power to demand risk assessments or to hold the White House accountable for dealing arms to high-risk entities. The Iran-Contra scandal under the Reagan Administration highlighted the use of the proceeds of arms sales to Iran to fund anti-communist rebels (Contras) in Nicaragua, who became a violent and authoritarian regime.[7]

The U.S. government also provided arms and other military supplies to former Iraqi leader Saddam Hussein, creating Hussein's dictatorial regime, which the United States then ended in the 2003 invasion of Iraq. Investigations of government documents have since revealed that the Reagan administration continued to support Hussein even after having direct knowledge that Hussein was using the nerve gas sarin, which is prohibited as a cruel and unusual weapon under international law.[8]

Following the 9/11 terrorist attacks on the United States, the United States has intensified its involvement in arms dealing in an effort to supply governments engaged in the process of fighting terror. However, evidence suggests that U.S. arms dealing has instead fueled human rights crises and contributed to the destabiliza-tion of nations and regions. This has created a significant anti-arms-dealing lobby within the United States. Significant attention has been paid to how the arms deals conducted by the Reagan and Bush administrations, in particular, escalated many of the global conflicts still relevant today.

A 2018 research report from Cato Institute looked at the history of U.S. arms deals since the 9/11 terrorist attacks and found that U.S. policy has resulted in many extremely high-risk arms deals with the potential to increase instability and human rights issues. Researchers found that most of the revenues from arms deals conducted by the United States have been with high-risk countries like Iraq, Ye-men, the Sudan, Afghanistan, Egypt, and the Philippines, countries where it is more likely that weapons will fall into the hands of bad actors or violent regimes.[9]

The risks associated with arms dealing and the role that U.S. arms have played in violent conflicts around the world have resulted in a small number of politicians, social activists, and human rights organizations lobbying for restricting or prohibit-ing U.S. arms exports. On the other hand, the defense industry lobby promotes the idea that expanding arms dealing benefits the U.S. economy and populace, as well as arms trading being an essential way for the United States to gain leverage and influence overseas and so, theoretically, to prevent violent conflict. As of 2019, the American people have little influence over federal policies in regard to defense, and public opinion has not been a predominant factor in the defense policies estab-lished under the Trump administration.

Works Used:

"American Civil War Viewpoints: It Was British Arms That Sustained the Confed-eracy." *Military History*. Mar 3, 2011. *Military History*. Retrieved from https://www.military-history.org/blog/it-was-british-arms-that-sustained-the-confedera-cy-during-the-american-civil-war-peter-tsouras.htm.

Beck, Michael D., Cupitt, Richard T.t, Gahlaut, Seema, and Scott A. Jones. *To Sup-ply or To Deny*. New York: Kluwer Law International, 2003.

Harris, Shane, and Matthew M. Aid. "Exclusive: CIA Files Prove America Helped Saddam as He Gassed Iran." *Foreign Policy*. Aug 26, 2013. Retrieved from https://foreignpolicy.com/2013/08/26/exclusive-cia-files-prove-america-helped-saddam-as-he-gassed-iran/.

Hyde, Charles K. *Arsenal of Democracy: The American Automobile Industry in World War II*. Detroit: Wayne State University Press, 1945.

"The Iran-Contra Affair—1986–1987." *The Washington Post*. 1998. Retrieved from https://www.washingtonpost.com/wp-srv/politics/special/clinton/frenzy/iran.htm.

Kelly, Joe. "How British Businesses Helped the Confederacy Fight the American Civil War." *The Conversation*. The Conversation US. Mar 7, 2016. Retrieved from http://theconversation.com/how-british-businesses-helped-the-confedera-cy-fight-the-american-civil-war-52517.

"Lend-Lease and Military Aid to the Allies in the Early Years of World War II." *U.S.*

Department of State. U.S. Department of State. Milestones: 1937-1945. 2016. Retrieved from https://history.state.gov/milestones/1937-1945/lend-lease.

Sanchez, Casey. "When Native Americans Were Arms Dealers: A History Revealed in 'Thundersticks'." *Los Angeles Times.* Dec 23, 2016. Retrieved from https://www.latimes.com/books/la-ca-jc-thundersticks-20161223-story.html.

Thrall, A. Trevor, Caroline Dorminey. "Risky Business: The Role of Arms Sales in U.S. Foreign Policy." *Cato.* Cato Institute. Policy Analysis No. 836. Mar 13, 2018. Retrieved from https://www.cato.org/publications/policy-analysis/risky-business-role-arms-sales-us-foreign-policy.

Notes

1. Sanchez, "When Native Americans Were Arms Dealers: A History Revealed in 'Thundersticks'."
2. "American Civil War Viewpoints: It Was British Arms That Sustained the Confederacy," *Military History.*
3. Kelly, "How British Businesses Helped the Confederacy Fight the American Civil War."
4. Hyde, *Arsenal of Democracy,* 4–10.
5. "Lend-Lease and Military Aid to the Allies in the Early Years of World War II," *U.S. Department of State.*
6. Beck, Cupitt, Gahlaut, and Jones, *To Supply or to Deny.*
7. "The Iran-Contra Affair—1986–1987," *Washington Post.*
8. Harris and Aid, "Exclusive: CIA Files Prove America Helped Saddam as He Gassed Iran."
9. Thrall and Dorminey, "Risky Business: The Role of Arms Sales in U.S. Foreign Policy."

A World of Weapons: Historians Shape Scholarship on Arms Trading

By Kritika Agarwal

American Historical Association, September 1, 2017

During his first trip abroad as president of the United States, Donald Trump made a $110 billion arms deal with Saudi Arabia. Trump, of course, is just one among a long list of presidents who have brokered arms deals with foreign powers on behalf of American manufacturers. And the United States has long been the world's largest arms exporter—it accounted for more than half of all arms-transfer agreements in the world as recently as 2015. But historians interested in the subject will struggle to find relevant historiography. As Brian DeLay (Univ. of California, Berkeley) says, "the US arms trade, either domestically or more specifically internationally, is something that has been shockingly understudied by historians."

Emerging work, by DeLay and others, seeks to lay to rest the idea that large-scale arms trading in the United States and elsewhere is a recent phenomenon, originating in the post–World War II military-industrial complex. The trade in small arms and ammunition, these historians argue, has been a key feature of domestic and international commerce and politics since at least the early 17th century. Although military production and trading would soar with World War II and the Cold War, the sale of complicated air and naval systems isn't where this history begins.

Long before early 19th-century industrialization transformed arms manufacturing in the United States, the continent was flush with guns. According to David Silverman (George Washington Univ.), the earliest trade in firearms developed between European colonial powers and indigenous nations. His book *Thundersticks: Firearms and the Violent Transformation of Native America* (2016) shows that once the Dutch flintlock musket was introduced in the 1630s, Iroquois League nations began trading for them, becoming "the preeminent military power of the Northeast and Great Lakes regions." The threat posed by armed Iroquois peoples set off an arms race that spread to the Pacific Northwest by the 18th century. A great deal of weapons trading and stockpiling, Silverman writes, took place in Quebec, Jamestown, and Plymouth, before settlers even arrived in other colonies, such as Pennsylvania and Georgia.

The fact that indigenous nations had steady access to firearms markets and used guns in warfare contradicts a major tenet of Jared Diamond's "guns, germs, and steel" theory: that disease and technological superiority were behind the European conquest of the Americas. "There's a widespread assumption that Native people were subjugated by European Americans because of a disadvantage in arms, and that's just not true," says Silverman. "They routinely got the very best of firearms technology and used those guns more effectively than white settlers. And white governments routinely struggled to control the trade in arms to Native people." In his book, Silverman points to Crazy Horse's surrender of more than 200 firearms to US troops in 1877 and notes, "Clearly, a lack of weapons had nothing to do with the Lakotas' capitulation to the Americans."

Instead, Silverman argues, other factors contributed to the eventual undoing of Native military resistance: starvation, "war weariness," intertribal conflict, and decline in population compared to settlers, who benefited from high birth rates and migration. In fact, if it hadn't been for their adoption of firearms and participation in arms trading, Silverman notes, indigenous nations would not have been able to sustain resistance for as long as they did.

The ability to trade in firearms was similarly crucial to other resistance efforts, such as the American Revolution, on the continent. When the colonies began rebelling in 1765, they lacked the ability to manufacture significant quantities of firearms or gunpowder. Britain also forbade arms exports to the colonies; in 1775, for example, the colonial militia ran out of ammunition at the Battle of Bunker Hill and had to withdraw, despite inflicting severe damage on British forces. Only when the French began supplying the colonists with munitions did the tide of war shift.

As DeLay says, "What happens during the American Revolution is supremely important for the history of the arms trade." In research for a coming book, *Shoot the State*, he found that after the revolution, "the governing classes in the new United States agree across partisan lines that in order to endure and to grow in a world that is dominated by mighty empires, the United States has to rapidly become self-sufficient in firearms and war materiel." The federal government thus established state-run gun arsenals such as the one in Harper's Ferry and awarded contracts and tariff breaks to private manufacturers. This soon made the country autonomous with regard to arms manufacturing. Andrew Fagal (Princeton Univ.), who is writing a monograph on the development of the arms manufacturing industry, says that the United States went from being "largely dependent upon foreign sources for arms and ammunitions to a country that by the War of 1812 was largely self-sufficient and a net exporter of weapons."

This shift was monumental not just for the United States but for the entire Western Hemisphere, says DeLay: "For the first time, there was in the Western Hemisphere an independent republic that was under no obligation to other colonial powers, in terms of treaties and alliances, to restrain its own merchants." What developed was trade in firearms and munitions, both licit and illicit, which played a major role in decolonization efforts throughout the Americas. Fagal writes in his dissertation that by 1805, New York City merchants trading in guns and munitions were engaged in such brisk business throughout Latin America that French generals complained that it allowed Haitian revolutionaries easy access to firearms and the ability to keep up their struggle. Spain's fate in the Americas was also complicated by the arms trade: despite its efforts to control commerce at its Spanish American ports, DeLay notes, US merchants' illicit arms trading played a "critical role" in the success of the Spanish American wars of independence in the early 19th century.

The early history of firearms trading and manufacturing is thus transnational and complex, involving European imperial powers, anti-imperial revolutionary forces throughout the Americas, indigenous nations, private arms dealers and manufacturers, and other actors. But the early American republic wasn't an isolated arena for growth in arms trading; guns helped foster empire and spur the global political economy in the 18th and early 19th centuries.

Priya Satia (Stanford Univ.), who is writing a book titled *Empire of Guns: The Violent Making of the Industrial Revolution*, says that arms manufacturing and trading were not only major drivers of the Industrial Revolution in Britain, they were also what allowed "British armies, navies, mercenaries, traders, settlers, and adventurers to conquer an immense share of the globe." Pointing out that Britain was in a state of "continuous war" during the height of the Industrial Revolution, she says that nearly every industry in the country at the time "was in some way contributing to war." Britain "knew arms manufacture was triggering industrial revolution at home" and therefore quashed local arms-manufacturing industries in its colonies, such as those in South Asia. At the same time, the country "permitted voluminous gun sales" to them. Paralleling Silverman's thesis about indigenous nations, Satia concludes, "the conquest of India is not about British technological superiority." This progression from perpetual war to economic growth through arms trading sounds similar to the modern concept of the military—industrial complex. But in a subtle variation, Satia refers to 18th-century Britain as a "military-industrial society": every sector of the political, social, and industrial world was affected by weapons.

> **The early history of firearms trading and manufacturing is thus transnational and complex, involving European imperial powers, anti-imperial revolutionary forces throughout the Americas, indigenous nations, private arms dealers, and manufacturers.**

Despite this rich, expansive history, these scholars see little interest in it within the academic history community. Books, documentaries, and entertainment about warfare, firearms, and the military are in high demand among popular audiences, but according to Silverman, scholarship on these subjects lags. "Effectively, since World War II, and especially since the 1960s," he says, "academics have drifted away from those topics." DeLay also notes that the transnational nature of arms trading "doesn't fit easily alongside most of the established research priorities" in the discipline, which, he says, still organize "historical knowledge around nation states." Furthermore, as Satia notes, the illicit nature of much of the early trade in firearms makes it hard for historians to find sources, discouraging them from undertaking research on the topic.

Satia, however, sounds a call to historians: arms trading matters. In leaving the writing of the history of guns and the gun trade to those interested mainly in firearms' value as collectors' objects or in "celebrating the old American gun culture," she says, historians have ceded it to gun enthusiasts. Arms trading, she says, can tell historians much about "state economy and culture, society, international relations, and so on, that's lost in the fetishization of the particularities of old guns."

DeLay agrees. In addition to contributing to knowledge about foreign relations, "the arms trade also speaks to the history of capitalism" and state making in "pretty urgent and fascinating ways," he says. Finally, DeLay argues, studying the arms trade can help historians understand power relations: "If we reflect upon the power asymmetries and the patterns of domination and resistance and the inequalities within the United States and between the United States and other parts of the world, you'll see that guns are everywhere in those relationships, structuring those relationships." As the United States hurtles inevitably to more arms deals, it would be remiss for historians not to dig deeper.

Print Citations

CMS: Agarwal, Kritika. "A World of Weapons: Historians Shape Scholarship on Arms Trading." In *The Reference Shelf: U.S. National Debate Topic 2019-2020 Arms Sales*, edited by Micah L. Issitt, 9-12. Amenia, NY: Grey House Publishing, 2019.

MLA: Agarwal, Kritika. "A World of Weapons: Historians Shape Scholarship on Arms Trading." *The Reference Shelf: U.S. National Debate Topic 2019-2020 Arms Sales,* edited by Micah L. Issitt, Grey House Publishing, 2019, pp. 9-12.

APA: Agarwal, K. (2019). A world of weapons: Historians shape scholarship on arms trading. In Micah L. Issitt (Ed.), *The reference shelf: U.S. national debate topic 2019-2020 arms sales* (pp. 9-12). Amenia, NY: Grey House Publishing.

Where Did Iran Get Its Military Arms over the Last 70 Years?

By Kuang Keng Kuek Ser
Public Radio International, June 1, 2016

Will Iran regain its military might after the removal of international sanctions?

This question has become a point of international debate since the Iran nuclear deal was initiated several years ago.

To answer the question, perhaps one of the basic steps is to look at the history of Iran's arms imports and factors surrounding them.

According to the arms transfers database of the independent international think tank, Stockholm International Peace Research Institute (SIPRI), which compiled all transfers of major conventional weapons in the world since 1950, the US was the largest arms exporter to Iran from the 1950s to 1970s.

The supply of arms from the US started to climb in 1953 after Iran's democratically elected prime minister Mohammad Mosaddegh was overthrown in a coup engineered by the British and American intelligence services. The Iranian shah, Mohammad Reza Shah Pahlavi, returned from exile to rule and become a close ally of the US.

According to a Senate Committee on Foreign Relations staff report in 1976, Iran was the largest single purchaser of US military equipment then. Military sales had increased more than sevenfold from $524 million in 1972 to $3.91 billion in 1974.

SIPRI data shows that the amount rose and peaked in 1977.

The staff report stated that in 1972 President Richard Nixon and his then-national security adviser, Henry Kissinger, agreed for the first time to "sell Iran virtually any conventional weapons it wanted." With its oil revenue, Iran acquired some of the most sophisticated US military equipment and received training and technical assistance from American personnel.

The report explained the rationale behind the sales.

"Iran is and will remain an extremely important country to the US and its allies because of its geographical location and oil. Iran, on the other hand, places great importance on its relationship with the US, in large part because of the Iranian belief that the US may come to Iran's defense if it is threatened."

With that level of support from the US, Iran emerged as a dominant military power in the Middle East, paving the way for nuclear weapon development.

The US-Iran alliance collapsed in 1979 when the shah's authoritarian rule led to riots, protests and eventually the Iranian Revolution. The shah was again forced into exile. An Islamic fundamentalist force, led by anti-American cleric Ayatollah Ruhollah Khomeini, took power and turned Iran into an Islamic republic.

US arms export to Iran was ceased abruptly and earlier orders canceled after Islamic militants took 52 Americans hostage inside the US embassy in Tehran in November 1979.

China and the Soviet Union soon replaced the US, becoming [a] major supplier of arms to Iran from [the] 1980s until now.

The US still sold a small amount of weapons to Iran between 1984 to 1986. According to SIPRI database, those are arms were sold covertly and illegally by the US with the help of Israel despite an arms embargo against the Iran.

The US attempted to secure the release of hostages in Lebanon through the clandestine arms deals. The proceeds from the sales were used to fund guerrillas fighting against the left-wing government in Nicaragua in an effort to stop the spread of socialism in Latin America. The scandal would later be known as the Iran-Contra affair.

Following US sanctions in 1979 which were further tightened in the 1990s, Iran moved closer to Russia and China. Arms sales from Russia increased significantly in the 1990s.

The sanctions pushed Iran to build its own military industry. The republic produced its own tanks, armored personnel carriers, missiles, fighter jets and submarines. It also exported military equipment to countries like Syria and Sudan, according to SIPRI data.

Arms sales by Russia were greatly reduced when the United Nations Security Council imposed sanctions against Iran in 2007 over its failure to halt uranium enrichment, a crucial step in developing [a] nuclear weapon.

> **Following US sanctions in 1979, which were further tightened in the 1990s, Iran moved closer to Russian and China.**

China's arms sales to Iran however were not effected.

Due to their close financial ties with Iran, both China and Russia only supported the sanctions after parts of them were watered down. Russia was then building a nuclear power station in Bushehr, Iran, which would be completed in 2011.

The sanctions banned the supply of nuclear-related technology and materials and called on member states to "exercise vigilance and restraint" in the transfer of arms to Iran. A ban on major conventional weapons transfers was only imposed in 2010 when the UN tightened the sanctions.

From 2008 to 2015, China and Russia still maintained a smaller volume or arms trade with Iran.

The Iran nuclear deal has opened up a window for China and Russia to revive their arms relationship with Iran.

In April 2015, Russia lifted its self-imposed ban on the delivery of a powerful missile air-defense system to Iran when the Iran nuclear deal negotiation—of which Russia was a part—was yet to be completed.

The $800 million deal, signed in 2007, was suspended by Russia in 2010 due to the UN sanctions. Russia started the delivery of the missiles in April 2016, only three months after the implementation of the nuclear deal.

Print Citations

CMS: Kuang, Keng Kuek Ser. "Where Did Iran Get Its Military Arms over the Last 70 Years?" In *The Reference Shelf: U.S. National Debate Topic 2019-2020 Arms Sales,* edited by Micah L. Issitt, 13-15. Amenia, NY: Grey House Publishing, 2019.

MLA: Kuang, Keng Kuek Ser. "Where Did Iran Get Its Military Arms over the Last 70 Years?" *The Reference Shelf: U.S. National Debate Topic 2019-2020 Arms Sales,* edited by Micah L. Issitt, Grey House Publishing, 2019, pp. 13-15.

APA: Kuang, K.K.S. (2019). Where did Iran get its military arms over the last 70 years? In Micah L. Issitt (Ed.), *The reference shelf: U.S. national debate topic 2019-2020 arms sales* (pp. 13-15). Amenia, NY: Grey House Publishing.

"Merchants of Death": The International Traffic in Arms

By Jonathan Grant
Origins, December 3, 2012

In April 2012, Viktor Bout, perhaps the single biggest private arms trader in the world, was convicted in a New York court and sentenced to twenty-five years in prison.

Bout, a Russian citizen, began his private business as a military transporter and weapons supplier in the early 1990s following the collapse of the Soviet Union. He acquired a fleet of Soviet military aircraft including Antonov and Ilyushin cargo planes as surplus of the Cold War and employed them in operations to deliver weapons to various combatants in Africa.

By his own admission, he had flown weapons to anti-Taliban forces in Afghanistan during the 1990s and aided the French government in transporting goods and UN peacekeepers to Rwanda after the genocide there. According to UN documents, in exchange for illicit diamonds Bout had supplied former Liberian President Charles Taylor with weapons to help destabilize Sierra Leone.

Previously Bout had supplied arms to both sides in the Angolan civil war and also sold and delivered weapons to various warlords across Central and North Africa. Operating through Eastern Europe, Bout transported weapons through Bulgaria, Moldova and Ukraine to Liberia and Angola in the first years of the new millennium.

Indeed, there were few conflicts in the world over the past two decades where Bout's weapons were not present. So spectacular was his rise as an arms dealer that his story served as the basis for the 2005 film *Lord of War*.

In court, Bout was found guilty of conspiracy to kill Americans and U.S. officials by delivering anti-aircraft missiles and aiding a terrorist organization.

The case against Bout was built upon a sting operation with DEA agents posing as would-be buyers from FARC, the Revolutionary Armed Forces of Colombia. Bout was prepared to supply anti-aircraft missiles so that FARC could shoot down American pilots working with Colombian government officials.

The Lessons of Viktor Bout

Bout's experiences as a gunrunner illustrate important patterns in the history of the global arms trade since the advent of firearms in the early modern era: where weapons are sold and bought, who sells and buys them (individuals or states), which weapons (new or second-hand), and whether the weapons' sales are legal in the context of shifting national and international law.

Bout also exemplifies the reemergence of the leading role of private suppliers in the global arms business—as opposed to the country-to-country transactions that dominated the Cold War era.

To be sure, weapons sales by sovereign states have not disappeared. In 2011, the United States sold a record-shattering $66.3 billion in weapons globally (more than 75% of the world arms market that year) and considerably more than the previous record of $31 billion.

But, Bout is a descendent of a long line of private "merchants of death"—a pantheon that includes the likes of Basil Zaharoff, Prodromos Bodosakis-Athanasiades, and Samuel Cummings.

Bout's arrest also reflects a long line of efforts on the part of the international community to control and restrict the arms trade.

In one regard, Bout's activities mark a significant change in the history of the global arms trade: for first time, thanks to the collapse of communism, black market supplies are more plentiful and cheaper than newly produced weapons.

The global arms trade has long been spurred on by the development of new weapons, from matchlock to flintlock to breech loading to automatic weapons, for example. With each advance in weapons technology, arms dealers and military elites looked for places and peoples to sell their old, technologically inferior weapons to make room for the cutting edge technology that would win wars.

But the flood of second-hand, cold-war weapons into the market has made the last two decades unprecedented in private arms dealing.

The Global Arms Trade Is Born: Early Modern Europe and Africa

While the trade in weapons has blanketed the planet, Bout's dealings in Africa reflect how that continent, more than others, has for centuries been saturated by the arms trade to disastrous effect.

Starting in the sixteenth century, European traders began trafficking arms into African, American, and, to a lesser extent, Asian markets.

While there was diffusion of firearms technology generally, and a number of locales developed production capabilities as gunpowder states, West European centers emerged as the main sources of arms across Europe and around the world.

Western European states dominated the trade in part because of advances in firearm and gunpowder technologies and also because of their burgeoning global trade networks. In particular, Europeans sought to leverage their advances in gun technology to increase their presence and profits in the slave trade out of Africa.

Among these western centers, Portugal acted as the chief conduit of firearms to Asia and Africa in the sixteenth century thanks to its global trade routes. Despite Papal bans on the sale of weapons to non-Christians first issued in 1179 and reiterated numerous times thereafter, the Portuguese initiated the arms traffic into the African Gold Coast in the sixteenth century—trade that brought great profit.

By the seventeenth century, the Dutch became probably the leading arms exporters internationally, with Amsterdam at the heart of the trade. Purchasers of Dutch weapons came from neighboring European states such as France and England, as well as customers further afield including from Sweden, Russia, Poland, Portugal, Venice, and Morocco.

As firearm technology changed on the European continent, European traders sought to sell off their old, less desirable weapons in Africa and elsewhere. And these weapons offered excellent goods for use in the slave trade.

In the period 1650-1700, a rising flow of new trade flintlock muskets together with older matchlocks released from European armies poured into West Africa: to the Gold Coast, Slave Coast, and rapidly spread out to Benin by the early eighteenth century and the eastern Niger Delta by 1750.

As a measure of the scale of operations, in 1700 Dutch establishments on the Gold Coast ordered 6,000 carbines. Additionally, the English Royal African Company sent 32,954 arms to West Africa between 1701 and 1704. In 1730, the Gold Coast and Slave Coast together imported 180,000 firearms.

English private commercial interests substantially joined the African arms traffic business by the turn of the eighteenth century. Private English arms exports to West Africa commenced in the late 1690s, with gun-making centers in London and (a little later) Birmingham, which completed its first order for "slave-trade guns" in 1698.

In large part, the increase of European firearms to the region was linked to increased European demand for African slaves as African traders found themselves in a position to demand more guns in exchange for slaves.

The second half of the eighteenth century witnessed a surge of English arms exports. Of the estimated 283,000-394,000 firearms annually imported into West Africa between 1750 and 1807, England accounted for about 45 percent. One firm in Birmingham by itself was manufacturing 25,000-30,000 guns a year for the West African market in 1754. As these figures indicate, the slave trade and the arms trade were inextricably bound.

Guns, Industry, and European Imperial Reach

The period 1860-1918 witnessed a profound expansion in the volume of arms trafficking. As industrialization picked up speed in Europe, more arms could be produced more quickly than ever before. Mass production and an unending series of technological advancements in weaponry generated obsolete castoffs and war surplus weapons on an increasing scale.

In the global context, the main players in the extra-European arms traffic were the French and Belgians, and the Italians to a lesser extent in the case of East Africa. Overwhelmingly, the weapons sold included older Remington and Gras rifles rather than the state-of-the-art weapons manufactured by Mauser and Steyr.

The prominence of the Belgian city of Liège as a chief supplier of firearms to Africa also reflected changes in the period. By the late nineteenth century, Liège had taken the African gun trade away from Birmingham, and the Belgian city accounted for some 67 percent of the African arms traffic by 1907.

Thanks to the imperial scramble for Africa in the last quarter of the nineteenth century, East Africa rose as the chief destination for imported firearms through trafficking and new private traders and state governments took on leading roles in the trade.

By the early 1880s, both the Italians and the French worked to supply Ethiopia with arms. Italian officials wanted to gain political influence over King Menilek of Ethiopia as part of their imperial efforts, whereas the French interest grew from private arms traders.

By the end of 1882, French rifles were arriving in Ethiopia from Marseilles. French traders delivered obsolete French and Belgian weapons, and often sold them with a markup between 400 and 500 percent. Not to be outdone, the Italians committed to deliver 4,000 rifles immediately and 50,000 Remingtons with 10 million cartridges over the next decade.

Beginning in the second half of the 1890s Belgian and French firms figured prominently in the arms traffic. And the arms trade was a consequential source of jobs for Europeans. At Liège more than 10,000 workmen engaged in the manufacture and repair of arms, of which about 3,000 worked at the large private factory of Herstal, which was supported by the Belgian government.

In 1895, Ethiopia's Menilek had sent a mission to Paris with the sole purpose of forwarding arms and ammunition via Djibouti. The fruits of this mission manifested in a major shipment of 40,000 arms and 5 million rounds of ammunition from Liège to Ethiopia conveyed by the Dutch steamer *Doelwijk*.

By 1898, no fewer than 300,000 guns and carbines had been exported from Belgium. A single French firm at St. Étienne had supplied 350,000 carbines for Ethiopia, of which 150,000 arrived in March 1900. These were Gras Mousqueton carbines recently discarded by the French artillery service.

Arming the Persian Gulf and Middle East

While the arms route into East Africa via Djibouti carried the most volume of traffic, another route flowed from the Persian Gulf into South and Central Asia beginning in the second half of the nineteenth century.

This route operated on various sections of the Persian Gulf littoral including Muscat, Bahrain, Kuwait, and the Arabian Peninsula. In particular, Muscat and Oman had served as central emporia for the arms traffic. The arms flowed freely into Muscat and from there throughout Persia and inland to Baluchistan and north to Afghanistan.

Local demand for these weapons was strong in Central Asia. The influx of new arms and ammunition permitted those who could access them to shift the balance of power not only with other local groups but also with the European colonial powers.

As had been the case with the East African traffic, French merchants from Marseilles along with Belgians imported arms into Muscat. Even with prohibitions against the arms trade decreed in Bahrain, Kuwait, and Qajar Persia, the region witnessed a large and increasing illicit traffic in arms. British colonial authorities in India estimated that 94,000 tribesmen on the Northwest Frontier had acquired breech-loading rifles by means of the illegal traffic.

Once consignments cleared the coast of Persia, it proved virtually impossible to catch the camel caravans that conveyed the arms to the interior. Local Persian officials were incapable of containing the traffic because the Afghans participating in the arms smuggling were almost always better armed than any opposition the Persians could manage.

In 1908 an estimated 30,000 rifles and 3 million rounds arrived in Afghanistan via Muscat, with an additional 40,000 rifles arriving in 1909. Undercover agents from British India discovered as many as 250,000 rifles in store at Muscat.

Afghans purchasing weapons from Muscat could sell them in the Kabul market within nine weeks of landing the guns at Makran. Ultimately, these weapons found their way into the hands of tribal leaders and regional strongmen in Afghanistan, affecting local power struggles.

Basil Zaharoff, Arms Dealer Extraordinaire

Although the second-hand arms trade proved vast—and the illegal trade in weapons very hard to control—the big money was found in the manufacturing and selling of the new weapons to governments. In that arena the major military industrial producers included Krupp (Germany), Schneider-Creusot (France), and Vickers (Britain).

Sir Basil Zaharoff, the infamous sales agent for Vickers, was probably the world's best-known arms dealer through World War I. Zaharoff once boasted to a London paper, "I made wars so that I could sell arms to both sides. I must have sold more arms than anyone else in the world."

His first important achievement was the sale of submarines to Greece and Turkey in the late 1880s. Calculating that if he could sell to one of these countries, then the rival country would feel compelled to keep pace, Zaharoff offered one submarine to the Greeks.

After the Greeks had purchased their submarine, Zaharoff turned to the Ottoman Turks alerting them to the new danger now emanating from Greece. To counter the perceived threat, the Turks subsequently acquired two submarines themselves from Zaharoff. In this way he managed to create a one-man arms race in the Eastern Mediterranean.

Such ploys paid off handsomely, and as Zaharoff built his fortune, he became a primary example of the "merchant of death" persona that captured the imagination and earned the opprobrium of the public during the interwar period of the 1920s and 1930s.

Regulating the Arms Trade between the Two World Wars

The notion that states should limit arms exports for the general sake of peace and the avoidance of war emerged out of the public disgust with the private arms trade following the First World War.

The newly formed League of Nations took up the cause of controlling the arms traffic as part of its larger mission of general disarmament during the interwar era. However, these efforts at regulating the weapons trade all-too-often foundered.

The European colonial powers recognized the danger of the arms trade to the stability and control of their empires, and thus found a common interest in strictly regulating the arms traffic. However, the smaller states rejected this course of action on the grounds that their sovereignty would be reduced and their security eroded by the de facto control of the arms trade by the few Great Powers.

Despite the failure to achieve effective international control over the arms trade through an officially accepted Arms Traffic Convention, the interwar period did see some principles of arms control established, including the licensing of arms exports and publication of export figures.

Thus, by the end of the 1930s, Belgium, Sweden, France, Britain, and the United States had established the peacetime licensing of arms exports as normal practice.

The attempts to control arms exports gained their greatest momentum during the two decades following the First World War. In particular, the arms embargo on warlord China from 1919 to 1929 represented the most sustained effort of this kind.

Initiated by the United States and then joined by Britain and France, the purpose of the Chinese arms embargo was to end

> With each advance in weapons technology, arms dealers and military elites looked for places and peoples to sell their old, technologically inferior weapons to make room for the cutting edge technology that would win wars.

internal fighting and prevent any further disintegration of the country. However, many other countries did not sign on and private firms pursued a brisk business. Nevertheless, the China arms embargo did mark the first international embargo against a single country.

Although warlord China did not serve as the most important arms market in terms of size (China ranked fifteenth globally as an arms importer), the demands of 1,300 warlords waging 140 provincial and inter-provincial wars between 1912 and 1928 did generate lucrative opportunities for a variety of arms traffickers.

Official arms traders could be found working within the various foreign legations in Beijing, but the majority of the arms dealers worked as independent contractors lacking formal connections with a foreign government or a private armaments maker. Included in the ranks of these private middlemen were South Asians, Russians, Japanese, overseas Chinese, and entrepreneurs in Canada and United States who smuggled arms from North America.

Bodosakis, Göring and the Spanish Civil War

In the decade following the end of the arms embargo in China, the Spanish Civil War (1936-1939) between the Nationalists (under General Franco) and the Republicans proved a boon for arms trafficking, and the lure of Spanish gold attracted all sorts of odd political bedfellows to the Spanish arms market.

Perhaps the most dissonant case involved the Greek arms dealer Prodromos Bodosakis-Athanasiades.

Bodosakis was the chief shareholder and executive of the Greek Powder and Cartridge factory, the main gunpowder and firearms factory in Greece. Bodosakis' pecuniary motives led him to supply both the Nationalists and the Republicans, and he arranged shipments so that the best and latest weapons went to Franco while the oldest and least serviceable arms were delivered to the Republicans.

The Greek factory was in business with the German armaments firm Rheinmetall-Borsig, an enterprise in which Hermann Göring, head of the German Luftwaffe, had personal financial interests. Even as Nazi Germany officially backed the Nationalists and German pilots were flying missions on behalf of the Nationalist cause, the Republicans purchased arms from Nazi Germany through the personal agency of Göring.

In this instance, Göring, who was free-lancing the sales for personal profit, arranged a secret arms deal to the Republicans that included 19,000 rifles, 101 machine guns and 28 million cartridges shipped from Hamburg. When Bodosakis received Spanish requests for arms, he passed them on to Rheinmetall. The Greek government then provided end-user certificates stating that these arms were for the Greek army.

When the shipment reached Greece from Germany, Bodosakis then transferred the cargo to another vessel supposedly bound for Mexico. However, the vessel actually went to Spain. In 1937 and 1938 the Republic's purchases of weapons from Nazi Germany reached their peak.

As a key participant in this arms trafficking, Bodosakis' company was taking shipments from Rheinmetall worth up to 40 million Reichmarks (£3.2 million) at a time. These consignments were almost all for Republicans, and generated payments to Göring and members of the Greek government.

Bodosakis even worked with the Soviet Union. In November 1937 he signed a contract with the Soviets to provide the Republicans with ammunition worth £2.1 million.

Samuel Cummings and the Private Arms Trade after World War II

During the Cold War era (1945-1989) arms trafficking again received a huge boost thanks to the vast quantities of war surplus equipment located in depots around the world following World War II.

Precisely at this time Samuel Cummings emerged as the world's biggest small-arms dealer. He founded his private company, Interarms, in 1953 and managed to control 90 percent of world's private trade in guns.

Cummings ran a legitimate and open business selling to the American civilian market of hunters, sportsmen, and collectors as well as to governments. He built his gun business from the debris of World War II by amassing the German Army surplus littering the battlefields in Western Europe. He also offered to buy surplus weapons from government arsenals.

In his first deal, Cummings made $20,000 by purchasing 7,000 weapons from the surplus of the Panamanian government and selling them on the U.S. civilian market.

After touring Europe he bought up German surplus left in bunkers in Holland and sold the material to the government of West Germany. Cummings ultimately bought and sold more rifles and ammunition than Eisenhower needed for the invasion of Normandy and the defeat of the Wehrmacht.

By end of the 1950s, Cummings had approximately 2 million weapons in England alone. By his tally he bought 4.5 million weapons and 500 million bullets in Europe in the period 1953-1968.

Avowedly apolitical and neutral, Cummings' business did $100 million annually with factory and arms depots in Manchester, England and Alexandria, Virginia. He supplied guns to overthrow the Guatemalan government in 1954, sold arms to Castro and Batista, and to both sides in the Costa Rican Civil War.

By far his biggest arms deals came from Spain. Over the course of two purchases in 1959-60 and 1965-66, Cummings bought up the entire surplus from the Spanish Civil War, thereby acquiring 1 million weapons and 250 million rounds of ammunition.

Scrupulously law-abiding, Cummings paid all his taxes, and every sale was licensed and approved by British and American governments. Interarms even abided by a UN arms embargo to South Africa 1963.

The Cold War and State-Level Arms Dealing

The Cold War rivalry between the Communist world and the West greatly contributed to the expansion of the global arms trade.

In general the supply of arms and military equipment became one of the most powerful weapons in international diplomacy, and both the United States and the Soviet Union gave a high proportion of their foreign aid in this form.

For the first time in modern global history, country-to-country transactions came to typify the arms trade.

Whereas Sam Cummings' arms business dominated the private trade in the millions of dollars, the Cold War arms bonanza of government-to-government weapons trade operated in the billions of dollars.

Prior to 1970 world military exports rarely exceeded $5 billion annually and less developed countries accounted for less than half of those sales.

In the period 1973-1980, however, the two Super Powers (USA and USSR) together supplied two-thirds of all arms imported by less developed countries, and arms exports dramatically shot up thanks to the petro-dollars generated by the oil shocks of the 1970s.

From 1978 to 1985, Third World countries ordered $258 billion worth of arms and ammunition including 13,960 tanks and self-propelled artillery, 27,605 armored personnel carriers, 4,005 supersonic aircraft, and 34,948 surface-to-air missiles.

In terms of technical changes, World War II had stimulated tremendous advancements in light automatic weapons. Most famous of these is the AK47, the Soviet automatic machine-gun which was engineered during the war but would come to dominate the light weapons traffic globally in the Cold War and post-Cold War eras. Approximately 70-100 million AK47s have been produced worldwide since 1947.

In 1975 Communist Vietnam became heir to huge numbers of arms available following the Communist victory and American withdrawal from the war in Southeast Asia, including roughly 2 million small arms (M16s) and 150,000 tons of ammunition.

Many of these abandoned American weapons found their way back to Central America in the 1980s, as the Vietnamese traded them to the Cuban government in exchange for foodstuffs. The Cubans then trafficked the weapons into Central America to support the spread of revolution by supplying the Sandinistas in Nicaragua and the FMLN in El Salvador.

Vietnamese trading of American war surplus from the Vietnam War led to the largest illicit arms shipment ever intercepted in transit from the United States to Mexico.

In March 1997 U.S. federal agents discovered containers of leftover American automatic rifles and rifle parts which had been shipped from Ho Chi Minh City (Vietnam) to Singapore, then to Bremerhaven (Germany), and thence through the Panama Canal to Long Beach, California for delivery in Mexico.

Back to Africa

Since 1945, conflicts in Africa have caused on the order of 6.5 million deaths, with most of these casualties due to light weapons, especially automatic weapons. Following the collapse of the Soviet Union in 1991, vast numbers of light weapons were released from controls and entered the international arms market.

Estimates of the total value of legal exports of light weapons globally reach $5 billion, while the value of the illicit trade may range from $2 billion to $10 billion. Africa is so saturated with weapons that an AK47 can be purchased for $10.

Since the 1990s, West Africa experienced some of the most devastating armed conflicts in the world. The United Nations Development Program (UNDP) has estimated some 8 million illicit small arms and light weapons are already present in West Africa.

Nigerian sources worry that 1 million such arms may be in Nigeria alone. Liberia used a series of questionable end-user certificates to acquire military equipment from former communist countries in 2000-2001, and Viktor Bout's Russian company transported much material from Ukraine.

Bout and the 21st-Century Arms Trade

Just as Zaharoff, Bodosakis, and Cummings were emblematic of the arms trade in their respective eras, Viktor Bout's business career as an arms transporter reveals much about globalization in the post-Soviet, post-Cold War world.

Working with the abandoned military surplus of the Soviet bloc that unpaid or underpaid soldiers and commanders were only too eager to sell for ready cash, Bout funneled the wares through an intricate web of supply chains involving up to 30 different companies and superficially legitimate end-user certificates to deliver arms around the globe.

In learning from Bout's case, however, it would be a gross misunderstanding to view the current problems of gun-running and weapons trafficking as recent developments or as primarily resulting from the international consequences of Cold War rivalries.

The preceding five centuries of firearms trafficking around the world shows that the gun markets are deeply embedded in the international landscape.

And as with previous efforts to control the weapons trade, the various recent UN arms embargoes have largely failed to limit access to weapons.

Since 1990, arms embargoes have been imposed to end civil wars in the former Yugoslavia (1991 and 1998), Somalia (1992), Liberia (1992 and 2001), Rwanda (1994), and Sierra Leone (1997). The embargo in Somalia has been in place for many years now, yet warlords and private militias remain well equipped with AK47s and other weapons.

Each successive historical period has brought forth bigger waves of the supply and demand for firearms, which have overwhelmed the attempts to monitor and control the trade through export licensing schemes and international agreements.

And one thing is clear. The easy accessibility of weapons, especially in the developing world, and the ineffective efforts to control the trade have contributed significantly to the devastating violence we see in the world today.

Print Citations

CMS: Grant, Jonathan. "'Merchants of Death'": The International Traffic in Arms." In *The Reference Shelf: U.S. National Debate Topic 2019-2020 Arms Sales,* edited by Micah L. Issitt, 16-25. Amenia, NY: Grey House Publishing, 2019.

MLA: Grant, Jonathan. "'Merchants of Death'": The International Traffic in Arms." *The Reference Shelf: U.S. National Debate Topic 2019-2020 Arms Sales,* edited by Micah L. Issitt, Grey House Publishing, 2019, pp. 16-25.

APA: Grant, J. (2019). "Merchants of death": The international traffic in arms. In Micah L. Issitt (Ed.), *The reference shelf: U.S. national debate topic 2019-2020 arms sales* (pp. 16-25). Amenia, NY: Grey House Publishing.

Let's Talk about George H.W. Bush's Role in the Iran-Contra Scandal

By Aran Gupta
The Intercept, December 7, 2017

The effusive praise being heaped on former President George H.W. Bush— "a calm and vital statesman" who exuded "decency, moderation, compromise"—risks burying his skeletons with him. One of the most notable skeletons that has gotten scant attention in recent days is his role in the Iran-Contra scandal.

As CIA director in the mid-1970s and as Ronald Reagan's vice president, Bush helped forge a world of strongmen, wars, cartels, and refugees that continues today. In particular, he was deeply involved in the events that became known as the Iran-Contra scandal, a series of illegal operations that began with a secret effort to arm Contra fighters in Nicaragua in the hopes of toppling the leftist Sandinista government; this effort became connected to drug trafficking, trading weapons for hostages with Iran, and banking scandals.

In 1987, Arthur Liman, chief counsel for the Senate Select Committee on Secret Military Assistance to Iran and the Nicaraguan Opposition, described it as a "secret government-within-a-government ... with its own army, air force, diplomatic agents, intelligence operatives and appropriations capacity." Independent counsel Lawrence Walsh, tasked with investigating Iran-Contra, concluded that the White House cover-up "possibly forestalled timely impeachment proceedings against President Reagan and other officials." Bush was a central figure in this.

Bush's spy history is murky. According to Russ Baker, author of *Family of Secrets*, a history of the Bush family, in the late 1950s, Bush allegedly allowed the CIA to use an offshore oil rig he owned near Cuba as a staging ground for anti-Castro Cubans to raid their homeland. In 1967, Bush visited Vietnam as a freshman member of Congress, and Baker claims that Bush was accompanied by his business partner, a CIA agent, to investigate the Phoenix Program, the CIA torture and assassination operation that killed more than 20,000 Vietnamese by 1971.

These pieces come together when Bush served as CIA director from January 1976 to January 1977. During his tenure, he met his future national security adviser, Donald Gregg, who was involved in operations linked to the Phoenix Program as a former CIA station chief in Saigon. There, Gregg fought alongside Cuban exile and CIA agent Felix Rodriguez, who helped track down and kill Cuban revolutionary Che Guevara.

Bush was at the CIA during the height of Operation Condor, an international "kidnap-torture-murder apparatus" run by six Latin American dictatorships and coordinated by Washington. In an Operation Condor plot carried out in October 1976, Chilean secret police assassinated former Chilean diplomat Orlando Letelier and American Ronni Moffitt with a car bomb in Washington, D.C. Bush misled an FBI investigation about Chile's responsibility. Also as spy chief, Bush met his Panamanian counterpart, Manuel Noriega, already suspected at the time of drug trafficking. (As president, Bush ordered the invasion of Panama in 1989 to remove Noriega from power, who was the country's ruler by that point.)

As vice president, Bush became an architect of the "secret government" that came into being for the Iran-Contra operations. Official investigations of Iran-Contra are limited to the period after October 1984 when Congress banned military and intelligence services from providing direct or indirect support to the Contras. But Gary Webb's expose on CIA and Contra links to cocaine smuggling, *The Dark Alliance*, dates to 1981 the covert U.S. support for the Contras. Cobbled together from remnants of Nicaragua's defeated National Guard, the Contras were notorious for torture, assassination, and other atrocities. The Phoenix-Condor link reached Central America, as the CIA recruited veterans of Argentina's Dirty War to train the Contras, who ignited a decadelong war that killed an estimated 50,000 Nicaraguans.

Rolling Stone dates Bush's involvement in the Contra war to 1982, when he reportedly conspired with CIA chief William Casey in an operation they code-named "Black Eagle." Working under Bush, Donald Gregg managed finances and operations for the Contras, according to *Rolling Stone*. Rodriguez handled arms flights to Central America and negotiated with military commanders there. Historian Douglas Valentine has claimed that in 1981, Bush authorized these veterans of the Phoenix Program to initiate a "Pink Plan" terror war against Central American insurgents.

Black Eagle masked its operation by relying on the Israeli Mossad to acquire and ship weapons to Central America, employing Panamanian airfields and companies as fronts, according to the *Rolling Stone* story. But the planes, once emptied of their arms cargo in Central America, were repurposed by Noriega and the Medellín cartel to ship drugs back to the United States. The CIA allegedly stuck a deal with the Medellín cartel's primary contact, Barry Seal. In return for Seal hauling weapons to the Contras, the CIA protected him as his operations smuggled an estimated $3 billion to $5 billion in drugs into the United States.

The White House also leaned on Gulf State monarchies to cough up more than $40 million for the Contras, violating the 1984 congressional ban known as the Boland Amendment. In 1985, Lt. Col. Oliver North coordinated with Israel to ship more than 2,000 anti-tank missiles to Iran through Israel in exchange for Iran's assistance in freeing American hostages held in the region—and the profits were used to fund the Contras.

The maneuver, which violated the Arms Export Control Act, was extraordinarily cynical. Iran was mired in a brutal war with Iraq, which was backed by Bush and other senior Reagan administration officials beginning in 1982. Through the

BNL bank that would later collapse in scandal, Iraq received more than $4 billion of U.S. Department of Agriculture credits. Most of that money reportedly went to buy weaponry even as Iraq waged chemical warfare against Iran and its own Kurdish citizens.

Both the Contra weapons shipments and the arms-for-hostages deals were exposed in 1986.

Much is still not known about Iran-Contra because of document shredding, deceit, and cover-ups by Reagan-era officials. Congress handcuffed its inquiry by failing to subpoena Oval Office recordings and calling knowledgeable witnesses. Robert Parry, an *Associated Press* reporter who uncovered the arms-for-drugs trade years before Webb, criticized the media for failing to dig into the story and succumbing to White House pressure and perception management.

On Christmas Eve 1992, then-President Bush decapitated the investigation by Walsh. Bush pardoned six figures, including Secretary of Defense Caspar Weinberger, whose trial was about to begin, with Bush likely called to testify. Walsh was livid. Saying "the Iran-Contra cover-up ... has now been completed," he called Bush a "president who has such a contempt for honesty [and] arrogant disregard for the rule of law."

> **Bush helped forge a world of strongmen, wars, cartels, and refugees that continues today.**

Bush's pardons are newly relevant because Bush consulted his attorney general at the time, William Barr, who reportedly did not oppose the pardons. Barr has just been named by President Donald Trump as his nominee for attorney general, where he may once again confront the issue of presidential pardons of senior government officials caught in an illegal conspiracy.

Bush's role in the Iran-Contra scandal shows that his legacy is far darker than what is being reported amid his death and funeral. The truth is that he coddled dictators and death squads, undermined democratic institutions, and trashed the Constitution. He created the conditions that helped give rise to Donald Trump.

Print Citations

CMS: Gupta, Aran. "Let's Talk about George H.W. Bush's Role in the Iran-Contra Scandal." In *The Reference Shelf: U.S. National Debate Topic 2019-2020 Arms Sales,* edited by Micah L. Issitt, 26-28. Amenia, NY: Grey House Publishing, 2019.

MLA: Gupta, Aran. "Let's Talk about George H.W. Bush's Role in the Iran-Contra Scandal." *The Reference Shelf: U.S. National Debate Topic 2019-2020 Arms Sales,* edited by Micah L. Issitt, Grey House Publishing, 2019, pp. 26-28.

APA: Gupta, A. (2019). Let's talk about George H.W. Bush's role in the iran-Contra scandal. In Micah L. Issitt (Ed.), *The reference shelf: U.S. national debate topic 2019-2020 arms sales* (pp. 26-28). Amenia, NY: Grey House Publishing.

How British Businesses Helped the Confederacy Fight the American Civil War

By Joe Kelly

The Conversation, March 7, 2016

The American Civil War devastated the US, but it also had serious consequences for the world beyond. Among them was the Lancashire cotton famine, which plunged thousands of British subjects into poverty. But the war also provided great opportunities to others outside the US who were willing to exploit them.

The South's campaign against the North would have been impossible without the contribution made by British businesses—and particularly those in Liverpool.

The rebel states of the Confederate South began the American Civil War in desperate need of cash, ships and arms. Most American industry and banking was headquartered in the North, so southern leaders were forced to look across the Atlantic to find these vital instruments of war. In Liverpool, they would find exactly what they were looking for.

The links between Liverpool and the southern states stretched back to the early 19th century boom in cotton consumption and manufacture. Cotton was the South's main export, and it was through the port of Liverpool that it made its way to the mills of Manchester. It was these connections that saw the establishment of Fraser, Trenholm & Co., the Liverpool branch of a South Carolina shipping firm, which went on to act as the Confederacy's European bank.

Fraser, Trenholm & Co. was managed by Charles Prioleau, a proud South Carolinian who had married the daughter of prominent Liverpool merchant Richard Wright. From his home in Abercomby Square, Prioleau forged commercial connections

> **The links between Liverpool and the southern states stretched back to the early 19th century boom in cotton consumption and manufacture.**

crucial to the Confederate war effort. Now owned by the University of Liverpool, the square housed merchants, engineers, and even mayors of the city—all of whom would be vital in supplying the Confederacy's needs.

It was the industry and profit-seeking of Liverpool merchants that generated money for a cash-strapped South. The Confederacy had begun the war by attempting to blackmail Britain into recognising its independence by withholding cotton, on which thousands of mill workers' jobs depended. This policy failed spectacularly, and when the southern government needed to sell cotton to generate funds, it found its ports blockaded by the Union navy.

The war saw cotton prices skyrocket, and Liverpool's shipping interests were well-placed to benefit. Encouraged by Prioleau, Merseyside merchants knew large profits awaited them if they could get through the blockade to purchase southern cotton, often providing arms in exchange. The war, which was responsible for immense suffering, also provided commercial opportunities for those with enough capital and ingenuity.

Made in Merseyside

Along with cash, the Confederacy needed warships—and Liverpool, with its bustling port, was happy to comply. The Mersey was home to innovative shipbuilders Laird Brothers and the engineers Fawcett, Preston & Co. Both companies were approached by Confederate agent James Bulloch to build the most notorious vessel of the war, the CSS *Alabama*.

The Alabama terrorised the Union navy from its launch in 1862 to its sinking in the summer of 1864. Northern politicians were understandably outraged by the construction of a Confederate vessel in a British port, not least because in 1862 the British government had issued a declaration of neutrality.

Technically it was illegal for British subjects to arm warships for either the North or the South, yet little official scrutiny was afforded to the building of the Alabama. It did not escape the attention of Thomas Dudley, Union consul in Liverpool, who hired a team of detectives to try and catch Bulloch in the act of arming a confederate vessel.

To avoid detection, the Confederate agent arranged for the Alabama to leave Merseyside under a false name and be armed offshore. This act of subterfuge would have been impossible without the help of the British shipbuilders, and possibly even the dock officials.

The launching of the Alabama was incredibly embarrassing for the foreign secretary, Lord John Russell, and from 1863 onwards the government took firm actions to stop this sort of thing. Several vessels under construction by Merseyside shipbuilders were seized over the next few years, but it was too little too late. The Alabama went on to sink an estimated 62 ships throughout the war, and after 1865, the furious US government brought a series of legal actions against Britain known as the Alabama Claims.

Liverpool's intimate links with the Confederacy are reminders of just how international the American Civil War really was. The merchants, shipbuilders and engineers of Liverpool seem to have been untroubled by the moral questions raised by aiding the South. The British government was committed to a strict policy of neutrality, but as the case of the Alabama shows, that position was easily undermined by individual desire for profit—a phenomenon all too familiar today.

Print Citations

CMS: Kelly, Joe. "How British Businesses Helped the Confederacy Fight the American Civil War." In *The Reference Shelf: U.S. National Debate Topic 2019-2020 Arms Sales,* edited by Micah L. Issitt, 29-31. Amenia, NY: Grey House Publishing, 2019.

MLA: Kelly, Joe. "How British Businesses Helped the Confederacy Fight the American Civil War." *The Reference Shelf: U.S. National Debate Topic 2019-2020 Arms Sales,* edited by Micah L. Issitt, Grey House Publishing, 2019, pp. 29-31.

APA: Kelly, J. (2019). How British businesses helped the Confederacy fight the American Civil War. In Micah L. Issitt (Ed.), *The reference shelf: U.S. national debate topic 2019-2020 arms sales* (pp. 29-31). Amenia, NY: Grey House Publishing.

As the US Entered World War I, American Soldiers Depended on Foreign Weapons Technology

By David Longenbach
The Conversation, March 31, 2017

On April 6, 1917, the United States declared war against Germany and entered World War I. Since August 1914, the war between the Central and Entente Powers had devolved into a bloody stalemate, particularly on the Western Front. That was where the U.S. would enter the engagement.

How prepared was the country's military to enter a modern conflict? The war was dominated by industrially made lethal technology, like no war had been before. That meant more death on European battlefields, making U.S. soldiers badly needed in the trenches. But America's longstanding tradition of isolationism meant that in 1917 U.S. forces needed a lot of support from overseas allies to fight effectively.

In Europe, American combat troops would encounter new weapons systems, including sophisticated machine guns and the newly invented tank, both used widely during World War I. American forces had to learn to fight with these new technologies, even as they brought millions of men to bolster the decimated British and French armies.

Engaging with Small Arms

In certain areas of military technology, the United States was well-prepared. The basic infantrymen of the U.S. Army and Marine Corps were equipped with the Model 1903 Springfield rifle. Developed after American experience against German-made Mausers in the Spanish American War, it was an excellent firearm, equal or superior to any rifle in the world at the time.

The Springfield offered greater range and killing power than the U.S. Army's older 30-40 Krag. It was also produced in such numbers that it was one of the few weapons the U.S. military could deploy with to Europe.

Machine guns were another matter. In 1912, American inventor Isaac Lewis had offered to give the U.S. Army his air-cooled machine gun design for free. When he was rejected, Lewis sold the design to Britain and Belgium, where it was mass-produced throughout the war.

With far more soldiers than supplies of modern machine guns, the U.S. Army had to adopt several systems of foreign design, including the less-than-desirable French Chauchat, which tended to jam in combat and proved difficult to maintain in the trenches.

Meeting Tank Warfare

American soldiers fared better with the Great War's truly new innovation, the tank. Developed from the need to successfully cross "No Man's Land" and clear enemy-held trenches, the tank had been used with limited success in 1917 by the British and the French. Both nations had combat-ready machines available for American troops.

After the U.S. entered the war, American industry began tooling up to produce the French-designed Renault FT light tank. But the American-built tanks, sometimes called the "six-ton tank," never made it to the battlefields of Europe before the Armistice in November 1918.

Instead, U.S. ground forces used 239 of the French-built versions of the tank, as well as 47 British Mark V tanks. Though American soldiers had never used tanks before entering the war, they learned quickly. One of the first American tankers in World War I was then-Captain George S. Patton, who later gained international fame as a commander of Allied tanks during World War II.

Chemical Weapons

Also new to Americans was poison gas, an early form of chemical warfare. By 1917 artillery batteries on both sides of the Western Front commonly fired gas shells, either on their own or in combination with other explosives. Before soldiers were routinely equipped with gas masks, thousands died in horrific ways, adding to the already significant British and French casualty totals.

Scientists on both sides of the war effort worked to make gas weapons as effective as possible, including by devising new chemical combinations to make mustard gas, chlorine gas, phosgene gas and tear gas. The American effort was substantial: According to historians Joel Vilensky and Pandy Sinish, "Eventually, more than 10 percent of all the chemists in the United States became directly involved with chemical warfare research during World War I."

Naval Power for Combat and Transport

All the manpower coming from the U.S. would not have meant much without safe transportation to Europe. That meant having a strong navy. The U.S. Navy was the best-prepared and best-equipped of all the country's armed forces. For many years, it had been focusing much of its energy on preparing for a surface naval confrontation with Germany.

But a new threat had arisen: Germany had made significant progress in developing long-range submarines and devising attack tactics that could have posed severe threats to American shipping. German Navy U-boats had, in fact, devastated British

> One of the first American tankers in World War I was then-Captain George S. Patton, who later gained international fame as a commander of Allied tanks during World War II.

merchant fleets so badly by 1917 that British defeat was imminent.

In May 1917, the British Royal Navy pioneered the convoy system, in which merchant ships carrying men and materiel across the Atlantic didn't travel alone but in large groups. Collectively protected by America's plentiful armed escort ships, convoys were the key to saving Britain from defeat and allowing American ground forces to arrive in Europe nearly unscathed. In fact, as military historian V.E. Tarrant wrote, "From March 1918 until the end of the war, two million U.S. troops were transported to France, for the loss of only 56 lives."

Taking to the Skies

Some of those Americans who made it to Europe climbed above the rest—right up into the air. The U.S. had pioneered military aviation. And in 1917, air power was coming into its own, showing its potential well beyond just intelligence gathering. Planes were becoming offensive weapons that could actively engage ground targets with sufficient force to make a difference on the battlefield below.

But with fewer than 250 planes, the U.S. was poorly prepared for an air war in Europe. As a result, American pilots had to learn to fly British and French planes those countries could not man.

Despite often lacking the weapons and technology required for success, it was ultimately the vast number of Americans—afloat, on the ground and in the air—and their ability to adapt and use foreign weapons on foreign soil that helped turn the tide of the war in favor of the Allies.

Print Citations

CMS: Longenbach, David. "As the US Entered World War I, American Soldiers Depended on Foreign Weapons Technology." In *The Reference Shelf: U.S. National Debate Topic 2019-2020 Arms Sales,* edited by Micah L. Issitt, 32-34. Amenia, NY: Grey House Publishing, 2019.

MLA: Longenbach, David. "As the US Entered World War I, American Soldiers Depended on Foreign Weapons Technology." *The Reference Shelf: U.S. National Debate Topic 2019-2020 Arms Sales,* edited by Micah L. Issitt, Grey House Publishing, 2019, pp. 32-34.

APA: Longenbach, D. (2019). As the US entered World War I, American soldiers depended on foreign weapons technology. In Micah L. Issitt (Ed.), *The reference shelf: U.S. national debate topic 2019-2020 arms sales* (pp. 32-34). Amenia, NY: Grey House Publishing.

Losing by "Winning": America's Wars in Afghanistan, Iraq, and Syria

By Anthony H. Cordesman
Center for Strategic & International Studies, August 13, 2018

The U.S. has now reached the point where the third Administration in a row is fighting wars where the U.S. often scores serious tactical victories and makes claims that it is moving toward some broader form of victory but cannot announce any clear strategy for actually ending any given war or bringing a stable peace. Once again, a new Administration seems to have focused on the tactical level of conflict and called this a strategy but has failed to have any clear strategy for ending the fighting on favorable terms.

More than that, the new Administration seems to have accepted the legacy of the previous Administration by largely abandoning the civil side of each war. It is dealing with major insurgencies and civil war as if they were limited terrorist movements. It has no clear civil-military strategy, plans for stability operations, or options to create the level of governance and development that could bring a lasting peace. It has no grand strategy and is fighting half a war.

Losing by "Winning": Afghanistan

The new Taliban offensives in Afghanistan are yet another warning of the fact that the U.S. is involved in a war of attrition that it has no guarantee of winning at the military level, and where it has no apparent strategy for dealing with Afghanistan's lack of political unity, leadership, and failure to give its people economic progress and freedom from corruption.

The U.S. has made progress in creating more effective Afghan forces and has provided enough train and assist personnel to provide serious help to the Afghan Army. It also provided more air support. Combat air support increased from a low of 411 sorties per year that actually fired munitions in 2015 to 1,248 in 2017. Put differently, the US. increased the number of sorties actually firing munitions per month from an average well under 100 sorties in 2008 to over 500 in the first five months of 2108.

That said, the recent fighting has not shown these steps are making the country more secure or that they can halt the slow growth of Taliban influence and control over given districts. Pakistan remains a problem, and Iran and Russia now seem ready to deal with the Taliban on their own. The US. and Afghan government forces may not be losing, but there is no clear evidence that they approach any form of winning.

Moreover, the U.S. is doing a far worse job of trying to fight the civil half of the war. It has virtually halted any major efforts at nation building and may be planning on major cuts in the limited stability and civil-military operations it still conducts. This simply is not a viable approach in what is effectively a failed state war.

Afghanistan's weak and divided central government has made some progress under President Ghani, but it is far from clear that the next election can be any more successful than the last one, or bring the level of united, honest, and effective government the country desperately needs to keep Taliban influence from growing and raise the level of popular support to the point where it has really won hearts and minds.

Seventeen years on, the U.S. has no real strategy in Afghanistan other than hoping that the Taliban will be exhausted first and be willing to negotiate on the government's terms, or somehow be willing to split the country, and accept a division that gives it control over a substantial portion at the government's expense. The U.S. not only can't answer the question of, "how does this war end?" The U.S. cannot answer the question of "why should this war end?"

Losing by "Winning": Syria

Afghanistan, however, is scarcely the only case in point. The war in Syria has become an Assad victory. The U.S. has largely defeated ISIS as a protostate or Caliphate, but has empowered Assad in the process. A combination of state terrorism, Russian airpower, and Iranian and Hezbollah support, have given the Assad regime a second life. It already controls some 75% of the remaining population and is steadily winning more control every day.

For all the talk of defeating terrorism in Syria, the latest START statistic on terrorism also show that ISIS has only been responsible for less than 30% of the terrorist acts in both Syria and Iraq between 2012 and 2017. It has only been responsible for 31% of the incidents in Syria alone—even if all Assad regime acts of state terrorism are excluded. Moreover, the Assad regime faces a major new fight against the remnants of the Syrian rebel forces in Syria's northwestern region of Idlib. Turkey is actively intervening against Syria's Kurds—the same groups that were the key to the U.S. supported fighting on the ground.

The civil side of the war is even worse than it is in Afghanistan, in part because Syria was a far more developed country when the war began. World Bank studies show that Syria's economy is devastated, and the UN estimated at the start of this year that that nearly half the country was at risk from the impact of war. No one knows how to accurately estimate the cost of rebuilding and recovering from the war—even if Syrian's could agree on how to do it and find the money. Worse, World Bank studies also show Syria has lost the equivalent of a decade of development, and there is no credible source of the far higher levels of aid it would need to allow its economy to recover and meet the needs of its people and heal the anger and massive political and economic divisions between Arab and Kurd, Sunni and other sects, and its regions.

Once again, the US cannot answer either the question of why the fighting should end or can end in a stable peace. In fact, at least the public side of American strategy seems to consist largely focusing on tactical victories against ISIS and pretending that the rest of Syria and the region do not exist or will magically become peaceful and stable because of some formal peace negotiations. Unlike Afghanistan, there is not even the shell of a plan to shape the future structure of the U.S.-back military forces in Syria or its security. There has never been a stability plan or meaningful civil-military operations. The U.S. hasn't just been just fighting half a war, it at best has been fighting less than a third of the enemy.

For all the talk about "peace" talks and negotiations, a divided country with rebel and largely Kurdish enclaves cannot have a real or stable peace. However, even a total Assad victory would then mean an Alawite dictator trying to rule over a largely hostile Sunni population that has lost some 400,000 civilians, been terrorized by barrel bombs and chemical weapons, and seen millions displaced or driven out of the country. It would also leave Israel, Turkey, and Syria's Arab neighbors to deal with Russia, the impact of Iranian and Hezbollah influence, and the spillover of the almost inevitable rebirth of some form of ISIS or rise of other new Sunni Islamist extremism resistance.

Losing by "Winning": Iraq

And then, there is Iraq. The U.S. has done better militarily the second time around than it did between 2003 and 2011. As was the case in Afghanistan, the U.S. finally began to concentrate on truly serious efforts to build-up combat-effective ground forces in 2015. It then sent train and assist forces forward to support them in actual combat. It also accepted the fact that there was no chance of success in fighting the Taliban in Afghanistan, or ISIS in Iraq-Syria without massive amounts of U.S. airpower.

The Military Side

The end result has been a success, at least in fighting ISIS to the point of destroying the its ability to occupy key Iraqi cities, and its "caliphate." At the same time, this success has come at the cost of a major expansion of Iran's military and security role in Iraq, and the rise of Shi'ite and Sunni militias.

The U.S. has not rebuilt Iraqi forces to a level where they have a credible capability to deter or defend against Iran, and tensions between the Arab forces under the control of the central government in Baghdad and the Kurdish Peshmerga in the North led to a major confrontation in 2018, where the government forces took back large areas the Pesh Merga had occupied, but the Arab and Kurdish forces remained as divided as ever.

Once again, "winning" at the military level has been largely a tactical success with no apparent strategy for winning even the military side of a stable peace. And here, it is useful to examine the overall U.S. approach to all three wars in the President's FY2019 budget request to Congress—requests which provide far more detail than the almost total lack of any specifics in the new National Defense Strategy.

The Administration asked for minimal civil aid of any kind but requested an increase in the cost of the Department of Defense's request for such operations for all three wars from $60.1 billion in FY2018 to $64.2 billion in FY2019—far lower than the peak of $187 billion in FY2008. It was also clear from the FY2019 budget request—and statements by the Secretary of Defense and senior U.S. officers—that it was seeking a significant increase in direct train and assist aid to Afghan, Iraqi, and Syria forces in the field.

The number of troops the U.S. actually sent forward to assist allied combat forces in each country was never made clear, and the current Department of Defense monthly reports on military and civilian personnel overseas does not include entries for Afghanistan, Iraq or Syria. However, the budget request for FY2019 did state that the U.S. planned to keep the total number of average military personnel actually deployed in Afghanistan, Iraq or Syria. at 12,000 (less some 3,000 to 6,000 more in "temporary" personnel.

This was a massive cut from 187,000 in FY2008, but much higher that the low of 8,000 troops in FY2017. There also was a major increase in other levels of support although the Department did not provide a break out of the number of contractors or civilians, and the budget justifications do not provide any clear way to tie the Department of Defense reporting to the full State Department civil OCO effort.

Other reporting by AFCENT showed that the U.S. had again made massive earlier increases in its active air support for local ground forces. The U.S. increased air support from a low of 1,411 sorties per year that actually fired munitions in Iraq and Syria in 2014, to some 10,000-12,000 per year in 2015-2017. The U.S. sharply reduced the number of attack sorties per month in 2018, but only after making massive increases in such sorties in the fight to after liberate Mosul and inflict major defeats on ISIS in both Iraq and Syria.

Equally important, the FY2019 budget submission did not describe any form of plan or strategy for any of the three wars for the portion of U.S. wartime spending devoted to Overseas Contingency Operations (OCO) beyond the coming fiscal year. It made no attempt to define a strategy or real-world budget estimate for the remaining period of FY2020 to FY2023 in the Future Year Defense Plan. The Administration also has not made any such attempt since submitting its budget request, or described any plan to build-up Iraq forces, reduced Iranian influence, reduced the growing flow of Russian arms sales, or help create some nation-wide systems for the rule of law and local security.

The Civil Side

As for the civil side, the U.S. seems to have almost deliberately ignore the warning from the World Bank regarding the cost of rebuilding the areas damaged during the fighting with ISIS or the far higher costs of economic reform that can meet the needs of the Iraqi people and win their support for the central government. Just as the U.S. effectively abandoned serious efforts at nation building and stability operations in Afghanistan in 2014, and never tried to restore them

> **The administration is dealing with major insurgencies and civil war as if they were limited terrorist movements.**

when it renewed major military support; the U.S. ended such efforts in Iraq in 2011 and never renewed them as it effectively went nearly bankrupt under the combined pressures a massive need for structural reform, the cost of the fighting, and major reductions in petroleum export revenues.

Similarly, the U.S. seems to have done little to try to help Iraq raised one of the lowest ranked levels of governance in the world, or to shape an outcome of the 2018 election that would be any less divisive than the 2010 election that helped make Maliki a would-be authoritarian, renewed the divisions between Sunni and Shi'ite, and polarized and corrupted Iraq's military forces. In fact, it is a bit of a contest as to which of the three governments in the countries the U.S. currently is fighting in is ranked by the World Bank as have the lowest levels of governance. As for corruption, both Abadi and Ghani have made some progress in their respective countries, but Transparency International ranks Syria as the 3rd most corrupt country in the world, Afghanistan is still ranked 4th, and Iraq is ranked 11th.

The outcome of the Iraqi election remains unclear and may well remain so for some months, given the problems to both creating a coalition and making it actually operate. However, it is already clear that could easily empower Iran, re-divide Iraq between Shi'ite and Sunni, and/or leave a festering quarrel between the central government and the Kurds. Such an outcome might well turn the U.S. "victory" over the ISIS "caliphate" into a major victory for Iran and defeat for the United States, but it seems to be yet another aspect of the future than no one in the Administration is willing to publicly face or address.

Coming to Grips with Some Grim Realities

It is far easier to state these problems than it is to suggest the solutions, especially since all of the options involved now present major risks and uncertainties and none of the options are particularly good. One set of options is phasing down or phasing out of each such conflict. These options do need to be taken far more seriously, as do setting very clear conditions for continued U.S. military and aid support to Afghanistan and Iraq—conditions based on a serious understanding that the U.S. will actually act on if they are not met. Declaring victory and leaving is one thing. Setting the right conditions and leaving with full justification if they are not met is quite another.

Afghanistan

The strategic importance of each war and country also, however, needs to be taken into full account. Afghanistan is not the center of major international terrorist activity. It is only one country of many which might become a center of international terrorism. U.S. withdrawal might well simply transfer its problems in stability and security to Pakistan, Iran, Russia, and its Central Asian neighbors.

Changing conditionality in Afghanistan from rhetoric to reality, and making the price of staying political unity, success in developing local security forces, and economic reform may be demanding. However, the cost of staying in a failed state over time is all too high. Moreover, the political cost to the U.S. of having to act on such conditionality may well be far more acceptable than an open-ended commitment to partial Afghan success or eventual failure.

Seen from this perspective, some form of peace with Taliban participation in the Afghan government, or division of the country may also be an option. However, it is one that is all too likely to either divide the country into ethnic and sectarian factions, see the Taliban reemerge as the dominant faction, or create some new form of civil war. Peace negotiations all too often become a form of war by other means or the prelude to new forms of power struggles.

Syria

Syria is the worst of a range of bad options. It is effectively lost already except for the Kurdish areas that have supported the U.S. Backing a coalition of the Kurds and some Arabs in the northeast on a contingency basis may be worth it—particularly if Iraq merits U.S. aid in creating a strategic buffer. However, the U.S. should not provide open ended support if it means becoming involved in the broader Kurdish struggles with Turkey or supporting a Syrian Kurdish movement with a fundamentally unworkable set of ideological goals.

It is also far from clear that the U.S. and its allies should continue even humanitarian aid to an Assad/Russian/Iranian dominated Syria—much less support any development aid. It anything, the U.S. should begin now to evaluate the kind of aid it might give any renewed Sunni or other rebels faction both now in Idlib or later.

Iraq

Iraq presents the highest risk that U.S. tactical victories will end in major strategic losses that really matter to the U.S. Its location as a land bridge that Iran can use to expand its strategic influence, its status as a major oil power, and its role in shaping Gulf security and the secure flow of world oil exports all make it far more of a strategic interest than Afghanistan or Syria.

This makes offering Iraq sustained military aid and economic aid as well far more of a priority, along with creating a matching civil effort to provide aid and assistance to its government if its government emerges out of the present election as a serious potential strategic partner. At the same time, the U.S. needs to seriously study what would happen if Iraq tilts towards Iran and consult with its Arab partners over the options.

Broader Options

Finally, the U.S. should consider two broader options.

First, trying to create some kind of broad international effort that could be coordinated by the World Bank to offer conditional aid for serious economic, governance, and political reform. The United States does not have to be the leader in "nation building." Having a more neutral and international body do so—with specialized expertise—may be the best answer to not fighting only half a war in the future. One thing is clear, however, there really is no purely military answer to any of America's three current wars, to dealing with the causes of terrorism, and to dealing with other conflicts like the fighting in Yemen or various Sub Saharan states.

Second, the U.S. needs to build on the military lessons of its current wars in shaping its commitments to future "wars" that involve terrorism and counterinsurgency campaigns. Finding the best combination of train and assist efforts and the use of airpower is one critical lesson, and one that will allow the U.S. to focus on other strategic priorities like Russia and China. the most critical issue, however, may be to define the conditions that really do merit U.S. intervention. One way or another, the U.S. has become involved in three "failed state" wars. Backing real strategic partners is one thing. Letting hope triumph over experience is quite another.

Print Citations

CMS: Cordesman, Anthony H. "Losing by 'Winning': America's Wars in Afghanistan, Iraq, and Syria." In *The Reference Shelf: U.S. National Debate Topic 2019-2020 Arms Sales,* edited by Micah L. Issitt, 35-41. Amenia, NY: Grey House Publishing, 2019.

MLA: Cordesman, Anthony H. "Losing by 'Winning': America's Wars in Afghanistan, Iraq, and Syria." *The Reference Shelf: U.S. National Debate Topic 2019-2020 Arms Sales,* edited by Micah L. Issitt, Grey House Publishing, 2019, pp. 35-41.

APA: Cordesman, A.H. (2019). Losing by "winning": America's wars in Afghanistan, Iraq, and Syria. In Micah L. Issitt (Ed.), *The reference shelf: U.S. national debate topic 2019-2020 arms sales* (pp. 35-41). Amenia, NY: Grey House Publishing.

2
Economics of the Arms Trade

A U.S. Army sergeant stands guard near a burning oil well in the Rumaylah Oil Fields in Southern Iraq. America's arms sales and foreign policy are inextricably linked to oil production in the Middle East. During the Iraq Invasion of 2003, Saddam Hussein's regime set fire to several oil wells and laid a defensive minefield across the area that contained an estimated 100,000 mines.

Checks and Balance: The Economy of Warfare

The U.S. arms trade industry grew as a function of the American economy, rather than as a tool to secure the nation's foreign policy aims. It wasn't until World War II that U.S. politicians began attempting to use strategy in arms dealing as a way to secure American interests on the global stage. By this time, the United States already accounted for more than half of all arms dealing in the world, and the United States has remained one of the world's leading arms distributors. In the modern world, politicians frequently attempt to link U.S. arms deals to foreign policy goals, but economic benefit remains the predominant motivation.

Overview of the Field

Researcher Pieter D. Wezeman and colleagues from the Stockholm International Peace Research Institute (SIPRI) released a study in 2018 indicating that the international arms trade is continuing a trend of upward growth that began in the 2000s. This growth was fueled, to a large extent, by an expanded weapons market among countries struggling to contend with the rise of extremist groups, most of which utilize American or European-made weapons from the Cold War. The volume of weapons traded from 2013 to 2017 was estimated at 10 percent higher than the volume traded from 2008 to 2012.

In 2019, the United States controlled 34 percent of the global trade, with more than 25 percent growth since 2012. The year 2017 marked the highest level of arms export for a single year since 1998. Russia, France, Germany, and China, are the world's next five largest weapons dealers. Together, the top five weapons dealers control a full 74 percent of the global market. As of 2018, the United States' primary clients were Saudi Arabia, with 18 percent of all U.S. weapons sales, followed by the United Arab Emirates (UAE) and Australia.[1]

The United States deals weapons in two primary ways. While Foreign Military Sales (FMS) are negotiated between government representatives of the two governments involved, Direct Commercial Sales (DCS) can only be made when selling weapons approved for the U.S. Munitions List (USML), and are completed by negotiations between foreign agents and U.S. companies. According to the U.S. Department of State 2019 data, FMS sales accounted for approximately $40 billion annually, while DCS transactions amount to approximately $110 billion annually.[2]

Research from SIPRI released in December 2018 looked at the world's top arms producing corporations. It found that the top 100 companies together accounted for more than $398.2 billion in sales in 2017. Further, there was a 44 percent increase in corporate arms sales from 2016 to 2017. The U. S. is home to 42 of the top 100 arms companies, with more than 2 percent growth in 2017, resulting in a combined profit of $226.6 billion. Companies representing the world's second most prolific arms dealer, Russia, accounted for 9.5 percent of the global trade, followed by the UK, with 9.0 percent, then France, with 5.3 percent. By comparison, U.S. companies accounted for 57 percent of the private arms trade. The degree to which the UnitedStates has been able to out produce competitors led SIPRI researchers to contend that, "the USA will continue to be the world's largest producer of arms for the foreseeable future."[3]

Supporters of American arms dealing often argue that the United States must increase arms trading to compete with other countries, but this is a misconception; U.S. exports are 58 percent higher than the nearest competitor, Russia, and the U.S. industry is growing while most other countries are either decreasing or maintaining current levels. While U.S. arms sales increased by 10 percent between 2013 and 2017, Russian arms trading decreased by 7.1 percent over this same period.[4] U.S. economic dominance is such that the United States could cut arms trading by more than 50 percent without risking competition from another country.

U.S. company Lockheed Martin is, by a large degree, the world's largest corporate arms producer, with approximately $44.9 billion in sales in 2017, an increase of 8.3 percent from 2016, due to F-35 combat aircraft, missiles, and anti-missile defensive systems. U.S. company Boeing accounted for some $18 billion in arms sales in 2017.

Economic Benefit of the Arms Trade

The U.S. manufacturing industry and the defense industry are intimately linked and mutually dependent. Defense industry companies employ hundreds of thousands of Americans and the revenues from the industry flow into every aspect of the American economy. Reduction in the manufacturing of key exports, like ammunition, aircraft, guided missiles, ships, and armored vehicles, could result in up to a 10 percent reduction in American manufacturing, which would result in a loss of jobs, an argument for not reducing U.S. arms sales.

When examining the economics of the arms trade, it is important to understand that taxation fuels the industry. American arms manufacturers make most of their products for the American military and so tax revenues fuel the entire defense industry. Further, defense industry companies are considered an important community commodity and municipal governments utilize tax payer revenues to bid for company partnerships. In some cases, more than $100 million in taxpayer revenues may be spent to convince a company to locate a new factory within a certain community. Manufacturers then receive tax breaks and, in many cases, cheap or free land, and taxpayers often fund the cost of constructing facilities and other logistical costs. Municipalities shoulder this burden for the opportunity to bring jobs and, ultimately, revenues to their communities. Pro-corporate conservatives often support expanding defense spending and arms dealing, arguing that doing so supports American manufacturing, benefitting the working and middle class, but to what degree is unclear.[5]

In 2018 Lockheed Martin was ranked 56 among the companies in the "Fortune 500" rankings, with estimated revenues of $51 billion and profits of $5 billion.[6] The company employed roughly 105,000 people in 2018, a number that dropped from 126,000 in 2015.

President Trump's tax plan reduced taxes on Lockheed Martin from 28.8 percent to 14.9 percent, after which the company added approximately 5,000 employees.[7] However, the distribution of profit in Lockheed Martin demonstrates one of the primary economic criticisms of the arms industry. Politicians aligned with corporate interests highlight the impact of defense industry companies on the economy; however, in many cases, defense industry profits provide little in the way of public benefit. According to QZ, Lockheed Martin earned $5 billion in 2018, an increase of 150 percent from the previous year. The 5,000 new jobs notwithstanding, the company distributed $3.8 billion among the company's shareholders, including a series of executive salary increases. Thus, the 150 percent increase in profits primarily benefitted a group of investment corporations, such as State Street Corporation, which owns 16.8 percent of the company, and Capital World Investors, which owns 7.69 percent of the company's stock.[8] This pattern held true for the other defense industry companies that profited from the Republican-led tax reform bill, including General Dynamics, Raytheon, Boeing, and Northrop Grumman, all of which distributed increases in profit derived from tax changes among company executives and shareholders, while adding few new jobs and no increase in workers' pay.

Critics argue that companies receiving tax reductions should utilize increased revenues to hire more workers, increase existing workers' wages, provide additional skills training or benefits, or in some other way invest in the communities in which corporate manufacturing facilities are located. While many large corporations are criticized for similar decisions on how to distribute increased profit, defense contractors derive revenues directly from the federal government and so are indirectly funded by taxpayer revenue. Lockheed Martin, the nation's leading weapons manufacturer, receives some 60 percent of its profit directly from the Department of Defense. Given this, critics argue that companies should be made to reinvest more of their profit in ways that benefit communities, workers, and the U.S. public as a whole. Prior to the Trump tax bill, Lockheed Martin would have paid an additional 8.9 percent, or $500 to $600 million per year in tax revenue that could have been used to pay for citizen services or infrastructure.[9]

Indirect Impact

While weapons manufacturing is an important facet of the American economy, the impact of the industry as a whole is often overestimated. Lockheed Martin employs approximately 105,000 people, and is not one of America's larger employers. Discount retail chain Dollar General employs 130,000 people, JC Penny stores employ an estimated 114,000, and McDonald's employs more than 1.7 million. The nation's largest private employer, WalMart, employs over 2 million.[10] However, the full economic impact of the defense industry cannot be estimated by looking at employment alone, as defense industry spending spreads into other facets of the economy.

Revenues derived from payments for weapons might also support individuals or companies subcontracted by weapons manufacturers. Therefore, a company like Raytheon might indirectly support mining and material supply companies, security companies, construction and facilities maintenance companies, and a variety of other industries.

The indirect relationship between arms dealing and other facets of the American economy can be seen most clearly in the relationship between arms dealing and the petroleum industry. America's 75-year diplomatic relationship with the Saudi Arabian monarchy, for instance, has been based largely on Saudi interest in U.S.-made weapons and U.S. interest in Saudi Arabian oil. A 2018 study by Vincenzo Bove, Claudio Deiana and Roberto Nisticò, published in the *Journal of Law, Economics, and Organization* demonstrates that the volume of arms shipped to a country is positively correlated with the degree to which weapon exporters are dependent on oil production in that country. In some cases, nations may organize a direct oil-for-weapons exchange while, in other cases, arms exporters can use arms deals to achieve governmental favoritism or a promise of consideration that can lead to substantially better oil import deals. Whatever the strategy, there is a clear correlation between arms deals as a foreign policy tool and oil production.[11]

The U.S. oil industry is also an essential and controversial part of the American economy, and the fact that American arms deals have been used to gain an advantage in the international oil market shows how the American economy is composed of interlinked segments; efforts to alter one segment of the economy often results in unintended impact in another. Ultimately, it is unclear whether or not arm deals provide any net benefit to the American economy, considering the economic cost of America's military activities. Around the world, radical groups, foreign armies, and rebel militias depend on American weapons and, in many cases, American military forces must combat groups armed with weapons that came from the American weapons trade. This is true, for instance, in the ongoing war in Syria, where the radical Islamic State utilizes weapons stolen or traded through American manufacturers. To fully calculate the benefit of the arms trade to the U.S. economy, economists would need to account for all the expenditures that the American military makes in combating groups armed with American weapons and weigh this against the revenues reaped from both arms sales and the peripheral economic activity that this industry generates. At present, this level of reckoning has yet to be done, and so it remains unclear whether or not weapons dealing provides any measurable economic benefit to the American people.

Works Used:

Bove, Vincenzo, Deiana, Claudio, and Roberto Nisticò. "Global Arms Trade and Oil Dependence." *The Journal of Law, Economics, and Organization*. Vol 34, No. 2, May 2018, 272–99.

Bowler, Tim. "Which Country Dominates the Global Arms Trade." *BBC News*. May 10, 2018. Retrieved from https://www.bbc.com/news/business-43873518.

Fleurant, Aude, Kuimova, Alexandra, Tian, Nan, Wezeman, Pieter D., and Siemon

T. Wezeman. "The SIPRI Top 100 Arms-Producing and Military Services Companies, 2017." *SIPRI*. Sipri Fact Sheet. Dec 2018. Retrieved from https://www.sipri.org/sites/default/files/2018-12/fs_arms_industry_2017_0.pdf.

Ingraham, Christopher. "The Entire Coal Industry Employs Fewer People Than Arby's." *The Washington Post*. Mar 31, 2017. Retrieved from https://www.washingtonpost.com/news/wonk/wp/2017/03/31/8-surprisingly-small-industries-that-employ-more-people-than-coal/?utm_term=.6a80be7f446b.

"Lockheed Martin." *Fortune*. Fortune 500. 2018. Retrieved from http://fortune.com/fortune500/lockheed-martin/.

"Number of Employees at Defense Technology Supplier Lockheed Martin 2000-2018." *Statista*. 2018. Retrieved from https://www.statista.com/statistics/268924/number-of-employees-at-defense-supplier-lockheed-martin/.

Timmons, Heather. "US Defense Giants Show How American Capitalism Fails Taxpayers." *QZ*. Quartz. Feb 4, 2019. Retrieved from https://qz.com/1537885/defense-companies-like-lockheed-martin-dont-share-tax-benefits-equally/.

Uchitelle, Louis. "The U.S. Still Leans on the Military-Industrial Complex." *The New York Times*. Sep 22, 2017. Retrieved from https://www.nytimes.com/2017/09/22/business/economy/military-industrial-complex.html.

"U.S. Arms Sales and Defense Trade." *U.S. Department of State*. Feb 4, 2019. Retrieved from https://www.state.gov/t/pm/rls/fs/2019/288737.htm.

Wezeman, Pieter D., Fleurant, Aude, Kuimova, Alexandra, Tian, Nan, and Siemon T. Wezeman. "Trends in International Arms Transfers, 2017." *SIPRI*. Stockhold International Peace Research Institute. March 2018. Retrieved from https://www.sipri.org/sites/default/files/2018-03/fssipri_at2017_0.pdf.

Whiteside, Eric. "Top 5 Shareholders of Lockheed Martin (LMT)." *Investopedia*. Mar 5, 2018. Retrieved from https://www.investopedia.com/articles/personal-finance/081416/top-5-shareholders-lockheed-martin-lmt.asp.

Notes

1. Wezeman et al., "Trends in International Arms Transfers, 2017."
2. "U.S. Arms Sales and Defense Trade," *Department of State*.
3. Fleurant et al., "The SIPRI Top 100 Arms-Producing and Military Services Companies, 2017."
4. Bowler, "Which Country Dominates the Global Arms Trade?"
5. Uchitelle, "The U.S. Still Leans on the Military-Industrial Complex."
6. "Lockheed Martin," *Fortune*.
7. "Number of Employees at Defense Technology Supplier Lockheed Martin 2000-2018," *Statista*.
8. Whiteside, "Top 5 Shareholders of Lockheed Martin (LMT)."
9. Timmons, "US Defense Giants Show How American Capitalism Fails Taxpayers."
10. Ingraham, "The Entire Coal Industry Employs Fewer People Than Arby's."
11. Bove, Deiana, and Nisticò, "Global Arms Trade and Oil Dependence."

How the Arms Trade Is Used to Secure Access to Oil

By Vincenzo Bove
The Conversation, May 4, 2018

UK arms exports to Saudi Arabia increased by 175% in the first nine months of 2017 according to an investigation by the Campaign Against Arms Trade. Similarly, France and the US are major exporters of arms to the oil-rich Gulf state—in 2017 alone, they were worth around US$2.6 billion.

Selling weapons is a lucrative business. As well as the money to be made, the arms trade is also a barometer of the quality of relationships between states and it creates an interdependence that gives current and future recipient governments incentives to cooperate with arms suppliers.

Oil dependency is another reason. Sometimes this idea is disregarded as a conspiracy theory, but colleagues Claudio Deiana, Roberto Nisticò and I recently researched the extent to which oil-dependent countries transfer arms to oil-rich countries. It turns out it's a lot.

The international transfer of weapons is one of the most dynamic and lucrative sectors of international trade. By one estimate, from the Stockholm International Peace Research Institute, global transfers of major weapons have grown continuously since 2004 and between 2012 and 2016 reached its highest volume for any five-year period since the end of the Cold War. The value of the global arms trade in 2015 was at least US$91.3 billion, roughly equal to the GDP of Ukraine, or half of Greece's GDP.

Since no country is self-sufficient in arms production—even the US—most of the countries in the world import weapons.

. . .

At the same time, the export of arms is a key part of national policy—and weapons are often given only to close allies. It is not unusual to observe arms transferred for free to allies, under the umbrella of military aid, such as US military support to Colombia to fight drug cartels and insurgent groups. Equally, the absence of trade in arms between two countries can reflect a desire to safeguard national security. For example, if there are fears that the importing nation can become a future threat.

The Oil Connection

To test the idea that energy dependence leads to a higher volume of arms transfers between countries, we assembled a large dataset with information on oil wealth (such as production, reserves and recent discoveries) and oil trade data, to measure energy interdependence and the potential damage of regional instabilities to oil supplies.

We found the existence of a "local oil dependence", which indicates that the amount of arms imported has a direct relationship with the amount of oil exported to the arms supplier. Speculatively, arms export to a specific country is affected by the degree of dependence on its supply of oil. The larger the amount of oil that country A imports from country B, the larger will be the volume of arms that country A will transfer to country B.

But we did not only find the existence of a direct oil-for-weapons relationship. Our results also reveal the presence of a "global oil dependence". The more a country depends on oil imports, the higher the incentives are to export weapons to oil-rich economies, even in the absence of a direct bilateral oil-for-weapons exchange. The idea is that by providing weapons, the oil-dependent country seeks to contain the risk of instabilities in an oil-rich country.

The oil-rich country does not necessarily need to be the oil-dependent's direct supplier, however, because disruptions in the production of oil are likely to affect oil prices worldwide. Violent events such as civil wars or terrorist incidents are often accompanied by surging oil prices, or more general insecurity in the supply of oil.

> **Speculatively, arms export to a specific country is affected by the degree of dependence on its supply of oil.**

This was the case in many recent wars, such as the Gulf War and the Iraq War, the political unrest in Venezuela in 2003, and the recent Iraq-Kurdistan conflict.

So it does not matter how much oil the UK directly imports from Saudi Arabia for it to want the country to remain stable, which in turn keeps oil prices stable. In line with this, we found that a country with a recent discovery of new oil fields will increase its import of weapons from oil-dependent economies by 56%.

Our results point consistently toward the conclusion that the arms trade is an effective foreign policy tool to secure and maintain access to oil. As such, the arms trade reveals national interests beyond simple economic considerations and the volume of bilateral arms transfers can be used as a barometer of political relations between the supplier and the recipient states. At the same time, we find that oil might play an even larger role in influencing economic and political decisions than is generally acknowledged.

Print Citations

CMS: Bove, Vincenzo. "How the Arms Trade Is Used to Secure Access to Oil." In *The Reference Shelf: U.S. National Debate Topic 2019-2020 Arms Sales,* edited by Micah L. Issitt, 51-53. Amenia, NY: Grey House Publishing, 2019.

MLA: Bove, Vincenzo. "How the Arms Trade Is Used to Secure Access to Oil." *The Reference Shelf: U.S. National Debate Topic 2019-2020 Arms Sales,* edited by Micah L. Issitt, Grey House Publishing, 2019, pp. 51-53.

APA: Bove, V. (2019). How the arms trade is used to secure access to oil. In Micah L. Issitt (Ed.), *The reference shelf: U.S. national debate topic 2019-2020 arms sales* (pp. 51-53). Amenia, NY: Grey House Publishing.

The Global Arms Trade Is Booming: Buyers Are Spoiled for Choice

The Economist, **August 18, 2018**

Only a few months ago, Canadians were earnestly debating whether or not the country's Liberal administration was right to go ahead with executing a $12bn contract to deliver armoured vehicles to Saudi Arabia. The government said it would, but acknowledged its critics' concerns by agreeing to adopt a version of an international treaty that limits arms sales to rogues.

However, things took a different turn. It was the Saudis who plunged the deal into uncertainty. After Canada's foreign minister urged the release of some political prisoners on Twitter, the Saudi government declared that all new business with Canada was suspended. This left Canadians unsure if the kingdom still wants the arms deal. And if the Saudis do walk away, plenty of other countries will be happy to supply armoured cars. "They could get their combat vehicles from Turkey, South Korea or Brazil," says Pieter Wezeman, a researcher at SIPRI, a Stockholm-based think-tank.

In the United States, meanwhile, Congress has been pressing the administration to implement the letter of a law that would force countries to make a hard, instant choice between buying American or Russian weapons. But the Pentagon is hinting that America's huge diplomatic power does not quite stretch that far. Defence officials argue it would be better to accept that some countries will go on buying Russian weapons for a while, in the hope they will gradually kick the habit.

Both these developments reflect the volatile (and from a Western viewpoint, barely controllable) state of the global arms market. Total demand is growing, the number of sellers is rising and the Western countries that have dominated the business are less confident of shaping the playing field. Above all, buyers are becoming more insistent on their right to shop around. For the likes of India, Saudi Arabia, Egypt and the United Arab Emirates, "this is a buyer's market," says Lucie Béraud-Sudreau of the International Institute for Strategic Studies, a London-based think-tank.

Speak Softly and Sell a Big Stick

The numbers show that the global commerce in conventional weapons is still dominated by the United States. But America feels strangely nervous about maintaining that role, and this year it has adopted a more aggressive sales posture. Under a policy proclaimed in April and mapped out in more detail last month, American diplomats have been told to promote weapons sales more actively and speed up procedures for approving them.

> **The jumpiness in Washington, DC, stems from the entry to the market of new competitors, especially China.**

At first sight, American apprehensions seem puzzling. There are several ways to measure the arms market, but America comes out on top of all of them. SIPRI has studied the volume of cross-border weapon transfers over the five years to December and compared them with the previous five years.

The size of the world market rose by 10% between the two periods. In the more recent one, America's slice of this expanding pie was 34%, up from 30% in the previous five years. America and its five nearest rivals (in descending order Russia, France, Germany, China and Britain), account for nearly 80% of total transfers.

Britain, meanwhile, claims that last year it jumped to third place among global arms exporters, as measured by the value of their sales. According to the Defence and Security Organisation, a government body, America bagged 53% of the global business, its "highest-ever market share". This left 16% for Russia and 12% for Britain, double the share taken by France.

In part, the jumpiness in Washington, DC, stems from the entry to the market of new competitors, especially China. In part it reflects new products and technologies where America will struggle to keep its lead. Both these challenges were highlighted by the appearance at last year's Paris Air Show of a Chinese military drone that looked very like the American unmanned aircraft that have been used for assassinations, for example in Pakistan. Hitherto, America has been willing to share these powerful drones only with close European allies. A new policy will broaden the range of customers and thus lessen the risk that China will dominate a market that could soon be worth $50bn a year.

China has long been better known as a buyer of arms, mainly from Russia, than as a seller. A big share of its arms deliveries have gone to close allies such as Pakistan. But it has enormously increased its capacity to make and sell its own weapons, including ships and submarines.

Meanwhile, American arms-export policy has been a delicate balance between, on the one hand, seizing economic and geopolitical opportunity and, on the other, being careful not to share technologies which could destabilise war zones or be used against the United States.

But such caution can be counter-productive. At a panel discussion in Washington this month, a defence-industry advocate lamented that, because of America's technology-transfer curbs, France had won from it a contract to sell airborne radar to India. "I like the French, but I like American industry even more," he grumbled.

In another Franco-American contest over technology, France is finding it hard to sell more Rafale combat aircraft to its prize arms customer, Egypt, because the accompanying Scalp cruise missile incorporates American know-how, the transfer of which to third parties is barred. France has promised to develop its own technology, but Egypt may not have the patience to wait. Egypt's government has also been a keen purchaser of Russian equipment, including aircraft and attack helicopters.

For defence-equipment manufacturers such as Britain and France, export sales matter ever more as a way to maintain their own industries. Britain's edge in military aviation may depend on its sales to Saudi Arabia. And the Royal Navy's ambitious building programme got a boost when Australia said it would buy British for a new range of frigates. France wants to develop a new air-to-air missile, but only, as Florence Parly, the defence minister, put it, if it can get foreign customers.

Such desperation adds to the frenzy of market competition. So does the utter indifference Russia and China display towards their customers' human-rights policies. So too does the growth in the number of countries that have graduated from being mainly buyers of weapons and knowhow to sellers—Turkey, the Emirates and South Korea, for example.

Japan, which boasts a huge defence industry, is entirely new to the market. It plunged in when the government lifted restrictions on arms exports in 2014. It competes, albeit from a fairly weak position, with China for Asia-Pacific customers.

As for Russia, SIPRI calculates that its share of the global market has slipped (to about 22% in 2013-17). But it offers a blend of tried-and-tested hardware and, to a few customers, superb know-how, especially in air defence.

That creates a dilemma for America, which hopes soon to sell weapons worth $6bn to India, but is dismayed by that country's determination to acquire S-400 air-defence systems from Russia: missiles that could ward off potential threats from China or Pakistan. Other countries intent on continuing to buy Russian include Indonesia and Vietnam.

Jim Mattis, America's defence secretary, has implored Congress not to be too harsh with Russia's customers, so long as they pledge gradually to reduce their reliance. In a letter leaked in July to Breaking Defense, a specialist news service, he told a congressman: "We are faced with a once-in-a-lifetime opportunity to decrease Russia's dominance in key regions." But that could only happen if America were free to sell its own weapons. For customers, that means that for the foreseeable future they can keep both American and Russian weapons in their arsenals.

It is telling that India has recently been admitted to the Missile Technology Control Regime, a group of countries which promises not to help pariah states obtain ballistic missiles. That will make it easier for both America and Russia to sell long-range rockets to India. The two arms-sales giants, who do not agree on much else, have welcomed India into the club.

Print Citations

CMS: "The Global Arms Trade Is Booming: Buyers Are Spoiled for Choice." In *The Reference Shelf: U.S. National Debate Topic 2019-2020 Arms Sales,* edited by Micah L. Issitt, 54-57. Amenia, NY: Grey House Publishing, 2019.

MLA: "The Global Arms Trade Is Booming: Buyers Are Spoiled for Choice." *The Reference Shelf: U.S. National Debate Topic 2019-2020 Arms Sales,* edited by Micah L. Issitt, Grey House Publishing, 2019, pp. 54-57.

APA: The Economist. (2019). The global arms trade is booming: Buyers are spoiled for choice. In Micah L. Issitt (Ed.), *The reference shelf: U.S. national debate topic 2019-2020 arms sales* (pp. 54-57). Amenia, NY: Grey House Publishing.

Defense Firms Say Trump's Saudi Arms Deal Will Create 500 American Jobs, While Trump Claimed as Many as 500,000

By Mike Stone

Business Insider, October 30, 2018

WASHINGTON (Reuters)—Every time President Donald Trump mentions the $110 billion arms deal he negotiated with Saudi Arabia last year, he quickly follows up, saying "It's 500,000 jobs."

But if he means new U.S. defense jobs, an internal document seen by Reuters from Lockheed Martin forecasts fewer than 1,000 positions would be created by the defense contractor, which could potentially deliver around $28 billion of goods in the deal.

Lockheed instead predicts the deal could create nearly 10,000 new jobs in Saudi Arabia, while keeping up to 18,000 existing U.S. workers busy if the whole package comes together—an outcome experts say is unlikely.

A person familiar with Raytheon's planning said if the Saudi order were executed it could help to sustain about 10,000 U.S. jobs, but the number of new jobs created would be a small percentage of that figure.

Lockheed Martin Corp declined to comment on the Saudi package. Raytheon Co's Chief Financial Officer Toby O'Brien said last week that hiring overall is growing, but he did not pin it to any particular program.

The White House did not immediately respond to a request for comment.

Jobs are important to Trump. He campaigned on his ability to create American jobs, especially high-paying manufacturing ones. Meanwhile he has limited his criticism of Saudi leadership over the killing of a prominent critic because he did not want to endanger the massive arms deal.

Trump's 500,000 figure has been greeted with widespread skepticism given the five biggest U.S. defense contractors, who make nearly every item on the Saudi list, now employ 383,000 people.

Documents seen by *Reuters* and interviews with defense industry sources familiar with the arms package suggest that between 20,000 and 40,000 current U.S. defense industry workers could be involved in Saudi-bound production if the whole $110 billion package goes through.

Existing workers typically are experienced, skilled, who can be redeployed more easily than new hires who would require significant upfront investment in their training.

One significant caveat to any predictions on job creation is whether all of the missile defenses and radars, ships, tanks, software, bombs and other equipment listed in the full Saudi package get delivered.

Saudi Arabia Jobs

Interviews with people familiar with other major defense contractors' plans and estimates reflect similar dynamic as Lockheed's and Raytheon's plans—relatively minor additions to their U.S. workforce and more significant build-up in Saudi Arabia.

Since Trump's trip to the Kingdom last year, little economic activity has taken place beyond Lockheed's work on four frigates the Saudis have ordered.

The order will yield nearly 10,000 jobs in the Saudi ports for maintenance workers, but only 500 new U.S. jobs will be created, according to documents seen by Reuters.

Executives at the several of top U.S. defense companies say Riyadh had wanted much of the military equipment as a way to both develop new domestic industry and to create new jobs and local expertise as a part of Crown Prince Mohammed bin Salman's Vision 2030 initiative to wean the country off oil dependency.

Saudi Arabia has set a goal of creating 40,000 defense industry jobs by 2030.

The arms package Trump announced in May 2017 came under renewed scrutiny after the Oct. 2 killing of *Washington Post* columnist Jamal Khashoggi in the Saudi consulate in Istanbul. The killing provoked international outrage and both the

> **Trump has limited his criticism of Saudi leadership over the killing of a prominent critic because he did not want to endanger the massive arms deals.**

administration and defense contractors have been working to prevent a backlash that could imperil what Trump has called a "tremendous order" and 500,000 jobs.

Industry executives have argued that without the Saudi package coming through they would have fewer orders to fill, but robust U.S. defense budgets, which account for the majority of their sales, coupled with a record backlog of orders suggest little risk that workers would face layoffs if the Saudi sales package failed to materialize.

Certainly for each defense manufacturing job, other adjacent jobs are supported indirectly by higher demand for defense products.

But Heidi Garrett-Peltier, a research fellow at the Political Economy Research Institute, estimated that for this type of industry the highest multiplier would be just below 3.2. Given that, 20,000 to 40,000 sustained or new jobs could generate between about 64,000 to 128,000 jobs in related industries, Reuters calculations show, bringing the total of sustained and new jobs to between 84,000 and 168,000.

In short, 500,000 jobs Trump keeps bringing up is at least three to five times higher than what one could expect from the Saudi deal, given the estimates from the companies themselves, plus the most generous use of the indirect multiplier.

By its own math, the U.S. State Department said in May 2017 that the Saudi deal could support "tens of thousands of new jobs in the United States."

Print Citations

CMS: Stone, Mike. "Defense Firms Say Trump's Saudi Arms Deal Will Create 500 American Jobs, While Trump Claimed as Many as 500,000." In *The Reference Shelf: U.S. National Debate Topic 2019-2020 Arms Sales,* edited by Micah L. Issitt, 58-60. Amenia, NY: Grey House Publishing, 2019.

MLA: Stone, Mike. "Defense Firms Say Trump's Saudi Arms Deal Will Create 500 American Jobs, While Trump Claimed as Many as 500,000." *The Reference Shelf: U.S. National Debate Topic 2019-2020 Arms Sales,* edited by Micah L. Issitt, Grey House Publishing, 2019, pp. 58-60.

APA: Stone, M. (2019). Defense firms say Trump's Saudi arms deal will create 500 American jobs, while Trump claimed as many as 500,000. In Micah L. Issitt (Ed.), *The reference shelf: U.S. national debate topic 2019-2020 arms sales* (pp. 58-60). Amenia, NY: Grey House Publishing.

Trump to Unleash More Global Arms Sales

By Bryan Bender and Tara Palmeri
Politico, September 29, 2017

President Donald Trump is preparing to ease some restrictions on U.S. weapons sales overseas, sparking concerns about further flooding the international market with high-tech weapons and inflaming feuds in hot spots like the Middle East.

The changes, which could include enlisting the State Department and Pentagon to more actively advocate on behalf of American arms manufacturers, are set to be included in an executive order or presidential memorandum that Trump will issue this fall, according to three administration officials involved in the deliberations.

The U.S. is already the global leader in weapons exports, accounting for more than half the world's annual arms deals. The new "arms transfer initiative," being run out of the White House National Security Council, aims to make U.S. companies more competitive when allies are shopping for fighter jets, ground vehicles, warships, missile defenses and other military gear in an intensely competitive market, the officials told *Politico*.

Those efforts would include establishing a more active government role in pushing U.S. products, beyond what military and diplomatic officials already do to help defense firms sell their wares internationally. This could also strengthen the defense industrial base and create jobs on production lines that Pentagon investments don't fully support.

"It is about making sure we are doing everything we can to promote the competitiveness of American trade," said a State Department official involved in the discussions who, like the other sources, was not authorized to speak publicly. "The message from the NSC is we can certainly be doing more."

The changes, which officials insist are also intended to enhance Americans' interests around the world, would be the latest in a series of moves by Trump to relax former President Barack Obama's restrictions on U.S. military activities.

The Trump administration recently launched a review of export regulations governing drone technology that had been put in place in 2015, and is also reported to be taking steps to make it easier for American arms manufacturers to sell to international buyers.

It has also green-lighted sales of precision-guided munitions to Saudi Arabia that the Obama administration held up over concerns they have been used to kill civilians in the offensive against rebels in Yemen. In addition, Trump has reversed restrictions on arms sales that were in place for Bahrain and Nigeria.

Overall, new data show that in the first eight months of 2017, the total value of U.S. arms transfer notifications has nearly doubled—to $48 billion—compared with the same period in 2016. Those figures are for arms sales conducted directly between the companies and foreign customers—known as direct commercial sales—as well as those conducted through the Foreign Military Sales process, which is overseen by the Pentagon's Defense Security Cooperation Agency.

"Do they want to move from a position to where U.S. companies dominate the world market, to where they are crushing the competition?" asked William Hartung, director of the Arms and Security Project at the Center for International Policy, a Washington think tank. "I don't know how much of a bigger footprint they could have."

The administration's new push involves the departments of State, Defense and Commerce, which have authority over the export of military equipment and are drawing up proposals for White House review. Two officials said they expect an order from Trump as early as October.

Among the areas under review, the officials said, are revamping the Conventional Arms Transfer Policy, which lays out the criteria for selling military-grade weapons to foreign nations. The administration is also seeking to make "more user friendly" the International Traffic in Arms Regulations, which have not been significantly rewritten since 1984, another State Department official said.

Streamlining the process by which U.S. companies can obtain export licenses for weapons sales has long been a major lobbying objective of the defense industry, whose advocates complain that even recent changes in the process are not enough to ensure they remain competitive.

Some leading industry associations express concern that the U.S. lead is at risk of slipping.

"While the United States dominates the global aerospace and defense export market, a shifting business and political landscape, coupled with domestic acquisition hurdles, are constricting industry's competitive edge," maintains the National Defense Industrial Association, which represents many leading arms manufacturers.

Tina S. Kaidanow, the acting assistant secretary of State who runs the Bureau of Political-Military Affairs, recently hinted at the administration's objectives.

"We are developing this initiative because the Administration believes that strengthening the defense capabilities of U.S. allies bolsters our ability to protect the United States by being a force multiplier for the U.S. warfighter, and ultimately benefits U.S. industry by driving new innovation and creating high-quality American jobs," she told a Capitol Hill event hosted by the Aerospace Industries Association.

Another potentially controversial step the administration is considering would develop new ways to leverage U.S. diplomacy to help companies get a leg up on foreign contracts. The U.S. government already plays a role in helping American companies compete, including deploying security assistance officers from the Pentagon and State Department who work out of U.S embassies.

In a response to questions from *Politico*, the NSC said the administration "has undertaken a review of our policy on arms sales and wherever possible is working to remove unreason-

Any moves to make it easier for U.S. companies to sell arms is likely to raise concerns, especially in conflict zones or in countries with shoddy records on democracy and human rights.

able constraints on the ability of our companies to compete."

But it also stressed that removing constraints cannot come at the expense of U.S. foreign policy interests. Those include ensuring that sensitive technologies do not fall into the wrong hands, become used for unintended purposes or are used against American troops or interests.

"The Trump Administration is pursuing a deliberate approach to our arms export policy, ensuring that such sales better align with our national security and foreign policy objectives as well as economic imperatives for American jobs," the statement said. "The Administration is intent on ensuring that U.S. industry has every advantage in the global marketplace, while at the same time ensuring the responsible export of arms and dual-use technologies."

But any moves to make it easier for U.S. companies to sell arms is likely to raise concerns, especially in conflict zones or in countries with shoddy records on democracy and human rights.

"The questions I would have are what are the motivations?" said Rachel Stohl, who directs the Conventional Defense Program at the Stimson Center, a nonpartisan think tank. "The United States is the world's largest arms exporter. Are there markets closed to the United States? Yes. Are there reasons they are closed? Yes. Are those reasons good? I think they are."

She added: "While you can always improve bureaucratic process, those fundamental goals of supporting our foreign policy and supporting democracy and human rights need to be recognized. My concern is there is such an emphasis on selling more that we are losing the notion of restraint and why that restraint exists. I don't believe the argument that 'if we don't sell to them, someone else will,' is reason to go into a new market.

Hartung, another skeptic of increased foreign arms trade, said he believes the move "is about jobs, jobs, jobs. I think Trump is more focused on that than Obama was."

He noted that many of the big-ticket weapons the United States is pushing are those the U.S. doesn't purchase anymore or buys only in small numbers, "like F-15s and F-16s."

"More of it is domestic pork-barrel politics dressed up as national security," Hartung said.

The White House insists such sentiments are off the mark.

"President Trump knows that success of our companies in the global marketplace means job creation at home and better economic benefits overall for the

United States," the NSC said. "While some policy changes are likely forthcoming, it is important to remember that there are reasons for limiting the sales of certain types of systems to certain potential customers. We need to make sure that these systems are sold to and operated by those who are able to use them properly and for legitimate purposes, such as counterterrorism, and are not used to deliver weapons of mass destruction or otherwise undermine our interests."

Print Citations

CMS: Bender, Bryan, and Tara Palmeri. "Trump to Unleash More Global Arms Sales." In *The Reference Shelf: U.S. National Debate Topic 2019-2020 Arms Sales,* edited by Micah L. Issitt, 61-64. Amenia, NY: Grey House Publishing, 2019.

MLA: Bender, Bryan, and Tara Palmeri. "Trump to Unleash More Global Arms Sales." *The Reference Shelf: U.S. National Debate Topic 2019-2020 Arms Sales,* edited by Micah L. Issitt, Grey House Publishing, 2019, pp. 61-64.

APA: Bender, B., & T. Palmeri. (2019). Trump to unleash more global arms sales. In Micah L. Issitt (Ed.), *The reference shelf: U.S. national debate topic 2019-2020 arms sales* (pp. 61-64). Amenia, NY: Grey House Publishing.

Arming the World: Inside Trump's "Buy American" Drive to Expand Weapons Exports

By Matt Spetalnick and Mike Stone
Reuters, April 17, 2018

WASHINGTON (Reuters)—In a telephone call with the emir of Kuwait in January, U.S. President Donald Trump pressed the Gulf monarch to move forward on a $10 billion fighter jet deal that had been stalled for more than a year.

Trump was acting on behalf of Boeing Co (BA.N), America's second-largest defense contractor, which had become frustrated that a long-delayed sale critical to its military aircraft division was going nowhere, several people familiar with the matter said.

With this Oval Office intervention, the details of which have not been previously reported, Trump did something unusual for a U.S. president—he personally helped to close a major arms deal. In private phone calls and public appearances with world leaders, Trump has gone further than any of his predecessors to act as a salesman for the U.S. defense industry, analysts said.

Trump's personal role underscores his determination to make the United States, already dominant in the global weapons trade, an even bigger arms merchant to the world, U.S. officials say, despite concerns from human rights and arms control advocates.

Those efforts will be bolstered by the full weight of the U.S. government when Trump's administration rolls out a new "Buy American" initiative this week aimed at allowing more countries to buy more and even bigger weapons. It will loosen U.S. export rules on equipment ranging from fighter jets and drones to warships and artillery, the officials said.

Reuters has learned that the initiative—which industry sources said will be announced on Thursday—will provide guidelines that could allow more countries to be granted faster deal approvals, possibly trimming back to months what has often taken years to finalize.

The strategy will call for members of Trump's cabinet to sometimes act as "closers" to help seal major arms deals, according to people familiar with the matter. More top government officials will also be sent to promote U.S. weapons at international air shows and arms bazaars.

Shares of major U.S. defense contractors added to gains after the news and Raytheon hit an all-time high.

Human rights and arms control advocates warn that the proliferation of a broader range of advanced weaponry to more

> **The Trump administration stresses that the main aims are to help American defense firms compete better against increasingly aggressive Russian and Chinese manufacturers.**

foreign governments could increase the risk of arms being diverted into the wrong hands and fueling violence in regions such as the Middle East and South Asia.

The Trump administration stresses that the main aims are to help American defense firms compete better against increasingly aggressive Russian and Chinese manufacturers and give greater weight than before to economic benefits of arms sales to create more jobs at home.

One Trump aide, speaking on condition of anonymity, said the new initiative is also intended to ease human rights restrictions that have sometimes led to an effective "veto" over certain arms deals.

"This policy seeks to mobilize the full resources of the United States government behind arms transfers that are in the U.S. national and economic security interest," a White House official said, responding to a request for comment on the story.

"We recognize that arms transfers may have important human rights consequences," the official said. "Nothing in this policy changes existing legal or regulatory requirements in this regard."

One of the main architects of the new policy has been economist Peter Navarro, a China trade skeptic ascendant in Trump's inner circle. His effort to boost arms exports has drawn little resistance within the White House, officials said.

"Whole of Government"

The initiative has been in the works for months and some of its expected components have already been reported. But with the rollout nearing, more than a dozen industry sources and current and former U.S. officials have provided Reuters with the most complete picture yet of Trump's policy, though they caution that last-minute changes are still possible.

The policy will call for a "whole of government" approach—from the president and his cabinet on down to military attaches and diplomats—to help drum up billions of dollars more in arms business overseas, U.S. officials said.

It will also call for cutting red tape to secure faster deal approval on a broader range of weaponry for NATO members, Saudi Arabia and other Gulf partners as well as treaty allies such as Japan and South Korea, among others, they said. Many details will remain classified.

Companies that stand to benefit most include Boeing and the other top U.S. defense contractors, Lockheed Martin Corp (LMT.N) , Raytheon Co (RTN.N), General Dynamics Corp (GD.N) and Northrop Grumman Corp (NOC.N). All of their shares have surged by double-digit percentages, led by the doubling of Boeing's stock price, since Trump took office in January 2017.

Trump's aides also want more senior officials to attend major international arms shows, including cabinet members such as Defense Secretary Jim Mattis and Commerce Secretary Wilbur Ross, to promote U.S.-made weapons the way countries such as France and Israel pitch their companies' wares.

"If you go to the Paris air show, you see the French foreign minister standing in front of the Airbus pavilion," one U.S. official said. "We're getting outplayed so we have to change our culture."

In addition to the broad arms export initiative, Trump is expected to sign a separate document easing exports of military drones, an item high on foreign governments' shopping lists, officials said.

U.S. foreign military sales totaled $42 billion last year, according to the U.S. Defense Security Cooperation Agency. Experts say exports from Russia, the largest U.S. competitor, are typically half those of the United States.

The Aerospace Industries Association trade group said it had first lobbied Trump during the 2016 presidential campaign on the need for "bolstering U.S. manufacturing" and encouraging allies to take more responsibility for their own security.

Salesman-in-Chief

While many presidents have helped promote the U.S. defense industry, none is known to have done so as unabashedly as Trump, a former real estate developer who seems sometimes at his most comfortable when he is promoting U.S. goods.

Trump regularly discusses specific arms sales with foreign leaders in meetings and on the phone, according to White House statements. And on a trip to Japan last November, he publicly urged Prime Minister Shinzo Abe to buy more American weapons.

More recently, at an Oval Office meeting with Saudi Crown Prince Mohammed bin Salman last month, Trump held up posters with pictures of U.S. jets, ships and helicopters and other armaments sold to Saudi Arabia. "We make the best military product in the world," he boasted to reporters as the prince sat smiling beside him.

Other presidents, including Richard Nixon, Bill Clinton and George W. Bush stressed the need to strengthen the defense industrial base, but they did it more subtly, said William Hartung, director of the arms and security project at the Center for International Policy, a non-partisan think tank.

"Nobody's been as blatant about it as Trump," he added. "Nobody has yelled it from the rooftops."

Former President Barack Obama would sometimes talk to allied leaders about weapons systems that he felt suited their security needs, but aides said he preferred to keep weapons salesmanship at arm's length.

The Trump administration's plan to overhaul the Conventional Arms Transfer policy, the framework for evaluating foreign sales, goes well beyond Obama's relaxation of rules in 2014 that enabled U.S. arms contractors to sell more overseas than ever before. Obama drew a clear line, however, requiring each sale to meet strict human rights standard—though he was criticized at times for allowing some controversial sales.

Trump has already gone ahead with several deals that Obama blocked, including the sale of $7 billion in precision-guided munitions to Saudi Arabia despite human rights groups' concerns they have contributed to civilian deaths in the Saudi-led campaign in Yemen's civil war.

Anatomy of a Trump-Era Deal

How Boeing's Kuwait deal got on Trump's agenda for the Jan. 17 call with Kuwait's Emir Sheikh Sabah Al-Ahmad Al-Jaber al-Sabah illustrates how seriously the administration is taking the arms export push.

The State Department granted approval in November 2016, in the final months of the Obama administration, for Kuwait to buy 40 F/A-18 Super Hornet strike fighters.

But Kuwait, a U.S. Gulf ally, appeared to drag out negotiations, U.S. officials and industry sources said, and the purchase was still not finalized by the time the emir visited Trump at the White House last September.

Trump told reporters at the time that, at the Kuwaiti leader's request, he had intervened and won State Department authorization for the deal—a false claim since that approval had already been granted nearly a year earlier.

Months later, Boeing's request for a presidential nudge to Kuwait was channeled to National Security Council aides, who included it among Trump's "talking points" for the January phone call, two people close to the matter said.

This time, Trump did make a difference. Just days later, Kuwaiti state media reported the deal was done.

The Kuwaiti government did not respond to requests for comment. A Boeing spokesman declined comment.

Print Citations

CMS: Spetalnick, Matt, and Mike Stone. "Arming the World: Inside Trump's 'Buy American' Drive to Expand Weapons Exports." In *The Reference Shelf: U.S. National Debate Topic 2019-2020 Arms Sales,* edited by Micah L. Issitt, 65-68. Amenia, NY: Grey House Publishing, 2019.

MLA: Spetalnick, Matt, and Mike Stone. "Arming the World: Inside Trump's 'Buy American' Drive to Expand Weapons Exports." *The Reference Shelf: U.S. National Debate Topic 2019-2020 Arms Sales,* edited by Micah L. Issitt, Grey House Publishing, 2019, pp. 65-68.

APA: Spetalnick, M., & M. Stone. (2019). Arming the world: Inside Trump's "buy American" drive to expand weapons exports. In Micah L. Issitt (Ed.), *The reference shelf: U.S. national debate topic 2019-2020 arms sales* (pp. 65-68). Amenia, NY: Grey House Publishing.

Why Congress Supports Saudi Arms Sales

By Oleg Svet

The National Interest, **September 26, 2016**

Senators Rand Paul and Chris Murphy recently proposed a congressional resolution to stop a $1.15 billion arms sale to Saudi Arabia. Their measure failed on a 26-71 vote this past Wednesday. Their case rested in large part on the fact that Riyadh's intervention in Yemen—conducted with American-made weapons—has cost an untold number of innocent lives in the Arabian Peninsula. While their argument carried weight from a humanitarian perspective, it did not make sense in terms of the impact it would have on American jobs, U.S. companies, and the wider defense industry.

On a local level, hundreds of American jobs in the proposed sale are at stake. The most important aspect of the deal is the proposed purchase of Abrams tanks. Some of these tanks will be used as "battle damage replacement" for tanks lost by the Saudi military in Yemen. Riyadh also ordered a General Dynamics-produced system to recover tanks damaged on the battlefield. The Abrams tanks are produced by General Dynamics' Combat Systems division in a plant in Lima, Ohio. About a decade ago the Lima plant employed 1,200 workers. Over the past few years, with declines in Defense Department purchases of weapons produced at the plant (including a 7 percent decrease in sales this quarter compared to the same period last year), the number of workers in the plant has dropped to four hundred. Stopping the sale to Saudi Arabia of such tanks would not only have put in jeopardy the remaining jobs at the Lima plant, but also put at risk larger deals with Saudi Arabia and our other Gulf allies, which themselves carry billions of dollars in revenue for American companies and are associated with tens of thousands of jobs in nearly every state in America.

When considering this particular sale it is important to keep in mind the big picture of U.S. defense exports and their contribution to America's defense industry. Over the past six years, as U.S. defense spending has faced considerable budgetary pressures, American defense companies have struggled to maintain employees and keep production lines open. With tightening defense budgets, highly-skilled manufacturing jobs on the line, and the prospect of production lines for advanced U.S. weapons being phased out, American exports of defense articles and services have become and will continue to be ever more important.

Saudi Arabia has emerged as the dominant purchaser of American arms. In 2010 Riyadh signed a record $60 billion deal to buy defense articles made by American companies. Under the deal, it agreed to spend $30 billion up front on fighter jets, helicopters, and other systems. That purchase is equivalent to a large chunk of the U.S. defense budget. In fact, the contribution is much larger, relatively speaking, when one looks at how it benefits the smaller defense companies that service American and foreign defense customers. The 2010 deal with Saudi Arabia entailed purchasing American jet fighters that will help manufacturers in forty-four states and aid in protecting seventy-seven thousand jobs.

Importantly, the 2010 Saudi deal included the purchase of eighty-four new F-15 fighters. The prime contractor was Boeing, a hundred-year-old American multinational company that consistently ranks as one of the world's most admired companies. Until recently, Boeing produced only one F-15 per month, and the production line for F-15s was on the verge of being closed, that is, until the deal with Saudi Arabia. Riyadh's purchase helped save thousands of jobs for Americans working on Boeing's F-15 production line on the outskirts of Lambert-St. Louis International Airport. Boeing also makes Apache helicopters, and the Saudi deal included the purchase of seventy Apaches. As *Fortune* reported, "Production lines for Boeing's F-15, Harpoon missile, and Apache helicopter are sustained by exports, which support thousands of high-paying, highly skilled manufacturing jobs." Saudi purchases help keep highly-skilled manufacturing jobs in the United States.

Maintaining a robust security cooperation relationship with Saudi Arabia also helps America's defense industry in the region as a whole. Saudi Arabia is the most important member of the Gulf Cooperation Council (GCC), which includes five other large purchasers of American defense articles: Bahrain, Kuwait, Oman, Qatar, and the United Arab Emirates. These countries are gradually creating a multinational, interoperable force that requires all of the countries to maintain similar weapons systems.

> **When Saudi Arabia purchases U.S. defense articles, other countries in the Gulf follow suit.**

When Saudi Arabia purchases U.S. defense articles, other countries in the Gulf follow suit. For example, a $7 billion deal to sell three dozen F-15 jets to Qatar and twenty-eight Boeing F/A-18E/F Super Hornets to Kuwait is currently in the works. Furthermore, in the crucial period from 2011 to 2015 (when U.S. defense spending was especially under strain), the UAE was the second-largest importer of U.S. defense articles, after Saudi Arabia. In 2015, the United States sold $33 billion in defense articles and services to the GCC countries. For large American defense companies, such exports are crucial. In recent years an estimated one-quarter of Raytheon's sales came from foreign purchases. A few years ago, the UAE's $3.3 billion order enabled Raytheon to restart the Patriot production line and add new features. Such purchases save highly-skilled manufacturing jobs in the United States, and, by adding advanced capabilities, will help win new customers unless Congress blocks them from happening.

If Senators Paul and Murphy would have succeeded in their measure, Riyadh would almost certainly have gone to another large military supplier, possibly Russia. Saudi and other GCC officials fear that Iran, which is not only ideologically and theologically diametrically opposed to the Kingdom, but also has a population and territory several times the size of Saudi Arabia, poses an existential threat. The uncomfortable truth is that Yemen is a proxy war in the Saudi-Iranian competition. Riyadh feels that it must win in Yemen against the Houthi rebels (who the Saudis are convinced are sponsored by Iran), and the only way to win is through military power. Saudi Arabia does not have an indigenous military industry to support the war; it has to find military suppliers to sustain its war effort. Had the sale been blocked and Saudi Arabia shifted to Russia, China, or other suppliers for military purchases, other Gulf States would have followed suit, putting in jeopardy an additional tens of billions of dollars in sales by American multinational companies and thousands of highly-skilled manufacturing jobs. Going forward, when considering whether to block arms sales to Saudi Arabia, therefore, Congress should not only worry about the particular sale in question. It should also consider the wider negative implications that a suspension would have on tens of thousands of high-skilled manufacturing jobs all across America, tens of billions of dollars in revenues for U.S. companies, and the wider defense industry.

Print Citations

CMS: Svet, Oleg. "Why Congress Supports Saudi Arms Sales." In *The Reference Shelf: U.S. National Debate Topic 2019-2020 Arms Sales,* edited by Micah L. Issitt, 69-71. Amenia, NY: Grey House Publishing, 2019.

MLA: Svet, Oleg. "Why Congress Supports Saudi Arms Sales." *The Reference Shelf: U.S. National Debate Topic 2019-2020 Arms Sales,* edited by Micah L. Issitt, Grey House Publishing, 2019, pp. 69-71.

APA: Svet, O. (2019). Why Congress supports Saudi arms sales. In Micah L. Issitt (Ed.), *The reference shelf: U.S. national debate topic 2019-2020 arms sales* (pp. 69-71). Amenia, NY: Grey House Publishing.

3
Arms and Foreign Policy

By April Brady, POMED, via Wikimedia.

Saudi journalist and *Washington Post* columnist Jamal Khashoggi was assassinated at the Saudi Arabian embassy in Istanbul in October of 2018 by agents of the Saudi government. The murder drew international censure and brought the Trump administration's proposed arms deal with Saudi Arabia into the spotlight.

Guns and Diplomats: The Arms Trade and Foreign Policy

It is often argued that the U.S. arms trade enables the United States to achieve international influence that ultimately enhances the nation's foreign policy objectives. Since World War I, the United States has used foreign arms deals to build or strengthen alliances and to strengthen the defensive capabilities of allied nations. Supporters believe that this ultimately decreases the likelihood that the United States will need to engage in direct military action. It is also argued that the United States must maintain its role in the international arms trade environment or risk allowing countries like China and Russia to fill any void. Such a situation would open the potential for these competing governments to increase their global influence to the perceived detriment of the United States and, some argue, the world.

According to the U.S. Department of State:

> Arms sales and defense trade are key tools of foreign policy with potential long-term implications for regional security. For this reason, the United States takes into account political, military, economic, arms control, and human rights conditions in making decisions on the provision of military equipment and the licensing of direct commercial sales to any country. Each proposed transfer is carefully assessed on a case-by-case basis and approved only if found to further U.S. foreign policy and national security interest.[1]

Despite this statement, research has called the foreign policy benefits of arms dealing into question. In the twenty-first century, most of the countries to which the United States has chosen to sell weapons are countries that do not mirror U.S. attitudes on human or political rights and there is little evidence to suggest that the U.S. arms trade stabilizes unstable regions. This is, in part, because the United States does not tie arms trades to human rights or political objectives and, instead, tends to deal weapons based more on economic than foreign policy considerations.[2]

Stabilization and the Support of Weak States

In a 1994 article in *Foreign Affairs*, conservative economic analyst Ethan Kapstein argued:

> For the first time in modern history, one country is on the verge of monopolizing the international arms trade. Rising costs and declining defense budgets are putting pressure on the world's inefficient defense producers, and most of them are collapsing under the strain. Soon the worldwide armaments industry will be nearly unrecognizable. By the early 21st century, the United States will be the sole producer of the world's most

advanced conventional weaponry, as other countries discover, like the Soviets did, that the costs associated with financing new defense programs are too heavy to manage.

In the mid-1990s, prior to the September 11, 2001 terrorist attacks and the massive expansion of U.S. overseas military activity that followed, Kapstein and like-minded theorists envisioned a global environment dominated by the United States, who might utilize its control over the global military industrial complex to extend its influence. As Kapstein argued in 1994:

> If exploited properly, this monopoly will benefit not only the United States but international security as well. The past proves that countries that rely on American arms are less likely to start wars with their neighbors. Ironically, a U.S. monopoly would also be good for the world economy. With inefficient defense firms put out of their costly misery, governments will be able to put scarce resources to more productive pursuits.[3]

Kapstein's article reflects two of the most common arguments in favor of U.S. arms trade: arms trade increases American security by enhancing the military capability of allies; and arms trade can stabilize areas suffering from persistent military and political instability, like parts of Africa and the Middle East.

The vision that Kapstein had for America's future did not happen. The United States remained the world's largest arms exporter into 2019 by a large margin, but this did not prevent either Russia's return to a position of power, or Russia from engaging in hostile foreign policy. U.S. arms trade dominance did not stabilize the Middle East or Africa, and violence and instability in both regions intensified markedly in the twenty-first century.

As of 2019, the United States was involved in pseudo-military operations and/ or arms trading with 100 countries, with the intention to reinforce "weak states" so that those states become stable and provide an "anchor" that can stabilize unstable regions. The idea is that when a region is fraught with conflict because of many powers competing for influence, the U. S. uses military agreements and arms trading to create a leading power. This leading power then helps develop the entire region according to the U.S. vision, which is ultimately based on what interests the United States has in the region. Arms trades to Saudi Arabia, therefore, are intended to maintain Saudi Arabia's military dominance in the Middle East, which grants U.S. diplomatic access to the region and secures America's primary interest in the region—access to oil.

Research indicates that arms trading is an ineffective way to create regional stability, largely because the problems contributing to regional instability are complex and cannot be solved by building up the militaries of the states in question. In societies plagued by deep economic, social and humanitarian issues, strengthening militaries or arming rebel groups tends to decrease stability and increase internal discord. Critics argue that the United States and other arms-dealing nations need to invest in fostering deeper economic changes within these countries and link arms trades to more substantive demands in terms of recipient behavior with regard to the use of those weapons.[4]

In 2018 and 2019, U.S. arms exports to the United Arab Emirates (UAE) and Saudi Arabia were among our most pressing national controversies. In the summer of 2018, it was revealed that the UAE and Saudi Arabia both made secret deals with the Al-Qaeda radical group, providing them with weapons, military equipment, and money, in an effort to recruit or influence members. The U. S. classifies Al-Qaeda as a terrorist group, and an enemy of the state, so weapons trades to the UAE and Saudi Arabia have inadvertently supported U.S. enemies in the region.[5] Further, the flow of weapons from America's arms-trade allies to radical sects may further destabilize the region by granting power to agents that seek to undermine America's influence and oppose existing governments supported or recognized by the United States throughout the region.

Global Influence

Another primary argument in favor of the U.S. arms trade is that it enables the United States to influence the foreign policy of other nations. For example, the World War II "Lend-Lease" policy had the United States providing arms and material support to World War II allies in return for "consideration," from the recipient nation of the objectives of the United States in terms of future economic or foreign policy decisions. The Lend-Lease program was a major factor in the United States' global influence during the Cold War, and the potential for arms dealing to grant influence over foreign nations remains one of the primary justifications for the continued practice among supporters.

Examining the U.S. alliance with Saudi Arabia provides an interesting test case for this theory. This alliance stretches back 70 years, to the founding of the Saudi Arabian kingdom, when Standard Oil Company of California (which became Chevron) began exploring for oil in the region, leading to a 1933 economic alliance between the United States and Saudi Arabia. During World War II, the United States began providing weapons to Saudi Arabia as a way to counter the growth of Iran and to maintain access to Saudi oil. Since 1950, the United States has transferred $90 billion in arms to Saudi Arabia, which has been touted as an important dimension to U.S. foreign policy as it enables the United States to maintain an ally in the region and provide a military counter against aggression by another Middle Eastern country.[6]

Over the years since the United States began its strategic alliance with the Saudi kingdom, stability in the Middle East has been an elusive goal, and U.S. economic interests in the region have been, in many cases, at odds with its strategic or diplomatic goals. For instance, weapons delivered to Saudi military were used to fight against the Soviet occupation of Afghanistan from 1979 to 1989, thus helping to influence foreign policy in Saudi Arabia in support of U.S. goals, specifically preventing Soviet powers from taking control of Afghanistan. The use of Saudi Arabia to help control the expansion of communism is an example of how the United States has used arms deals to meet foreign policy goals.

On the other hand, Saudi Arabia is also a source of instability in the region. Osama bin Laden, the son of the founder of Saudi Arabia's largest construction company, fought in the war with Russia in Afghanistan in the 1980s and broke with his family and the Saudi government over their alliance with the United States. Bin Laden's perception of America, as an indirect empire utilizing economic dominance and weapons dealing to exert its influence over the world, helped inspire the radical group Al-Qaeda, which then conducted the attacks on the United States on September 11, 2001. In the 2010s, it was discovered that Saudi Arabia had harbored anti-U.S. radicals in the 9/11 era.[7] The practice of dealing arms to Saudi Arabia and then using this influence to convince Saudi Arabia to participate in America's war against communism helped inspire the rise of radical Islamism and thus fueled the rise of extremism that poses the single greatest threat to national security in the twenty-first century. Saudi Arabia therefore is an example of both how arms dealing can be a tool to accomplish America's foreign policy goals, and how the arms trade inadvertently create new threats that ultimately undermine that policy.

Conflict and Controversy

In 2019, arms deals with Saudi Arabia and the UAE are just two that have drawn criticism. The United States also faces difficult arms trade issues Taiwan, a country mired in a decades-long power struggle with China. America's Taiwanese arms trades have been praised by those who consider Taiwanese independence a worthy goal, but have raised concern from those seeking to avoid conflict with China. Further, America's diplomatic activities between the Trump administration and North Korea have posed further diplomatic problems. Progress in diplomacy with North Korea hinges on U.S. military and arms support for allies like Japan and South Korea, both of which perceive a direct threat from the North Korean state.

The arms trade provides a significant boon to nations lacking the infrastructure to invest in domestic arms production, and the United States has been able to utilize the needs of other nations to exert a significant influence over foreign affairs. However, it is unclear whether this effort benefits the United States over the longer term. Ultimately, the economic and foreign policy goals of the arms trade may be incompatible. Were arms trades to significantly reduce global strife, demand for American weaponry would be reduced, thus reducing the economic benefit. Likewise, where instability increases, the arms trade thrives. Because the arms trade is both an industry and a foreign policy tool, those responsible for arms trading, both at the corporate and governmental level, face an industry marked by opposing forces that are never completely in balance.

Works Used:

Kapstein, Ethan B. "America's Arms-Trade Monopoly." *Foreign Affairs.* May/June 1994. Retrieved from https://www.foreignaffairs.com/articles/1994-05-01/americas-arms-trade-monopoly.

Karlin, Mara. "Why Military Assistance Programs Disappoint." *Brookings.* Nov/Dec 2017. Retrieved from https://www.brookings.edu/articles/why-military-assistance-programs-disappoint/.

Meshal, Sheikh and Hamad Al-Thani. "The United Arab Emirates and Saudi Arabia Are Aiding Terrorists in Yemen." *The Washington Post.* Aug 29, 2018. Retrieved from https://www.washingtonpost.com/news/global-opinions/wp/2018/08/29/the-united-arab-emirates-and-saudi-arabia-are-aiding-terrorists-in-yemen/?utm_term=.7119c03534ab.

Thrall, A. Trevor, and Caroline Dorminey. "Risky Business: The Role of Arms Sales in U.S. Foreign Policy." *Cato.* Cato Institute. Policy Analysis No 836. Mar 13, 2018. Retrieved from https://www.cato.org/publications/policy-analysis/risky-business-role-arms-sales-us-foreign-policy.

"U.S. Arms Sales and Defense Trade." *U.S. Department of States.* Bureau of Political-Military Affairs. Feb 4, 2019. Retrieved from https://www.state.gov/t/pm/rls/fs/2019/288737.htm.

"U.S.-Saudi Arabia Relations." *CFR.* Council on Foreign Relations. Dec 7, 2018. Retrieved from https://www.cfr.org/backgrounder/us-saudi-arabia-relations.

Wright, Lawrence. "The Twenty-Eight Pages." *The New Yorker.* Sep 9, 2014. Retrieved from https://www.newyorker.com/news/daily-comment/twenty-eight-pages.

Notes

1. "U.S. Arms Sales and Defense Trade," *U.S. Department of State.*
2. Thrall and Dorminey, "Risky Business: The Role of Arms Sales in U.S. Foreign Policy."
3. Kapstein, "America's Arms-Trade Monopoly."
4. Karlin, "Why Military Assistance Programs Disappoint."
5. Meshal and Al-Thani, "The United Arab Emirates and Saudi Arabia Are Aiding Terrorist in Yemen."
6. "U.S.-Saudi Arabia Relations," *CFR.*
7. Wright, "The Twenty-Eight Pages."

The Trump Administration Has a Plan to Compete with Russia and China over Weapon Sales

By Dave Majumdar
The National Interest, August 9, 2018

The Trump Administration is hoping to boost the export prospects for American weapons systems to allied countries by modifying policies and streamlining the bureaucratic process. The Trump Administration announced a revised conventional arms transfer policy in April, but that is just the first step. There are more policy changes coming down the line.

"The new policy reflects the priorities of the president's National Security Strategy," Ambassador Tina Kaidanow, Acting Assistant Secretary of State for Political-Military Affairs, said on Aug. 8 at the Center for Strategic and International Studies.

"Which are, namely, to preserve peace through strength by reforming regulations to facilitate the exports of U.S. military equipment; to strengthen partners and allies; to facilitate U.S. economic security and innovation."

Under the new policy, the United States hopes to make its export bureaucracy more proactive and cut red tape in the process.

"These steps are among the first in what we hope will be a series of efforts to streamline the arms transfer process," Kaidanow said.

"I can assure you that my colleagues and I at the State Department, but also again more broadly in the USG, will continue exploring ways to cut red tape and give U.S. industry every advantage in an increasingly competitive global marketplace, while continuing to ensure the responsible export of arms."

The United States is making these policy changes with great power competition with China and Russia in mind.

"We're trying to improve our ability to compete with our adversaries by providing our partners with viable alternatives to foreign products in order to maintain influence in key regions throughout the world," Laura Cressey, Deputy Director for Regional Security and Arms Transfers at U.S. Department of State, said.

"We're going to be working with our partners and allies to identify critical capability requirements that they have and then trying to expedite transfers to support these essential foreign policy and national security objectives."

However, writing the policy guidance is the easy part. Implementing the policy will be far more challenging.

"The release of the new policy was only the first step in a series of what we believe will be very practical results-focused initiatives to transform the way that the U.S. government works to support and grow our defense industrial base," Kaidanow said.

"Through that memorandum, the president also directed the secretary of state, in coordination with the secretaries of defense, commerce, and energy, to submit an implementation plan within 60 days."

As part of the effort, the United States is looking at reforming export hurdles such as the International Traffic in Arms Regulations, which has been a vexing problem for the defense industry for decades.

"We'll look at streamlining the International Traffic in Arms Regulations, or ITAR, and also continuing to revise the U.S. Munitions List and the Commerce Control List," Cressey said.

Additionally, the State Department and Defense Department will try to speed up the bureaucratic processes involved in weapons exports.

"We will also be looking at the day-to-day processes to ensure that we are as efficient, as streamlined, and as effective as possible," Cressey said.

"So some of the things that we're looking at, and that folks in industry and associations have asked us to look at, is: establishing milestones and timelines for the foreign military sales process; improving and speeding up our contracting process—processes within the Defense Department; trying to increase the competitiveness

> **Those nations that are unable to purchase American weapons could find that China or Russia are more than willing to supply them with comparable systems.**

of U.S. defense items and systems by building in exportability to the design and development; and also by expanding support for what we call non-program-of-record systems. We're looking into potential financing options that could make our systems more attainable for our foreign partners. And we're also examining existing polices to ensure that they don't unnecessarily detract from our ability to compete in international—in the international marketplace."

Without the changes, the United States is increasingly in danger of losing its market share as China, in particular, increasing develops and produces evermore-capable weapons for the export market. One example is the Unmanned Aerial Systems (UAS) market, which the United States dominates, but which is also threatened by Chinese competition and by Washington's tight export regulations.

"By removing some of the previous administration's artificial barriers to the transfer of arms to critical partners, the UAS export policy being one example, this administration is both strengthening our hand in the ongoing strategic competition while also stimulating economic growth at home, as well as job creation," Alex Gray, Special Assistant to the President for the Defense Industrial Base, said.

"It should be noted that the U.S. aerospace and defense industries contribute almost $1 trillion annually to the U.S. economy and they support about 2.5 million American jobs. Just as one point, the international—UAS export market alone is estimated to be worth more than $50 billion a year within the next decade. Those are the stakes we're competing for."

Those nations that are unable to purchase American weapons could find that China or Russia are more than willing to supply them with comparable systems.

"We are witnessing China—as an example, not alone—but China filling voids the U.S. left with a denial to a friend or ally," Keith Webster, president of the Defense and Aerospace Export Council at the U.S. Chamber of Commerce, said.

"The consequence of a denial filled by China or others is as follows: The U.S. loses market share that is not easily recaptured, and in some cases will never be re-captured. The U.S. loses control of the capability. The U.S. loses the opportunity to train, influence, and maintain a military relationship with foreign forces, who now are introducing into their inventory a Chinese—Korean, Israeli, et cetera—capability."

There are some immediate examples that Webster said he could point to. "We never answered India's request for ballistic missile defense capability."

"That ask of the U.S. went unanswered for a number of years. And now, India has been forced to consider and has—may potentially go buy, potentially, the Russian S-400 system. Similar to what Turkey's buying—or said they were going to buy. Now we are rushing to put together a proposal for BMD for India to counter that situation."

Print Citations

CMS: Majumdar, Dave. "The Trump Administration Has a Plan to Compete with Russia and China over Weapon Sales." In *The Reference Shelf: U.S. National Debate Topic 2019-2020 Arms Sales,* edited by Micah L. Issitt, 81-83. Amenia, NY: Grey House Publishing, 2019.

MLA: Majumdar, Dave. "The Trump Administration Has a Plan to Compete with Russia and China over Weapon Sales." *The Reference Shelf: U.S. National Debate Topic 2019-2020 Arms Sales,* edited by Micah L. Issitt, Grey House Publishing, 2019, pp. 81-83.

APA: Majumdar, D. (2019). The Trump administration has a plan to compete with Russia and China over weapon sales. In Micah L. Issitt (Ed.), *The reference shelf: U.S. national debate topic 2019-2020 arms sales* (pp. 81-83). Amenia, NY: Grey House Publishing.

After Khashoggi, US Arms Sales to the Saudis Are Essential Leverage

By Bruce Riedel

Brookings Institution, October 10, 2018

Eighteen months ago, Donald Trump visited Saudi Arabia and said he had concluded $110 billion dollars in arms sales with the kingdom. It was fake news then and it's still fake news today. The Saudis have not concluded a single major arms deal with Washington on Trump's watch. Nonetheless, the U.S. arms relationship with the kingdom is the most important leverage Washington has as it contemplates reacting to the alleged murder of Jamal Khashoggi.

Follow the Money

In June 2017, after the president's visit to Riyadh—his first official foreign travel—we published a *Brookings* blog post detailing that his claims to have sold $110 billion in weapons were spurious. Other media outlets subsequently came to the same conclusion. When Saudi Crown Prince Mohammad bin Salman visited the White House this year, the president indirectly confirmed that non-deal by chiding the prince for spending only "peanuts" on arms from America.

The Saudis have continued to buy spare parts, munitions, and technical support for the enormous amount of American equipment they have bought from previous administrations. The Royal Saudi Air Force (RSAF) is entirely dependent on American and British support for its air fleet of F15 fighter jets, Apache helicopters, and Tornado aircraft. If either Washington or London halts the flow of logistics, the RSAF will be grounded. The Saudi army and the Saudi Arabian National Guard are similarly dependent on foreigners (the Saudi Arabian National Guard is heavily dependent on Canada). The same is also true for the Saudis allies like Bahrain.

> **Saudi Arabia's war is alienating people around the world.**

Under President Obama, Saudi Arabia spent well over $110 billion in U.S. weapons, including for aircraft, helicopters, and air defense missiles. These deals were the largest in American history. Saudi commentators routinely decried Obama for failing to protect Saudi interests, but the kingdom loved his arms deals.

But the kingdom has not bought any new arms platform during the Trump administration. Only one has even been seriously discussed: A $15 billion deal for THAAD, terminal high altitude area defense missiles, has gotten the most attention and preliminary approval from Congress, but the Saudis let pass a September deadline for the deal with Lockheed Martin. The Saudis certainly need more air defenses with the pro-Iran Zaydi Shiite Houthi rebels in Yemen firing ballistic missiles at Saudi cities.

The three and a half year-old Saudi war in Yemen is hugely expensive. There are no public figures from the Saudi government about the war's costs, but a conservative estimate would be at least $50 billion per year. Maintenance costs for aircraft and warships go up dramatically when they are constantly in combat operations. The Royal Saudi Navy has been blockading Yemen for over 40 months. The RSAF has conducted thousands of air strikes. The war is draining the kingdom's coffers. And responsibility for the war is on Mohammed bin Salman, who as defense minister has driven Riyadh into this quagmire. Shaking the arms relationship is by far the most important way to clip his wings.

Avenging Khashoggi

Congress now has the power to make a serious decision, halting arms sales and the logistics train for the kingdom in the wake of the reported murder of Saudi critic Jamal Khashoggi in the Saudi Consulate in Istanbul Turkey last week. The outrageous attack on Jamal deserves serious reaction, and given Trump's dereliction of duty on the matter, it is up to Congress to act. The president may try to override a Senate arms stand-down but it would be a painful setback for the prince.

Jamal's last opinion piece before his death was about the war in Yemen. He called for an immediate Saudi ceasefire and blamed the war on Mohammed bin Salman. At stake, Jamal argued, is Saudi "dignity" and its role as a leader in the Islamic world. It has rightly been seen as an ineffectual bully. Saudi Arabia's war is alienating people around the world. Across the Muslim world, the Saudi brand has been damaged. Khashoggi compared Mohammed bin Salman to Syrian President Bashar Assad as a war criminal. His death only further darkens Mohammed bin Salman's standing. Much of the world is likely to treat him and his henchmen as pariahs.

The prince's goal in Istanbul was to intimidate any opposition or criticism no matter how peaceful. The more blatant and gruesome the intimidation, the more likely it will chill dissent. But it will also polarize the country and encourage the deep conspiracies that could violently and suddenly change the kingdom in very unexpected ways. These are very dangerous waters for the House of Saud.

Print Citations

CMS: Riedel, Bruce. "After Khashoggi, US Arms Sales to the Saudis Are Essential Leverage." In *The Reference Shelf: U.S. National Debate Topic 2019-2020 Arms Sales,* edited by Micah L. Issitt, 84-86. Amenia, NY: Grey House Publishing, 2019.

MLA: Riedel, Bruce. "After Khashoggi, US Arms Sales to the Saudis Are Essential Leverage." *The Reference Shelf: U.S. National Debate Topic 2019-2020 Arms Sales,* edited by Micah L. Issitt, Grey House Publishing, 2019, pp. 84-86.

APA: Riedel, B. (2019). After Khashoggi, US arms sales to the Saudis are essential leverage. In Micah L. Issitt (Ed.), *The reference shelf: U.S. national debate topic 2019-2020 arms sales* (pp. 84-86). Amenia, NY: Grey House Publishing.

US Remains Top Arms Exporter, but Russia Is Nipping at Its Heels

By Terrence Guay

The Conversation, March 24, 2015

One of the features of the 21st century, particularly since the 2008 financial crisis, has been the increasing number of rankings in which the United States is no longer number one. Title of top arms exporter, however, is not one of them—at least not yet—with the US maintaining its number one spot almost every year since the Cold War ended.

At last month's International Defense Exhibition in Abu Dhabi, around 1,200 companies from 56 countries showcased their hardware, trying to sell their high-resolution surveillance satellites, Reaper drones and Kalashnikov rifles to the government officials and military brass in attendance. Plenty of American arms makers were on hand in hopes of maintaining their global dominance.

The US controlled 31% of the global market for weapons exports from 2010 to 2014, up from 29% from 2005 to 2009, according to the Stockholm International Peace Research Institute (SIPRI), the world's best-known collector of defense spending and weapons trade statistics. Russia came a close second with 27%, a significant increase from 22% in the prior period, followed by China, Germany and France each with a 5% share of the arms market.

The fast-rising wealth of emerging markets like India and countries in Africa that are gobbling up a growing share of weapons is rapidly changing the arms market, particularly as global instability seems to grow year after year. The surge in conflicts involving non-state actors in the Middle East and Africa is also forcing more countries to stock up, creating more demand for tanks, advanced weapons systems and especially light arms.

And regional rivalries between India and its neighbors Pakistan and China, as well as Saudi Arabia and the Gulf states with Iran, continue to simmer. Government coffers, filled with earnings from oil, manufactured goods and other exports, can readily be tapped to purchase weapons from abroad, even if spending on education, health and infrastructure might provide greater long-term benefits. The US Congressional Research Service estimates that global arms transfers rose from about $51 billion in 2004 to $85 billion in 2011, totaling more than $500 billion over the eight-year period.

US Corporate Dominance

At the moment, the global defense industry remains an area of US corporate dominance. Six American companies placed among the top eight global firms, based on defense-related revenues. Lockheed Martin topped the list with $35 billion in arms sales, with Boeing in second place ($31 billion). Raytheon ($22 billion), Northrop Grumman ($20 billion), and General Dynamics ($19 billion) ranked fourth through sixth, while United Technologies ($12 billion) took eighth.

Obviously, a large portion of the revenues generated by these firms comes from the US Department of Defense. But exports are essential, since it allows the companies to produce larger quantities of fighter planes, tanks, and other weapons systems, thereby driving down the per unit cost, which ultimately benefits the Pentagon and American taxpayers.

So while arms exports help achieve national security and foreign policy goals, they provide significant economic benefits as well, particularly for the workers and communities where production is located.

Who's Buying

Buyers in Asia and Oceania snared the most US weapons, or 48%, while recipients in the Middle East purchased 32%. Another 11% went to Europe. Meanwhile, Russia's biggest buyers were India, China and Algeria, which consumed 60% of its arms exports. Overall, it sold arms to 56 countries and the rebels it backs in Ukraine, according to SIPRI.

One of the most interesting, and perhaps disturbing, global trends is the increased defense spending and weapons trade by emerging market economies. India was the largest importer of weapons from 2010 to 2014, accounting for 15% of all global arms imports, followed by Saudi Arabia, China, and the United Arab Emirates.

As countries in Asia and Africa get richer, larger sums are being spent on defense, particularly weapons imported from the world's largest producers.

Africa, which has experienced some of the world's most impressive economic growth over the past decade, saw arms imports increase 45% over the past five years. Part of this is due to windfall revenues earned by oil-producing countries, while inter-state rivalries between Algeria and Morocco and intra-state conflicts in Nigeria and Cameroon drive additional demand.

China, whose economy recently surpassed that of the US on a purchasing power parity basis, has moved into third place in weapons exports for the first time, signifying the country's growing importance in international affairs. It also shows off China's rapidly rising defense budget, which concerns many of its neighbors, as well as the US.

The Illicit Arms Market

Traditionally, countries have been the primary buyers of armaments. However, the rise of non-state actors such as Al-Qaeda, Boko Haram and ISIS has raised concerns about weapons falling into their hands. Organizations such as these rarely purchase weapons directly from the leading arms-exporting countries—certainly not planes, tanks and heavy artillery.

Terrorist and guerrilla groups typically acquire weapons in two ways. The first is the illicit trade of small arms and light (man-portable) weapons such as assault rifles, grenades, mortars and land mines. Many of these weapons have been in circulation for decades, the result of US and Soviet support for their respective allies during the Cold War.

Such weapons are easily smuggled across borders today, facilitated by all of the financial, logistic and communication benefits that globalization provides to legitimate international commerce. When countries like Libya collapse into civil war, their supply of weapons is quickly acquired by factions within the country, or enters the illicit global arms market.

The second way that non-state organizations acquire weapons is from soldiers they defeated in battle, or military supplies from areas they conquered. So, for example, Boko Haram benefits from sympathizers in the Nigerian military who have facilitated the transfer of weapons to the terrorist group, as well as porous borders that make it easy to transport weapons from neighboring countries.

> **One of the most interesting, and perhaps disturbing, global trends is the increased defense spending and weapons trade by emerging market economies.**

ISIS obtained many light weapons from the battlefield where it defeated Iraqi forces, and more sophisticated weapons when it overran Iraqi military bases. It is an unfortunate fact that far more people around the world, especially non-combatants, are killed by these light arms and weaponry than the far more expensive weapons systems associated with major defense contractors like Lockheed Martin or UK-based BAE Systems.

The Post-9/11 Arms World

In the post-9/11 world, military leaders are prioritizing command, control, communications, computers, intelligence, surveillance and reconnaissance over more traditional weapons systems like aircraft, ships and tanks. As a result, less well-known companies such as L-3 Communications, Exelis and Leidos are quickly moving up the global rankings by producing high-tech avionics, drones, encryption devices, sensors, night vision goggles and information technology services.

In response to cuts in US defense budgets in the years following the Iraq and Afghanistan draw-downs, most defense firms have diversified their sales to more non-defense applications, or to other countries by way of exports. These trends have made competition for Pentagon weapons contracts even more intense, since fewer and higher-priced items are being acquired.

But this appears to be shifting in light of heightened levels of global insecurity from the likes of terrorist groups, provocations by Russia, rivalries in Asia and nuclear ambitions in Iran and North Korea. In recent weeks, Congress has called for increases in defense spending. And other countries are using their growing economic power to build up their military power as well so they can better protect their interests and increase their regional and global influence.

At the end of the day, the main winners of global insecurity are likely to be defense companies.

Print Citations

CMS: Guay, Terrence. "US Remains Top Arms Exporter, but Russia Is Nipping at Its Heals." In *The Reference Shelf: U.S. National Debate Topic 2019-2020 Arms Sales,* edited by Micah L. Issitt, 87-90. Amenia, NY: Grey House Publishing, 2019.

MLA: Guay, Terrence. "US Remains Top Arms Exporter, but Russia Is Nipping at Its Heels." *The Reference Shelf: U.S. National Debate Topic 2019-2020 Arms Sales,* edited by Micah L. Issitt, Grey House Publishing, 2019, pp. 87-90.

APA: Guay, T. (2019). US remains top arms exporter, but Russia is nipping at its heels. In Micah L. Issitt (Ed.), *The reference shelf: U.S. national debate topic 2019-2020 arms sales* (pp. 87-90). Amenia, NY: Grey House Publishing.

U.S. Approves New Military Sale to Taiwan, Drawing China's Ire

Bloomberg News, September 25, 2018

The U.S. approved the sale of military equipment to Taiwan on Monday, drawing China's ire as tensions escalate between the world's two largest economies.

Taiwan welcomed the package, estimated by the Pentagon to be worth $330 million, which was proposed by its government last year and includes spare parts for F-16, C-130 and indigenous defense fighter aircraft. It represents the smallest stand-alone offering to the self-ruled island since President George W. Bush approved a $125 million sale of anti-ship missiles in 2007, according to a report by the Congressional Research Service.

"This case-by-case approach in military sales could be more efficient than previous practices of big packages," Chen Chung-chi, spokesman for Taiwan's Ministry of National Defense, said by phone on Tuesday. "We hope military purchases in the future can be discussed case by case in order to enhance efficiency."

The sale may further hurt U.S.-China relations, which have deteriorated as President Donald Trump's use of tariffs stokes fears of a long-term competition for global power between the nations. The Chinese government has already called off a planned round of bilateral trade talks with the U.S., according to people familiar with the matter, and the countries imposed a new round of tariffs on each other on Monday.

Trump's relationship with Taiwan has been a hot issue for China.

"Strongly Opposed"

China's military "is strongly dissatisfied and strongly opposed to this," Defense Ministry spokesman Ren Guoqiang said in a statement, adding that it has launched "stern representations" with the U.S.

"We are resolutely opposed to the U.S. sale of weapons to Taiwan," Ren said. China demanded that the U.S. cancel the sales as well as its military contacts with Taiwan "in order to avoid the next step in damaging China-U.S. military relations and peace and stability in the Taiwan strait."

Trump's relationship with Taiwan has been a hot issue for China since he accepted a congratulatory phone call from President Tsai Ing-wen after his election and questioned why the U.S. recognizes Beijing instead of Taipei, a policy that underpins China-U.S. relations.

"Punished by History"

Since then, the U.S. has approved $1.3 billion in arms sales to Taiwan, and Trump has signed legislation to encourage senior U.S. officials to visit the island, a move that would raise its diplomatic status. The U.S. has also agreed to provide technology for the island's submarine-building program.

In a March address to China's parliament, President Xi Jinping warned that efforts to widen divisions with Taiwan would be "punished by history." The government has ordered all airlines to stop referring to Taiwan and the former colonies of Hong Kong and Macau as countries, something the White House described as "Orwellian nonsense."

"Strong self defense will help Taiwanese people to be more confident when they face more severe security challenges," said Alex Huang, spokesman for the president. Enhanced capabilities for the island would help ensure "cross-strait and regional peace and stability," he added.

Print Citations

CMS: "U.S. Approves New Military Sale to Taiwan, Drawing China's Ire." In *The Reference Shelf: U.S. National Debate Topic 2019-2020 Arms Sales*, edited by Micah L. Issitt, 91-92. Amenia, NY: Grey House Publishing, 2019.

MLA: "U.S. Approves New Military Sale to Taiwan, Drawing China's Ire." *The Reference Shelf: U.S. National Debate Topic 2019-2020 Arms Sales*, edited by Micah L. Issitt, Grey House Publishing, 2019, pp. 91-92.

APA: Bloomberg News. (2019). U.S. approves new military sale to Taiwan, drawing China's ire. In Micah L. Issitt (Ed.), *The reference shelf: U.S. national debate topic 2019-2020 arms sales* (pp. 91-92). Amenia, NY: Grey House Publishing.

U.S. Policy in the Arabian Peninsula: An Evaluation

By Michael Singh

The Washington Institute for Near East Policy, **February 6, 2019**

Chairman Engel, Ranking Member McCaul, and distinguished members of the Committee, thank you for inviting me to testify on this timely and important topic. My testimony will consist of four parts: the U.S. policy context, the regional context, obstacles to U.S. objectives, and a way forward for U.S. policy.

U.S. Policy Context

The United States is in the midst of a broad strategic shift, away from a focus on the "global war on terrorism" and toward an emphasis on great-power competition, particularly with Russia and China. While the discrete policy choices attending this shift are often contentious, the change in strategic direction is one which has been pursued by successive administration and reflects a deepening bipartisan consensus.

Less clear, however, is precisely what this strategic shift implies for American policy in the Middle East. Some have argued that it requires a rebalancing of resources away from the Middle East and toward Asia and Europe, not only because the latter regions are of increasing importance, but because the past two decades of heavy U.S. engagement in the Middle East have produced few clear successes despite a tremendous investment of resources.[1]

Any such effort at a pivot faces two obstacles, however. First, vital American interests remain at stake in the Middle East, and there are no regional or external powers to which we can entrust them. These include countering terrorism, preventing the proliferation of nuclear weapons, ensuring the free flow of energy and commerce, and ensuring the access of the U.S. military. Second, securing these interests is vital to great-power competition itself. Both China and our allies in East Asia, for example, are highly dependent on energy imports from the Middle East.

The challenge the United States faces in the Middle East is how therefore to secure our interests in the region and prevent rivals from gaining at our expense, while at the same time reallocating resources from Middle East commitments toward other priorities. The most straightforward answer, and one already being implemented to an extent, is to work as much as possible through regional allies, supplementing their efforts with limited American support. Yet this approach is complicated in practice.

Regional Context

The Middle East is in the midst of a prolonged period of flux. Since 2011, the region has undergone what I have termed a "double collapse"—the collapse, first, of states and institutions, and second, of the de facto U.S.-centered regional security architecture.[2] This double collapse has had a num-ber of consequences.

First, the center of gravity in the Arab world has shifted from where it tradition-ally resided—Egypt and Syria, first and foremost—to the Arab Gulf states, especial-ly Saudi Arabia and the United Arab Emirates.[3] This has had a number of reverbera-tions, including the shift in Arab states' focus from issues like the Israeli-Palestinian conflict to Iran and Islamism.

Second, the relative disengagement of the United States has, in the absence of any other great power ready to take the baton as America did from Britain in the 1950s, contributed to intensifying regional competition. Three ad hoc blocs have emerged in this contest for preeminence—one comprised of conservative powers like Saudi Arabia, the UAE, Egypt, Jordan, and, tacitly, Israel; a second headed by states that support political Islamism, primarily Turkey and Qatar; and a third, anti-American bloc led by Iran and supported by its non-state proxies and affiliates and Assad's rump Syria, and sustained externally by the revisionist states, Russia and China. The United States is most closely identified with the first bloc, but in fact has very strong military, economic, and diplomatic ties with the first two but hostile relations with the third. These groupings are necessarily simplified, but the regional fault lines are real.

Third, the collapse of states has created vacuums that non-state actors—includ-ing those affiliated with Iran—have been keen to exploit. This has been evident in eastern Syria and western Iraq, where the Islamic State took advantage in the relative absence of any central government authority acceptable to local citizens; in Yemen, where the Houthi movement in 2014 ousted the internationally-recognized transitional government that replaced the Saleh regime; and in Lebanon, where the Iranian proxy Hezbollah has accumulated power due in large part to the weakness and disorganization of the state.

These phenomena have contributed to a burst of interventionism by regional powers. Saudi Arabia and the UAE, supported by the other Gulf Cooperation Council (GCC) states, intervened in Yemen and Bahrain. The UAE, largely to sup-port its Yemen intervention and compensate for the feared U.S. departure from the region, has become increasingly active in East Africa. The UAE and Qatar inter-vened in Libya, supporting different factions in that country's civil war. Turkey has intervened in Syria, Iraq, and Qatar, and opened its largest overseas military base and embassy in Somalia. Iran has intervened in Iraq, Syria, and Yemen, and has a vise-grip on Lebanon. At the same time, other external powers have made increas-ing inroads into the region. The clearest case of this today is Russia, but over the longer run China is likely to be more active, and indeed has already stepped up its military engagement in the Middle East.[4]

The overall result of this competition, with limited exceptions, has been to add to regional instability, undermine U.S. interests, create an environment of insecurity for the region's smaller states, and, most ominously, increase the risk of wider regional conflict.

Obstacles to a New U.S. Strategy

Under different circumstances, the United States might find itself welcoming the increased willingness of our partners to address problems and conflicts within their own region. Pushing our allies to share burdens has been a global theme for the Trump administration, just as it was to a lesser degree for the Obama administration. Harnessing allies' willingness to act to advance U.S. interests, however, faces a number of obstacles.

Limited Military Effectiveness

Despite the tens of billions of dollars that the United States has invested over decades in building up the militaries of our regional partners, those forces' effectiveness remains limited,[5] as demonstrated by the struggles of the GCC in Yemen and Turkey in Syria. This is not strictly a matter of capabilities (regional militaries have spent enormous sums on the latest military hardware) but rather of transforming those capabilities into battlefield results. Nor is the problem strictly one of operational effectiveness; more important, arguably, are failures of strategic planning—setting realistic objectives and devising a plan to achieve them expeditiously—most evident in Yemen. Others among our partners have capable forces, but limited ability to project power beyond their borders.

Limited Cooperation among Partners

Despite facing common challenges, our partners in the region have coordinated poorly and even clashed with one another. This is most evident in the intra-GCC dispute that has pitted Saudi Arabia, Bahrain, Egypt, and the UAE against Qatar. But even where these partners are ostensibly working together—for example, the GCC intervention in Yemen—they appear to be working more in parallel than in effective combination. This lack of cooperation is not limited to the military sphere, but also extends to the diplomatic and economic arenas. Traditional regional coordination mechanisms like the GCC and Arab League have diminished in importance and effectiveness, and the Middle East remains less economically integrated than virtually any other region of the world.[6] By all accounts, our partners' advance coordination with Washington on major initiatives affecting our interests also remains poor.

Human Rights Deficits

The assassination of Jamal Khashoggi in October 2018 and the detention of women's rights activists in Saudi Arabia that same year have brought increased scrutiny of Riyadh's human rights record. While these incidents are indeed egregious, they are also representative of endemic human rights problems across the region. As the Khashoggi affair demonstrates, our partners' lack of respect for human rights creates a tension between U.S. interests and values, and erodes U.S. public support for these partnerships.

But human rights deficits are also a problem for U.S. interests, period—repression gives sustenance to extremism, as does a lack of non-violent channels for the expression of dissent. It can also erode business confidence in partners in need of foreign direct investment. Furthermore, the marginalization of certain communities, like the Arab Gulf's Shia Muslim populations, creates an opportunity for Iranian interference. In Bahrain, for example, there is evidence that the government's crackdown on the Shia opposition has led to increased, rather than decreased, opportunity for Iran.[7] The same may be true in eastern Saudi Arabia.[8] An increase in repression may also be taken as a sign of regime fragility, and should raise questions among U.S. policymakers about the stability of partner governments.

Economic Deficiencies

In addition to poor regional economic integration, our regional partners suffer from a common set of domestic economic challenges that if unaddressed can pose a threat to their success and stability. Among Gulf oil exporters, these are primarily twofold: first, an overdependence on oil revenue, which given the increasing volatility of oil prices can give rise to unanticipated fiscal pressures; and second, a bloated public sector and underdeveloped private sector.[9,10]

Spoilers

Those parties in the region that oppose our partners—including both Iran and non-state actors like the Islamic State—have sought to exploit and exacerbate the problems noted above. Iran, for example, has reportedly supplied Yemen's Houthi rebels with advanced capabilities such as ballistic missiles and drones, which have fueled and escalated the conflict there. Iran likely does this in furtherance of a security strategy that involves sowing instability within and along foes' borders in order to keep them preoccupied and, presumably, unable to focus their attention on Iran proper. Per UN Security Council resolution 2231, the international prohibition on the sale of major offensive weapons systems to Iran will cease in 2020. It is not yet clear whether Iran, which to date has stressed self-sufficiency and asymmetry in its military strategy, will choose to purchase conventional arms from abroad, but the possibility will add to the security worries of U.S. partners in the near future.'

The increasing involvement of other external powers in the Middle East also poses a challenge for U.S. strategy. The presence of the forces or systems of other external powers could limit the U.S. military's freedom of action and, were the United States to return to an "over-the-horizon" posture, even limit our ability to respond quickly to crises. These powers' involvement also risks in-creasing the capabilities of hostile actors, not just with respect to conventional arms, but with respect to intelligence, surveillance, and reconnaissance (ISR) functions, cyber capacities, space launch, and other areas.

The Way Forward for U.S. Policy in the Arabian Peninsula

Amid outrage over the Khashoggi assassination and concern over mounting humanitarian problems in Yemen, U.S. partnerships in the Gulf—and particularly the U.S.-Saudi relationship—has faced new scrutiny. Some scholars have suggested that the partnership between Washington and Riyadh no longer serves U.S. interests, any more than it is consistent with U.S. values.[11]

In my view, it would be a serious mistake to jettison our partnership with Saudi Arabia or with our other Gulf allies, for three reasons. First, there is a defensive element to these alliances—the United States seeks to preserve close ties in Riyadh and elsewhere in order to maintain influence over these states' choices, and to ensure they remain stable. Second, as noted above, working through allies is the clearest way to secure our interests in the Middle East while shifting resources to other regions. Third, severing our partnerships in the region would force these states to look elsewhere for arms and other support, and increase the incentives for other external powers to deepen their involvement in the region.[12]

This is not to say, however, that the United States should simply be content with the status quo. Just as walking away from our regional partnerships would undermine our interests, so too would uncritically embracing them or resigning ourselves to the present state of affairs. Instead, the United States should concentrate its efforts in a number of areas:

Improve Allied Military Effectiveness

As noted above, much U.S. military aid in the Middle East has proven to be a poor investment—but not all. With willing partners and a long-term U.S. commitment, such aid can pay significant dividends, as in the cases of Israel, the Palestinian Authority security forces, and the UAE. To be effective, the United States should not focus solely on training and equipping, or on modeling regional forces after our own. Rather, as Dr. Mara Karlin has argued,[13] effective military aid must also address questions of doctrine and organization. And as Dr. Kenneth Pollack has argued, U.S. assistance should focus on enhancing positive qualities partner militaries already possess.[14] Congress and the administration should also consider the allocation of military aid within the region; excluding aid to Israel, the lion's share currently goes to support the purchase of major weapons systems by Egypt.

It is important, in my view, that the U.S. exercise care when imposing conditions on military aid or military sales, such as those now being debated with respect to Saudi Arabia. We should avoid, in my view, tying military assistance to unrelated issues, however compelling. The track record of this sort of conditionality is poor, likely because military assistance offers insufficient leverage to address deeper political and social problems in a partner state, and because our partners bristle at any perception that the United States is using assistance to impose our views on other matters. Tying multiple issues together means that progress on all will move at the pace of the most difficult among them; it is better to address our concerns separately and accept that progress will be fast in some areas and slow in others.

It is entirely appropriate, however, to tie assistance and sales to the conduct of partner militaries and the manner in which they wage war, as well as on stringent end-use verification. In addition, both Congress and the administration should bear in mind the systemic risks of steadily increasing arms sales to the region.[15] Arms sales and other military assistance can fuel interventionism, distort civil-military relations in recipient states, and result in proliferation in cases of instability or poor custody. Policymakers also need to continue to bear in mind the need to preserve Israel's qualitative military edge—despite warming relations between Israel and our Arab allies—as well as the possibility of conflict between U.S. allies more generally.

> **We should only support military actions that serve our mutual interests, are conducted in accordance with international norms, have clear and realistic objectives and timetables, and have a viable political strategy alongside any military plan**

Conditionality need not be explicit or Congressionally-mandated. It should instead be implicit in our security coordination with partners; we should only support military actions that serve our mutual interests, are conducted in accordance with international norms, have clear and realistic objectives and timetables, and have a viable political strategy alongside any military plan. This may produce difficult conversations in which we inform partners that we cannot support a particular operation, but this is likely less damaging to our partnerships than initially offering support to a dubious action only to walk away when it begins to falter.

This raises the specific case of Yemen. As Congress and the administration consider U.S. policy options in Yemen, they should bear in mind several points. First, Yemen is not, as it sometimes is portrayed, primarily a Saudi-Iranian conflict. The conflict has its roots in the disintegration of the Saleh regime in 2011—whose authority beyond Sanaa was already questionable—and the political turmoil which followed. The GCC states intervened only after the Houthi movement ousted the internationally-recognized transitional government and violated several power-sharing agreements, for which the Houthis were condemned by UN Security Council resolution 2216. Iran's involvement has reportedly remained modest, if pernicious. Iran's exports of arms and fuel to the Houthis have helped to sustain and escalate the fighting. However, it is not clear that Tehran has the necessary influence to shape Houthi decision-making, and in any event, it is unlikely Iran would wish to encourage the Houthis to stand down since its interests are arguably better served if Saudi Arabia and the UAE remain bogged down in the conflict. There is a silver lining to this, as it also implies that the Saudis and Emiratis could influence the Houthis directly, and Iranian influence is not necessarily permanently entrenched in Yemen.

Second, the withdrawal of U.S. support to the GCC coalition, or the suspension of U.S. arms sales to Saudi Arabia or the UAE, are unlikely to end the conflict or ease humanitarian conditions in Yemen. Despite the Stockholm Agreement, the path to a political agreement between the Houthis and Yemeni government forces remains difficult, as the Director of National Intelligence recently noted[16] and as violations of the ceasefire have so far demonstrated.[17] Nor is this the only of Yemen's conflicts; the country is also experiencing a renewed north-south split which may jeopardize its unity, which dates back only to 1990.[18]

The best course of action for the United States and its partners is to boost our support for UN efforts at mediation between the Houthis and pro-government forces.[19] Even if these falter, the United States should discourage its partners from pressing an attack on the port city of Hodeida, which could have significant humanitarian consequences. Instead, the United States should en-courage its partners to remain focused on negotiations and improving humanitarian access, in part by addressing the problems identified in the most recent report of the UN Panel of Experts.[20] The coalition's military aims going forward should be modest and focused on direct threats, including countering Iranian proliferation to Yemen, deterring Houthi missile and rocket attacks on neighboring countries and international shipping lanes, protecting areas liberated from Houthi control, and continuing to degrade al-Qaeda in the Arabian Peninsula and the Islamic State. While continued offensive military assistance to our allies should be contingent on a shared strategy, we should resist the temptation to walk away from our partners while U.S. interests remain at stake.

Improve Coordination among Partners

While discussion of an "Arab NATO" remains ambitious, the Trump administration is nevertheless right to press our Gulf partners for more and better multilateral coordination, which is embodied in the Middle East Strategic Alliance, or MESA, initiative. One model for such multilateral engagement is the Bush administration-era Gulf Security Dialogue, or GSD.[21] The GSD was organized around six pillars: defense capabilities and interoperability, regional security issues and conflicts, counter-proliferation, counter-terrorism and internal security, critical infrastructure protection, and Iraq.

A retooled GSD might have a different membership—states such as Egypt and Jordan could be included, as they are in the MESA concept. In addition, the pillars might be expanded to include regional economic integration, which is not strictly a security matter but is no less important to regional stability and prosperity. Such a construct could offer a structured framework for the United States and others to engage likeminded states on long-term security issues, and provide a mechanism for more veteran regional leaders to influence those who are less experienced, and encourage strategic planning by partners whose own domestic national security apparatuses do not necessarily lend themselves to it.

More multilateralism of this sort is not likely to solve the rift within the GCC, which is deep and longstanding, and has defied efforts at Kuwaiti mediation. The

United States should continue to support Kuwaiti efforts and add our own pressure on the parties to resolve a dispute that risks benefiting U.S. adversaries. In the meantime, the United States should continue to press Qatar to improve its performance on matters such as countering terrorist finance and other longstanding U.S. concerns.

Press for Domestic Reform

U.S. officials should elevate the human rights issue in bilateral and regional agendas and ensure that American messages on these issues enjoy clear, high-level diplomatic support. Making clear to partners that these issues will always be a topic of conversation when high-ranking U.S. officials visit, and that visiting officials' itineraries will include meetings with civil society representatives, can help rein in abuses and create space for civil society in the region, which is vital to our partners' prosperity and stability. When violations occur, the United States should be prepared to impose targeted costs, such as the sanctioning of seventeen Saudi officials following the assassination of Jamal Khashoggi. These steps, in turn, can contribute to sustaining domestic U.S. support for these relationships. The U.S. should be prepared to take a patient, case-by-case approach, focusing less on headline gains such as elections and more on the incremental work of building and strengthening the institutions that are vital to resilient states.[22]

As noted above, the United States should not focus merely or even primarily on political reform, but should also stress economic reform, which arguably is just as important for regional stability and individual dignity—and regarding which our partners are generally more open to U.S. advice. Ideally, this should take the form of supporting plans devised by our partners themselves, such as Saudi Arabia's "Vision 2030" plan, or recommendations formulated by the IMF and World Bank.

Reinvigorate Regional Diplomacy

At the moment, the United States has multiple regional ambassadorships vacant, and has no con-firmed Assistant Secretary of State or Defense for the Middle East region. As for our partners, they increasingly choose to deal with the United States through a small number of interlocutors, regardless of the issue. This dynamic presents significant risks, because such a small circle of people—who are also engaged on other foreign and domestic policy matters—can necessarily only devote so much attention to our regional partnerships. In Saudi Arabia, for example, it would be both to the U.S. and Saudi advantage to broaden our points of contact on security issues, particularly at the working level. The first step to encouraging delegation by our partners, however, is to practice it ourselves, by confirming and empowering a U.S. ambassador who can develop a broad set of relationships in Riyadh. If done in a spirit of friendship, our partners should see this not as a threat but as a step to strengthen our bilateral relationships.

Having personnel in place, however, is insufficient. In addition, the United States should ensure that we have a robust strategic planning process for devising our own regional policies, and should include as part of that process consists of consulting with partners. The United States is viewed as increasingly unpredictable, and our commitment to the region is increasingly called into question. Our partners should not be given a veto over our policy choices, but their views should be taken into consideration, and they should be given whatever advance warning they need to prepare for the consequences of our decisions.

Counter Spoilers

As noted above, where Iran and non-state actors such as the Islamic State have expanded their footprint, they have generally been taking advantage of preexisting conflicts rather than initiating them. While resolving these conflicts—especially in Syria and Yemen—can reduce these actors' room for maneuver, doing so is inordinately difficult. For this reason, the United States and our partners should also focus on denying them new opportunities to exploit by using diplomacy and deterrence to prevent conflict, pressing partner governments to embrace marginalized minorities, and address grievances and ideologies that can fuel extremism and conflict.

Such steps, however, will only accomplish so much in the face of actors who are determined, well-organized, and well-resourced. For this reason, the United States should continue to play a lead role in organizing regional and international partners to share intelligence on and counter the terrorism, proliferation, and associated financial threats posed by Iran and non-state actors. This is a role that we must continue to play ourselves, in part because our partners lack the international diplomatic and economic influence to do so, because these actors' activities are often global in scope, and because we possess the ability to respond to threats, such as Iran's maritime threat in the Gulf, which our partners do not. In order to do this effectively, the United States should retain a forward-deployed posture in the region; due to the increasing involvement of other external powers and the proliferation of anti-access/area-denial (A2AD) capabilities, we cannot otherwise be assured of the ability to quickly respond to threats to our interests in the region or surrounding regions.

To be most effective, U.S. efforts must be seen by partners in and outside the region as rooted in evidence, and proportionate to the threat. In the specific case of Iran, this implies a need to reach a modus vivendi with European and Asian allies regarding the JCPOA [Joint Comprehensive Plan of Action]—even if the United States continues to remain outside the agreement while those allies continue to abide by it—in order to refocus multilateral discussions on shared threats that are a matter of broader agreement, such as Iran's support for terrorism and non-state proxies, its cyber activities, and the advances in its ballistic missile and other advanced weapons programs.[23]

Notes

1. See for example Mara Karlin and Tamara Cofman Wittes, "America's Middle East Purgatory: The Case for Doing Less," *Foreign Affairs*, January/February 2019, https://www.foreignaffairs.com/articles/middle-east/2018-12-11/americas-middle-east-purgatory.

2. Michael Singh, "The Great Unraveling," The Washington Institute for Near East Policy, February 25, 2016, https://www.washingtoninstitute.org/policy-analysis/view/the-great-unraveling.

3. For a fuller discussion, see Marc Lynch, "The New Arab Order: Power and Violence in Today's Middle East," Foreign Affairs, September/October 2018, https://www.foreignaffairs.com/articles/middle-east/2018-08-13/new-arab-order.

4. Richard Fontaine and Michael Singh, "Middle Kingdom Meets Middle East," American Interest, April 3, 2017, https://www.the-american-interest.com/2017/04/03/middle-kingdom-meets-middle-east/.

5. Kenneth Pollack, "The U.S. Has Wasted Billions of Dollars on Failed Arab Armies," Foreign Policy, January 31, 2019, https://foreignpolicy.com/2019/01/31/the-u-s-has-wasted-billions-of-dollars-on-failed-arab-armies/.

6. Mustapha Rouis, "Regional Economic Integration in the Middle East and North Africa," MENA Knowledge and Learning Quick Notes Series, World Bank, https://openknowledge.worldbank.org/bitstream/handle/10986/20566/780730BRI0QN95onowledgeonoteoseries.pdf?sequence=1&isAllowed=y.

7. Michael Knights and Matt Levitt, "The Evolution of Shia Insurgency in Bahrain," CTC Sentinel (Vol. 11, Issue 1, January 2018), https://ctc.usma.edu/evolution-shia-insurgency-bahrain/.

8. Chris Zambelis, "The Kingdom's Perfect Storm: Sectarian Tension and Terrorism in Saudi Arabia's Eastern Province," CTC Sentinel (Volume 9, Issue 1, April 2016), https://ctc.usma.edu/the-kingdoms-perfect-storm-sectarian-tension-and-terrorism-in-saudi-arabias-eastern-province/.

9. "Regional Economic Outlook: Middle East and Central Asia," International Monetary Fund, October 2018, http://data.imf.org/?sk=4CC54C86-F659-4B16-ABF5-FAB77D52D2E6.

10. Michael Singh, "The Real Middle East Crisis is Economic," New York Times, Aug. 19, 2014, https://www.nytimes.com/2014/08/20/opinion/the-real-middle-east-crisis-is-economic.html.

11. See for example Emma Ashford, "The US-Saudi Alliance Was in Trouble Long Before Jamal Khashoggi's Death," War on the Rocks, October 22, 2018, https://warontherocks.com/2018/10/the-u-s-saudi-alliance-was-in-trouble-long-before-jamal-khashoggis-death/.

12. For a more extensive discussion of the US-Saudi relationship, see Michael Singh, "The United States, Saudi Arabia, and the Middle East in the Post-Khashoggi Era," War on the Rocks, December 10, 2018, https://warontherocks.com/2018/12/the-united-states-saudi-arabia-and-the-middle-east-in-the-post-khashoggi-era/.

13. Mara Karlin, "Why Military Assistance Programs Disappoint," Foreign Affairs, November/December 2017, https://www.brookings.edu/articles/why-military-assistance-programs-disappoint/.

14. Pollack.

15. See for example Trevor Thrall and Caroline Dorminey, "Risky Business: The Role of Arms Sales in U.S. Foreign Policy," Cato Institute Policy Analysis No. 836, https://www.cato.org/publications/policy-analysis/risky-business-role-arms-sales-us-foreign-policy.

16. Daniel Coats, "Statement for the Record: Worldwide Threat Assessment of the U.S. Intelligence Commit-tee," Testimony before the Senate Select Committee on Intelligence, January 29, 2019, https://www.dni.gov/files/ODNI/documents/2019-ATA-SFR---SSCI.pdf.

17. Michael Knights, "Protecting Yemen's Peace Process from Houthi Ceasefire Violations," The Washington Institute for Near East Policy, Policy Watch No. 3065, January 8, 2019, https://www.washingtoninstitute.org/policy-analysis/view/protecting-yemens-peace-process-from-houthi-ceasefire-violations.

18. For a fuller discussion, see Ariel Ahram, "The Stockholm Agreement and Yemen's Other Wars," Lawfare Blog, February 3, 2019, https://www.lawfareblog.com/stockholm-agreement-and-yemens-other-wars.

19. For several recommendations on how to do this, see Dana Stroul, "How to Build on the New Yemen Agreement," The Washington Institute for Near East Policy, December 13, 2018, https://www.washingtoninstitute.org/policy-analysis/view/how-to-build-on-the-new-yemen-agreement.

20. The report is not yet publicly available. For a summary, see Elana DeLozier, "In Damning Report, UN Panel Details War Economy in Yemen," The Washington Institute for Near East Policy, Policy Watch No. 3069, January 25, 2019, https://www.washingtoninstitute.org/policy-analysis/view/in-damning-report-un-panel-details-war-economy-in-yemen.

21. For background on the GSD, see "The Gulf Security Dialogue and Related Arms Sales Proposals," Congressional Research Service, October 8, 2008, https://fas.org/sgp/crs/weapons/RL34322.pdf.

22. This passage drawn from Michael Singh, "The United States, Saudi Arabia, and the Middle East in the Post-Khashoggi Era," *War on the Rocks*, December 10, 2018, https://warontherocks.com/2018/12/the-united-states-saudi-arabia-and-the-middle-east-in-the-post-khashoggi-era/.

23. For a fuller treatment of this issue, see Michael Singh, "How Trump Can Get a Better Deal on Iran," Foreign Policy, October 10, 2018, https://foreignpolicy.com/2018/10/10/how-trump-can-get-a-better-deal-on-iran-sanctions-european-union-pompeo-trump-missile-program/.

Print Citations

CMS: Singh, Michael. "U.S. Policy in the Arabian Peninsula: An Evaluation." In *The Reference Shelf: U.S. National Debate Topic 2019-2020 Arms Sales,* edited by Micah L. Issitt, 93-104. Amenia, NY: Grey House Publishing, 2019.

MLA: Singh, Michael. "U.S. Policy in the Arabian Peninsula: An Evaluation." *The Reference Shelf: U.S. National Debate Topic 2019-2020 Arms Sales,* edited by Micah L. Issitt, Grey House Publishing, 2019, pp. 93-104.

APA: Singh, M. (2019). U.S. policy in the Arabian Peninsula: An evaluation. In Micah L. Issitt (Ed.), *The reference shelf: U.S. national debate topic 2019-2020 arms sales* (pp. 93-104). Amenia, NY: Grey House Publishing.

Why Military Assistance Programs Disappoint: Minor Tools Can't Solve Major Problems

By Mara Karlin
Foreign Affairs, November/December 2017

Since the end of World War II, U.S. administrations of both parties have relied on a time-honored foreign policy tool: training and equipping foreign militaries. Seeking to stabilize fragile states, the United States has adopted this approach in nearly every region of the world over the last 70 years. Today, Washington is working with the militaries of more than 100 countries and running large programs to train and equip armed forces in such hot spots as Afghanistan, Iraq, Jordan, and Pakistan.

The logic behind this approach is simple. Fragile states jeopardize U.S. interests, but large-scale interventions are costly and unpopular. By outsourcing regional security in places where U.S. interests are not immediately threatened, Washington can promote stability without shouldering most of the burden itself. And heading off threats before they metastasize means that the United States can keep its eye on more sophisticated rivals such as China and Russia.

Among U.S. policymakers, this approach enjoys widespread popularity. Writing in this magazine in 2010, for example, Secretary of Defense Robert Gates called weak states "the main security challenge of our time" and made the case for dealing with them by "helping other countries defend themselves or, if necessary, fight alongside U.S. forces by providing them with equipment, training, or other forms of security assistance." And at a moment when public support for military intervention is falling and once coherent countries are dissolving, the prospect of stabilizing weak states cheaply and quickly is more alluring than ever. Indeed, these days, the commonly accepted narrative in Washington for security assistance in fragile states can be summed up in one word: "more"—more training, more equipment, more money, more quickly.

But history shows that building militaries in weak states is not the panacea the U.S. national security community imagines it to be. As examples that span the globe have demonstrated, in practice, American efforts to build up local security forces are an oversold halfway measure that is rarely cheap and often falls short of the desired outcome.

For decades, the United States has poured countless billions into foreign security forces—to the tune of nearly $20 billion per year these days. But the returns have been paltry. Sometimes, the problem is one of execution, and the United States can improve the way it conceives of and carries out military assistance. Often, however, the problems run deeper, and the United States must recognize that the game is simply not worth the candle.

Not Enough Strings Attached

The biggest problem with Washington's efforts to build foreign militaries is its reluctance to weigh in on higher-order questions of mission, organizational structure, and personnel—issues that profoundly affect a military's capacity but are often considered too sensitive to touch. Instead, both parties tend to focus exclusively on training and equipment, thus undercutting the effectiveness of U.S. assistance.

Such narrow-mindedness hampered U.S. support for South Vietnam, which began in earnest after the French withdrawal from Vietnam in 1954. Ngo Dinh Diem, South Vietnam's president from 1955 to 1963, sought to orient his military toward external threats, even though internal defense against communists should have been the primary concern, as many U.S. officials knew. Yet even after receiving nearly half a billion dollars in U.S. military aid between 1956 and 1960, Diem reorganized the South Vietnamese military according to his preferences, preparing it for a conventional external conflict with North Vietnam and leaving it ill equipped for the growing communist insurgency at home. To make matters worse, the military's leadership remained weak, its chain of command confusing, and its method of promotion based on loyalty rather than merit. When the security situation deteriorated throughout 1960 and Vietnam's military was incapable of dealing with the growing insurgency, it became evident that the country had a poorly led military that was oriented toward the wrong kind of threat.

Something similar happened in El Salvador, where the Carter and Reagan administrations supported the country's military in its fight against left-wing guerrillas. Despite U.S. officials' preference for a more humane approach to the rebels, the El Salvadorian military spearheaded an extremely violent counterinsurgency campaign characterized by death squads and civilian massacres. Things got slightly better once the United States decided to intervene in the military's internal affairs: after it temporarily conditioned arms transfers on respect for human rights in 1983, the military purged some right-wing officers, which resulted in a reduction in violence. But it was too little, too late. Although the military did prevent the guerrillas from taking over the state, more than 75,000 civilians died in the protracted conflict, mostly at the hands of government forces. And El Salvador today remains a fragile state with one of the world's highest homicide rates.

In Yemen, from 2007 to 2011, the U.S. government disbursed more than $500 million to assist the country's military in its fight against a mix of domestic insurgents and al Qaeda affiliates. In its narrow focus on counterterrorism, however, the United States failed to fully appreciate that Yemen's security challenges were only one of many problems facing the country. Its president, Ali Abdullah Saleh, had filled the military with friends and family members who grew rich while nearly everyone else in the country suffered from poverty, hunger, and unemployment. Moreover, Saleh used the U.S. funds and equipment intended for counterterrorism to enrich his family and bolster his personal security detail. In 2015, when Yemen descended into outright civil war, Pentagon officials admitted that they had lost track of millions of dollars' worth of military equipment and could not guarantee that U.S. weapons would not fall into the wrong hands.

U.S. efforts to build Mali's military have fizzled out for similar reasons. As General Carter Ham, the commander of U.S. Africa Command from 2011 to 2013 explained, military assistance to Mali "focus[ed] almost exclusively on tactical or technical matters." The U.S. approach consisted of ad hoc assistance programs, which failed to comprehensively strengthen Mali's military or address issues such as organization, discipline, and mission. As a result, most of the force collapsed in 2012, after a U.S.-trained officer staged a military coup and leaders of elite units defected, taking valuable U.S. materiel with them.

Although the situation is different in Afghanistan and Iraq—namely, the United States has put American boots on the ground—similar problems have emerged. In both countries, the United States has spent billions of dollars to build militaries composed of hundreds of thousands of troops. But it has largely sidestepped bigger-picture questions about these forces' mission, structure, and leadership in favor of a focus on training and equipment. Small wonder, then, that both militaries remain plagued by problems with recruitment, discipline, leadership, motivation, and corruption.

Despite receiving some $60 billion in aid since 2001, Afghanistan's military has suffered from chronic problems with morale and desertion, especially in regions of intense conflict, such as Helmand Province. And in Iraq, during the battle for Mosul against the Islamic State (or ISIS) that began in 2014, whole swaths of the Iraqi military deserted en masse, leaving behind U.S.-supplied equipment for ISIS to capture. The current fight against ISIS has been more successful, with the U.S.-trained Iraqi Counter Terrorism Service playing a key role in the liberation of Mosul in July 2017. But credit for success in the broader fight against the terrorist group also goes to the numerous Iranian-backed Shiite militias that have fought alongside—and often in place of—the Iraqi military.

Trying to Keep the Customer Satisfied

One might expect that Washington's tendency to avoid raising hot- button issues with its partners would placate them, but that is rarely the case. Almost always, partner states are disappointed by the quantity, quality, and timing of the assistance they receive. Because these countries are living with the threat every day, they usually want help as quickly as possible. But the U.S. system is not designed to work so fast, even in high-priority cases.

That was true of the $1 billion-plus U.S. program to build Lebanon's military after 2005, when Syrian forces withdrew from the country. Despite a consensus in Washington that Lebanon needed urgent help to exert control over its territory after almost 30 years of occupation, it took over a year for any military assistance to materialize. It took yet another year to set up a comprehensive military training program and upward of 18 months for vital equipment—including vehicles, light arms, sniper rifles, and night-vision devices—to arrive. Frustrated by these delays, the Lebanese did not shy away from criticizing U.S. assistance and even sought additional help from Russia.

But even under the best of circumstances, U.S. partners are rarely satisfied. In 2007, when the Lebanese military faced down Fatah al-Islam, an al Qaeda–affiliated group that had taken over a Palestinian refugee camp, the United States dispatched planeloads of materiel to the frontlines in just a few weeks. Lebanese officials nonetheless griped. "We didn't get anything but promises and best wishes and some ammunition," Michel Suleiman, the commander of the Lebanese armed forces, said. "It's as though [the Americans] are telling us, 'Die first and assistance will follow.'" This disappointment resulted in uncertainty about U.S. seriousness and staying power and made the Lebanese less amenable to U.S. guidance.

A House Divided

Another problem with U.S. military assistance concerns divisions on the American side. Washington does not always come to a consensus on the parameters and purpose of its help. This confusion undermines a program's efficacy and can result in unmitigated disaster.

Again, consider Vietnam. The man the Pentagon put in charge of assisting the South Vietnamese military from 1955 to 1960 was Lieutenant General Samuel Williams, a commander who had received a battlefield demotion during World War II due to incompetence. Williams repeatedly clashed with U.S. embassy officials in Saigon, kowtowed to Diem, and remained committed to building a conventional South Vietnamese military, contrary to the wishes of the White House and the CIA. At a time when there were more than enough problems among its Vietnamese allies, Washington was needlessly undermining its own efforts.

It repeated that mistake in Lebanon in the 1980s. In the wake of Israel's 1982 invasion of the country, the Reagan administration dispatched U.S. troops to serve in a multinational peacekeeping force and to professionalize Lebanon's military. But Washington failed to establish a consensus on the purpose of its involvement. What began as a 30-day mission to oversee the withdrawal of the Palestine Liberation Organization from Beirut turned into a vague and open-ended commitment to support Lebanese stability and security. Senior U.S. policymakers disagreed sharply over the scope of the U.S. role in Lebanon—in particular, the extent to which the United States should directly support Lebanon's military in combat operations. Not surprisingly, then, officials sent mixed messages. Although officially speaking, the U.S. government was invested in the stability and security of the Lebanese state, one senior U.S. policymaker broke ranks and encouraged the commander of the armed forces to lead a military coup.

This disunity laid the groundwork not only for a convoluted program but also for the deaths of hundreds of U.S. military and diplomatic personnel. Two spectacular attacks in 1983 on the U.S. embassy and marine barracks in Beirut illustrated that at least some actors saw the United States as a combatant in the conflict, despite efforts to characterize itself as playing a supporting role. By early 1984, portions of the Lebanese military had melted away amid increased violence, and the United States withdrew from Lebanon, having failed to make the state more stable or secure.

Three's Company

A final problem with assistance programs concerns the impact of antagonistic external actors. When Washington partners with foreign militaries, it too often fails to grapple with the third parties intent on exploiting a country's weakness. These actors have a vested interest in opposing policies designed to strengthen the state, but U.S. policymakers, often viewing the situation through a bilateral lens, tend to pay too little attention to their meddling.

In Lebanon, for example, U.S. efforts to build up the military in the 1980s were thwarted by all manner of foreign proxies and governments. Iran flooded the country with hundreds of Islamic Revolutionary Guard Corps personnel to establish Hezbollah, a group whose original purpose was to fight the Israeli occupation. Israel intimidated senior Leba-

> **By outsourcing regional security in places where U.S. interests are not immediately threatened, Washington can promote stability without shouldering most of the burden itself.**

nese political figures by parking tanks outside their homes. Syria had perhaps the greatest influence of all. As Donald Rumsfeld, Reagan's envoy to the Middle East at the time, quipped, "If [Amine] Gemayel [the president of Lebanon] fears Israel could eat him 'like a mouthful of bread,' the Syrians could do so like a potato chip." By refusing to work with Lebanon's fledgling government and empowering its opponents, Israel, Syria, and Iran undercut U.S. efforts to help Lebanon's military strengthen the state.

External meddling also poses a threat to U.S. objectives in Iraq, where Iranian-backed militias and politicians feed sectarian tensions. Countering Tehran in Baghdad is admittedly complicated, given Iran's help in the fight against ISIS, but if left unchecked, continued Iranian interference will undermine Iraqi sovereignty, posing further problems as Iraq's government struggles to achieve political reconciliation among the country's Shiites, Sunnis, and Kurds. With ISIS routed from Mosul, the United States should help Iraq meaningfully incorporate the Iranian-backed militias into the Iraqi military. In Afghanistan, likewise, Pakistan's support for the Afghan Taliban has weakened the government in Kabul and inhibited national reconciliation. U.S. efforts to pressure Pakistan—including through drone strikes within the country's borders—should be redoubled to stop the country from serving as a safe haven.

Better Building

History is not replete only with tales of failure, however. Under certain circumstances, the United States has succeeded in reforming foreign militaries. Perhaps the best example is the first: the U.S. program to build Greece's military after World War II. In 1946, communist insurgents began waging war against the Greek government. In the words of Dean Acheson, then the U.S. secretary of state, "Greece was in the position of a semiconscious patient on the critical list whose relatives and physicians had been discussing whether his life could be saved." Concerned about growing Soviet influence around the world, the administration of President Harry Truman quickly undertook a $300 million effort to strengthen the Greek economy and military.

Crucially, the United States deeply involved itself in all aspects of Greek military affairs. State Department officials even drafted the Greek government's initial request for aid. U.S. officials worked closely with Greece to reorganize the Hellenic Army's structure to align with the mission of defending the government against communist guerillas rather than foreign armies. And they made sure that capable military leaders were appointed to the right positions. The architect of the U.S. effort, General James Van Fleet, was himself a capable and charismatic leader committed to keeping Athens and Washington on the same page.

Under Van Fleet's leadership, U.S. advisers trained and equipped the Greek forces, provided tactical and strategic advice, planned operations to rout guerilla fighters, and made organizational and personnel changes. Van Fleet and his team oversaw a complete overhaul of military personnel, appointing a new chief of staff and compelling all of the Hellenic Army's lieutenant generals except one to resign. They then facilitated the promotion and placement of eight major generals and encouraged the removal of division and corps commanders who were reluctant or incapable of supporting the broader strategy.

In Washington, senior national security officials regularly assessed the program to ensure its purpose was clear, making necessary adjustments as the situation evolved. They held serious debates about the appropriate role for the U.S. military, including when and if the United States should consider becoming a co-combatant in Greece's civil war. And Truman responded promptly and decisively to signs of division among those administering the program. When a clash between Lincoln MacVeagh, the U.S. ambassador to Greece, and Dwight Griswold, who was in charge of the U.S. aid program in the country, proved insurmountable, the president removed MacVeagh.

There were challenges, to be sure. The most intense disagreements with the Greeks centered on the size of the Hellenic Army, which Athens wanted to increase beyond what the United States thought necessary for internal defense. After more than a year of debate, during which the Greeks kept expanding the military despite American displeasure, U.S. officials finally threatened to withdraw U.S. support. The threat had its intended effect: the Greeks dropped the issue, and the military stayed within its authorized limits.

All told, the program was a success. When Yugoslavia diminished its support for the communist insurgents as part of an effort to reposition itself away from the Soviet Union, the Greek military, thanks to the reforms instituted at the behest of Washington, was able to extend its control over the country. By 1949, thanks to U.S. support and training, government forces had defeated the guerillas, and the Greek state prevailed in one of the first proxy conflicts of the Cold War.

To Build or Not to Build

Past experience offers two key lessons for U.S. officials as they seek to strengthen the security sectors of weak states. First, like all state-building endeavors, these are political, not technical, exercises. Instead of focusing narrowly on training and equipment, U.S. policymakers responsible for implementing such programs must address the purpose and scope of the U.S. role and the mission, leadership, and organizational structure of the partner's military. In Saudi Arabia, for example, the U.S. military is running a handful of programs to train and equip the country's armed forces, but it stays far away from sensitive issues, in line with Saudi preferences. The United States should align these disjointed programs, assess the broader purpose of U.S. support, and use the findings to meaningfully engage on crucial but sensitive matters.

To be sure, increasing U.S. involvement in the details of a foreign country's military is rife with colonial undertones and therefore might be difficult to digest. To minimize pushback, U.S. officials should watch how they communicate and avoid creating the perception that they are bullying those they seek to assist. That said, it would be foolish not to acknowledge the reality of the relationship between the United States and its partners: as the provider of often irreplaceable military assistance, Washington has more influence than it may realize. Recent efforts to condition military aid to Pakistan on the country's cracking down on the militants within its borders, for example, are a good first step.

The second lesson for policymakers is that they cannot afford to ignore the destabilizing potential of third parties that pose a serious challenge to a newly equipped military. When and where possible, the United States should marshal its tools to limit external meddling. This might involve enhancing border security, going to the UN to leverage international pressure, or even, in extreme cases, attacking the third parties themselves.

At times, however, these recommendations may prove infeasible. A partner state may refuse to discuss those crucial, higher-order questions, motivated by some combination of distrust, a desire to pursue a different agenda, uncertainty about the American commitment, and the belief that it will receive U.S. aid no matter what. For example, officials in Egypt, one of the top recipients of U.S. military aid, appear to believe that Washington will continue to provide assistance in order to maintain the country's peace treaty with Israel regardless, which explains their reluctance to reform their corrupt military. Nigerian officials, likewise, seem to have calculated that the United States will help with their fight against Boko Haram despite the military's egregious human rights violations, and so they have refused to discuss changes to the Nigerian military's outdated defense strategy and inefficient organizational structure.

In other cases, improving an assistance program may be unworkable because the United States is unwilling to crack down on external actors, whose support it needs for higher-priority issues. In Syria, for example, where the United States supports a range of Syrian opposition forces, it may make sense for the United States to give up on trying to get Russia to lessen its meddling in the civil war and instead prioritize making progress on broader European security affairs.

In such scenarios, policymakers need to make a clear-eyed assessment about the goals and likely outcomes of U.S. military assistance. That will lead them to one of two conclusions. Sometimes, they may decide to move forward, recognizing that the effort to train and equip the foreign military will be just that: light security-sector reform. Limited train-and-equip programs can serve useful purposes, such as providing intelligence, professionalizing the military to make the force more respected, enabling some tactical and operational cooperation on mutually agreed threats, and giving U.S. personnel valuable experience working with foreign forces. But limited U.S. involvement will have a limited impact. Alternatively, policymakers may conclude that the costs outweigh the benefits. In those cases, better to submit to reality and deal with the problem some other way than throw good money after bad.

Print Citations

CMS: Karlin, Mara. "Why Military Assistance Programs Disappoint: Minor Tools Can't Solve Major Problems." In *The Reference Shelf: U.S. National Debate Topic 2019-2020 Arms Sales,* edited by Micah L. Issitt, 105-112. Amenia, NY: Grey House Publishing, 2019.

MLA: Karlin, Mara. "Why Military Assistance Programs Disappoint: Minor Tools Can't Solve Major Problems." *The Reference Shelf: U.S. National Debate Topic 2019-2020 Arms Sales,* edited by Micah L. Issitt, Grey House Publishing, 2019, pp. 105-112.

APA: Karlin, M. (2019). Why military assistance programs disappoint: Minor tools can't solve major problems. In Micah L. Issitt (Ed.), *The reference shelf: U.S. national debate topic 2019-2020 arms sales* (pp. 105-112). Amenia, NY: Grey House Publishing.

America Needs to Sell More Weapons

By Alexander Benard

The Wall Street Journal, July 1, 2018

America's arms-sales policies are too restrictive, leading even some pro-U.S. countries to buy weapons from Russia and China. This year's National Defense Authorization Act would give Defense Secretary Jim Mattis authority to waive certain new restrictions for specific countries enacted by Congress last year. But the problem is more fundamental: The U.S. arms-sale regime needs to be recalibrated to protect American influence in a highly competitive geopolitical environment.

The U.S. government blocks weapons sales to foreign countries for various reasons. Congress is often wary of selling arms to countries that could use them to undermine civil liberties. The Defense Department often worries the purchasing country could allow sensitive U.S. technology to fall into the wrong hands. The State Department arms-control bureau has a general aversion to any weapons proliferation on grounds that it could trigger an arms race.

These are valid concerns. But as Russia and China actively pursue weapons sales as part of an aggressive strategy to expand their spheres of influence, U.S. strategic interests must be given more weight.

Over the past decade, Russia has easily maintained its position as the world's second-largest weapons supplier, comprising 22% of global sales from 2013-17. Chinese arms exports increased by nearly 40% from 2013-17 compared with the previous four years, the largest increase for any large exporter country except Israel, according to the Stockholm International Peace Research Institute. Neither Russia nor China has qualms about selling weapons to even brazen human-rights violators. In fact they often provide the technologies authoritarian governments use to surveil and repress their citizens. And they are especially eager to peel off countries the U.S. has declined to arm.

Russia sells aircraft, submarines, antiaircraft systems and missiles. China has made strides in advanced missile systems as well as unmanned aerial vehicles. The sale of these sophisticated weapons poses a direct threat to U.S. security interests. It also creates challenges around interoperability. Technologies developed by the Russians and Chinese—such as advanced radars, sonars, sensors and communications platforms—cannot integrate effectively with U.S. technologies. The more a country purchases from Russia or China, the less able it is to purchase from the U.S. in the future, pushing a country further out of America's security orbit. The

> **Countries cut off by the U.S. will still be able to purchase advanced systems. Worse, they will be able to do so without depending on the U.S. for maintenance, ammunication or spart parts.**

lack of interoperability would also present major obstacles if the U.S. needed to fight a war alongside an ally whose advanced military equipment had been sourced from Russia or China.

Countries cut off by the U.S. will still be able to purchase advanced systems. Worse, they will be able to do so without depending on the U.S. for maintenance, ammunition or spare parts. This eliminates a key lever for U.S. influence in the event that human-rights abuses occur, for instance.

Take Turkey. In 2016 and 2017 it had been attempting to purchase helicopters and other technology from U.S. manufacturers, but was turned down due to concerns around deteriorating governance. Then in late 2017 it acquired a sophisticated missile-defense system from Russia for $2.5 billion, an unprecedented move for a member of the North Atlantic Treaty Organization.

Vietnam's relations with the U.S. have been pleasantly thawing, partly because of a common concern around China's aggressiveness in the Indo-Pacific region. The U.S. lifted its arms embargo on Vietnam in 2016, but residual concerns about human rights have largely limited sales to sonars and radars. In addition the U.S. has not provided meaningful military assistance to Vietnam to help offset costs. As a result, Vietnam continues to purchase much of its military equipment from Russia, which often subsidizes the transactions.

Or consider Thailand, traditionally one of America's closest security partners in Asia. A 2014 coup caused concern about the country's trajectory and led the U.S. to limit some weapons sales. China took immediate advantage, signing a deal to sell over $1 billion of submarines to the Thai navy. In late 2017 Bangkok announced plans to establish a joint naval center with Beijing to service those submarines, as well as a joint arms factory to produce and maintain other military equipment.

There are more examples around the world. As the U.S. moves into a phase of more intense competition with Russia and especially China, its approach to arms transfers must change. If not, its global security partnerships will be steadily eroded by more assertive and less scrupulous rivals.

Print Citations

CMS: Benard, Alexander. "America Needs to Sell More Weapons." In *The Reference Shelf: U.S. National Debate Topic 2019-2020 Arms Sales,* edited by Micah L. Issitt, 113-114. Amenia, NY: Grey House Publishing, 2019.

MLA: Benard, Alexander. "America Needs to Sell More Weapons." *The Reference Shelf: U.S. National Debate Topic 2019-2020 Arms Sales,* edited by Micah L. Issitt, Grey House Publishing, 2019, pp. 113-114.

APA: Benard, A. (2019). American needs to sell more weapons. In Micah L. Issitt (Ed.), *The reference shelf: U.S. national debate topic 2019-2020 arms sales* (pp. 113-114). Amenia, NY: Grey House Publishing.

Japan Wants Cruise Missiles (and That Should Terrify China or North Korea)

By Kyle Mizokami
The National Interest, June 9, 2018

North Korea's development of nuclear weapons has destabilized East Asia, with far-reaching consequences not only for its neighbors but the entire world. Japan, the only country in history subject to nuclear attack, now faces the possibility of new attacks. In response, the country is considering buying offensive missiles for the first time since the end of World War II. Those missiles would give Japan the ability to destroy nuclear-tipped missiles on the launching pad, before they are used.

Japan forsake war as a tool of the state and banned offensive weapons as a matter of policy in the aftermath of World War II. Aircraft carriers, ballistic missiles, bombers, and marine infantry were all prohibited on the grounds that they had purely offensive purposes. Since then, however, a growing number of formerly prohibited forces and formations, including marines, have been re-evaluated and cleared for use so long as they are used defensively or to pre-empt enemy offensive action.

Although Japan has a very good ballistic missile network, it has until now been unable to consider the most obvious way to avoid attack: striking first. The scenario most often presented is that of a Japanese satellite detecting a North Korean liquid-fueled, nuclear-tipped missile on the launch pad, fueling and preparing to attack. With hours before launch, most countries would have a window of opportunity to launch strikes with missiles or

> **The purchase of offensive missiles is an important policy shift that clears the way for a more serious approach to destroying enemy weapons before they can threaten Japan.**

tactical aircraft, blowing up the missile on the pad. Japan, however, does not have the capability, and can only watch and hope its ballistic missile defense network works properly.

The confirmation that North Korea has nuclear—and perhaps thermonuclear weapons—and is actively working to place them on missile warheads upps the level of risk to Tokyo. Recently the Japanese government has made clear its desire to purchase two cruise missiles: the American Joint Air-to-Surface Standoff Missile-Extended Range (JASSM-ER) and Norwegian/U.S. Joint Strike Missile (JSM). Both missiles will give Tokyo the ability to attack North Korean missiles on the launch pad or command and control sites that control the launch process. Politically, the missiles are justified as "offensive-defensive" missiles capable of carrying out pre-emptive strikes—but only against targets that present an imminent threat.

The JASSM-ER is an improved version of the JASSM missile used in a raid on Syrian chemical weapons facilities earlier this year. Launched from a B-1, F-16, and F-15 aircraft, the missile has a range of more than 575 miles. Adapted for use by Japanese F-15J or F-2 fighters, a JASSM-ER launched from the Sea of Japan could strike targets across North Korea. Each missile has a one thousand blast fragmentation warhead with a hard target smart fuse capable of penetrating underground facilities, and accuracy is within three yards of the designated target.

Originally, Japanese officials in and out of government floated plans to buy the Tomahawk land attack missile. U.S. officials, on the other hand, were reluctant to provide Japan with what has historically been a nuclear-capable missile. The JASSM-ER, however, is a purely conventional missile and the current presidential administration may have little qualms about providing it to a key ally.

The second offensive missile Japan plans to acquire is the JSM. JSM is an evolutionary development of the Kongsberg Naval Strike Missile, which was recently selected by the U.S. Navy as the over-the-horizon anti-ship missile for the Littoral Combat Ship. JSM is designed to fit internally in the weapons bay of the F-35 Joint Strike Fighter, of which Japan has forty-two on order. JSM can also be launched from the Mk.41 vertical launch silos on Japan Maritime Self Defense Force guided missile destroyers.

Japan is still a long way from being capable of executing a complex air and sea campaign against North Korean—or Chinese—cruise and ballistic missiles. Such a campaign would necessitate more intelligence/surveillance/reconnaissance assets, particularly drones, more aerial refueling tankers, and more airborne early warning and command and control aircraft. Still, the purchase of offensive missiles is an important policy shift that clears the way for a more serious approach to destroying enemy weapons before they can threaten Japan. North Korea's threats of destruction against Japan may end up creating a new, more capable Japanese military that neither Pyongyang or Beijing are prepared for.

Print Citations

CMS: Mizokami, Kyle. "Japan Wants Cruise Missles (and That Should Terrify China or North Korea)." In *The Reference Shelf: U.S. National Debate Topic 2019-2020 Arms Sales,* edited by Micah L. Issitt, 115-116. Amenia, NY: Grey House Publishing, 2019.

MLA: Mizokami, Kyle. "Japan Wants Cruise Missles (and That Should Terrify China or North Korea)." *The Reference Shelf: U.S. National Debate Topic 2019-2020 Arms Sales,* edited by Micah L. Issitt, Grey House Publishing, 2019, pp. 115-116.

APA: Mizokami, K. (2019). Japan wants cruise missles (and that should terrify China or North Korea). In Micah L. Issitt (Ed.), *The reference shelf: U.S. national debate topic 2019-2020 arms sales* (pp. 115-116). Amenia, NY: Grey House Publishing.

The New Iron Curtain: Russian Missile Defense Challenges U.S. Air Power

By Thomas Grove
The Wall Street Journal, January 23, 2019

HMEIMIM AIR BASE, Syria—North from Syria, along the borders of Eastern Europe and rounding the Arctic Circle to the east, Russia has built a ring of air defenses that threaten the reach of the U.S. military, forcing Washington to rethink its place as the world's undisputed air power.

Russia's S-400 antiaircraft missile system, a nettlesome and potentially deadly aerial shield, is changing the calculus of the U.S. and its allies in potential hot spots, beginning with its deployment in Syria.

Radar employed by the S-400, which Russia claims can detect the latest stealth aircraft, casts a net around western Syria that stretches from Turkey to the Mediterranean Sea to Israel.

While it hasn't been tested in battle, S-400 radar tracking has shooed away aircraft of the U.S.-led coalition in Syria "as soon as they see on their electronic indicators that they are being watched," Lt. Gen. Viktor Gumyonny, commander of Russia's air-defense forces, told a TV interviewer.

Russia's hybrid warfare tactics against the West, including election meddling and online disinformation campaigns, have drawn the most attention from lawmakers and the U.S. government. Proliferation of the S-400 system demonstrates how Russia is also investing heavily in traditional military firepower.

Airborne Defense

"We have to understand that the period of U.S. absolute dominance of the air is over," said Elbridge Colby, the director of the defense program at the Center for a New American Security, a nonpartisan defense think tank.

The Pentagon acknowledged that S-400 batteries in Syria have forced adjustments to coalition air operations, but it contended the U.S. in general still maintains freedom of movement in the air. "We can continue to operate where we need to be," a U.S. defense official said.

The White House revamped its National Security Strategy in late 2017 to account for the new challenge. Russia is "fielding military capabilities designed to deny America access in times of crisis and to contest our ability to operate freely," a report said. "They are contesting our geopolitical advantages."

A bipartisan commission established by Congress to evaluate President Trump's defense strategy echoed those fears in a paper released in November. Russia, the commission concluded, was "seeking regional hegemony and the means to project power globally."

The commission said Russia's actions were "diminishing U.S. military advantages and threatening vital U.S. interests."

The Kremlin has long opposed what it calls a U.S.-led world order. Through its increasingly aggressive foreign policy, Russia seeks a foothold in a world that would be divided into spheres of influence controlled by Moscow, Washington and Beijing.

Moscow isn't eager to confront U.S. forces head-on: Russia has a military budget about a 10th the size of the Pentagon's. Despite Russia's intervention in Syria and invasion of Crimea, its air force and navy capabilities fall far short of the U.S. and China's military.

In Syria, more Russian army personnel have been killed in plane crashes than enemy fire, according to official data. Russia's sole aircraft carrier, the *Admiral Kuznetsov*, is being overhauled. In October, a crane fell on the vessel, causing serious, possibly irreparable damage to the carrier.

The S-400's guided missiles are intended to give Russian President Vladimir Putin a lethal threat against Western military intervention should a crisis erupt on Russia's European borders, in the Middle East or North Korea.

The presence of the S-400 in Syria has been an effective sales tool, drawing interest among both American foes and allies. Purchases by China and India, as well as prospective deals with Turkey and Saudi Arabia, have raised alarms among officials in Washington and at the North Atlantic Treaty Organization.

> **Russia seeks a foothold in a world that would be divided into spheres of influence controlled by Moscow, Washington and Beijing.**

As Russia fills orders, the expanding S-400 footprint creates barriers that threaten decades of unchallenged U.S. air superiority in the Middle East, the Arctic and parts of Asia. By selling the S-400 to other countries, Russia spreads the cost of limiting U.S. forces.

"Russia doesn't want military superiority, but it has ended the superiority of the West or the U.S.," said Sergey Karaganov, a foreign-policy adviser to Mr. Putin. "Now, the West can no longer use force indiscriminately."

The Pentagon said Russian measures have yet to change America's position.

"The U.S. remains the pre-eminent military power in the world and continues to strengthen relationships with NATO allies and partners to maintain our strategic advantage," said Eric Pahon, a Pentagon spokesman. "The U.S. and our allies have quite a few measures at our disposal to ensure the balances of power remain in our favor."

Russia's Rise

After the breakup of the Soviet Union in 1991, the U.S. moved into the role of the world's unchallenged superpower.

Following the Sept. 11 terrorist attacks, the U.S. used its air superiority against foreign governments considered a threat. Afghanistan, Iraq and then Libya fell into the crosshairs.

In 2010, Mr. Putin announced a plan in to modernize Russia's military, saying his nation would spend the equivalent of $650 billion over a decade. The plan included replacement and upgrades of aging Soviet antiaircraft and antiship defenses.

Russia's preoccupation with defense is a product of its history, spanning past invasions by Napoleon Bonaparte's army in the War of 1812 to Nazi troops during World War II.

"The Russian military is configured very differently from expeditionary powers like the United States," said Michael Kofman, a research scientist at CNA, a nonprofit research group in Arlington, Va. "It's not meant to mirror powers like the United States, it's meant to counter them."

Buyers of the S-400 face possible U.S. sanctions under a 2017 law that penalizes allies that do business with the Russian defense industry.

China received an S-400 shipment last year, and its Equipment Development Department, which oversaw the purchase, was sanctioned in September.

India agreed in October to a $5 billion-plus deal for the S-400 antiaircraft system. It hopes to evade sanctions, saying that as a U.S. security partner it can counterbalance China's growing power. It is unclear whether Saudi Arabia's deal with Russia will be completed because of likely U.S. pressure.

The Pentagon has objected to Turkey's planned S-400 purchase, saying it would give Russia too close a view of NATO operations. Antiaircraft missile systems typically receive data from satellites as well as aircraft to detect attacks. Integration of the S-400 system on Turkish bases also would give Russia insight into radar-evading F-35 combat jets, U.S. officials said.

Missile Matchup

The S-400 deal could jeopardize the delivery of F-35 fighters bound for Turkey, U.S. officials have said.

Turkish officials said they need the antiaircraft system to shield the southern border with Syria. Washington installed U.S.-operated Patriot missiles in southern Turkey in 2013, after Syrian armed forces shot down a Turkish jet fighter killing two. The systems were removed in 2015 when the U.S. saw the threat from Syria fading.

The U.S. has since offered to sell Turkey its Patriot missile defense systems, and an American delegation was in Ankara last week to hash out the details. Still, Turkey said, it had no intentions of giving up the S-400 purchase.

Missile to Missile

On paper, the S-400 outperforms the Patriot missile system. Its radar system can track as many as 300 potential targets—missiles or aircraft—as far as 250 miles and at speeds close to 3 miles a second.

The Patriot can lock on to 100 potential targets and hit a target moving a maximum speed of just under a mile per second.

The basic S-400 unit has four launchers carried on a wheeled transport vehicle. It takes about eight minutes to push the 33-foot launching tubes into a vertical position, initiate tracking radar and lock onto targets.

The bulk of Russia's S-400s are deployed along the country's western border; S-400 divisions also defend the Black Sea peninsula of Crimea, which Moscow seized from Ukraine in 2014.

Several divisions are positioned on four of Russia's Arctic territories. As polar ice gives way to global warming, both Washington and Moscow see the far north as a new frontier for Arctic sea travel, potentially connecting Asia and Europe, as well as a spot for energy exploration.

Farther east, the S-400 is positioned to cover the northern end of the Kuril Islands, territory the Soviet Union seized at the end of World War II. Japan claims four of the islands at the southern end of the archipelago.

Russia has more than 300 of the air defense systems across the country, according to its defense ministry. The exact number and locations are secret.

Washington accuses Moscow of violating the Cold War-era Intermediate Range Nuclear Forces Treaty, saying the Russian 9M729 missile could fly at a range prohibited by the agreement. Russia says the missile doesn't violate the agreement.

Russia has deployed other defenses to discourage enemy forces from penetrating its sea and land borders. Antiship missiles reinforce Kuril Island defenses, and there are short-range ballistic Iskander missiles in the Russian exclave of Kaliningrad, between Lithuania and Poland.

Despite its economic downturn in the past several years, triggered by lower oil prices and Western sanctions, the Kremlin in November earmarked another 19 trillion rubles, more than $300 billion, over the next decade to spend on weapons research, development and production.

Looking ahead, Almaz-Antey, the Russian arms maker that builds the antiaircraft defense systems, is designing a more advanced S-500 model to counter next-generation hypersonic and intercontinental ballistic missiles.

The company has chosen two plants for large-scale manufacturing of the S-500, which is scheduled to start production in 2020.

Print Citations

CMS: Grove, Thomas. "The New Iron Curtain: Russian Missile Defense Challenges U.S. Air Power." In *The Reference Shelf: U.S. National Debate Topic 2019-2020 Arms Sales,* edited by Micah L. Issitt, 117-121. Amenia, NY: Grey House Publishing, 2019.

MLA: Grove, Thomas. "The New Iron Curtain: Russian Missile Defense Challenges U.S. Air Power." *The Reference Shelf: U.S. National Debate Topic 2019-2020 Arms Sales,* edited by Micah L. Issitt, Grey House Publishing, 2019, pp. 117-121.

APA: Grove, T. (2019). The new Iron Curtain: Russian missile defense challenges U.S. air power. In Micah L. Issitt (Ed.), *The reference shelf: U.S. national debate topic 2019-2020 arms sales* (pp. 117-121). Amenia, NY: Grey House Publishing.

The Uneasy Co-Existence of Arms Exports and Feminist Foreign Policy

By Srdjan Vucetic
The Conversation, April 8, 2018

In recent years, we've seen a number of depressing political shifts in the Euro-Atlantic area—but the rise of feminist foreign policies is not among them.

The trend was set in 2014 when Margot Wallström was named foreign minister in Sweden's new centre-left coalition government. First came the sound bites: Helping provide women everywhere with 3 Rs—resources, representation and rights, for example.

Four years later, there is an actual policy in place, one that is being closely watched, analyzed and in some cases imitated—one that contains lessons for Canada in its own efforts to enact feminist foreign policies.

The policy reads:

> Equality between women and men is a fundamental aim of Swedish foreign policy. Ensuring that women and girls can enjoy their fundamental human rights is both an obligation within the framework of our international commitments, and a prerequisite for reaching Sweden's broader foreign policy goals on peace, and security and sustainable development.

Some believe Sweden's feminist foreign policy is here to stay even if Wallström and her government are voted out of office later this year.

In opening up new political possibilities, Wallström's policies have often made headlines.

In February 2015, when Wallström stood up in Sweden's parliament to denounce the Saudi state for its oppression of women, the political and diplomatic world sat up and took notice.

Half-excited, half-shocked, Sweden's media swiftly linked this unprecedented move to the Swedish government's separate decision not to renew a memorandum on military collaboration and weapons technology exchange with the sheikdom.

Then, in June 2015, when a parliamentary committee recommended that Swedish arms exports should be made conditional on "democracy criteria," Wallström's speech was interpreted as a call for a "moratorium" on the arms deals with the Saudis.

The policy's critics, and not just those on the left, did not buy it, however.

Swedish Arms in Yemen

> **Some contend that responsible arms trade is an oxymoron while also adding that feminist foreign policy is the latest tool for co-opting female emancipation in the service of imperial and white masculinity.**

According to a 2017 report released by a group of 19 Swedish civil society organizations called Concord, Sweden never actually gave up on Riyadh. Svenska Freds, a 135-year-old Swedish arms control group, also notes that billions of Swedish arms have gone to Saudi allies in the bloody Yemen war.

What's happening in Sweden is directly relevant to Canada's own feminist foreign policy and the Liberal government's upcoming statement on that policy expected to be released this year.

For one, Canada's record of military exports is similar to Sweden's in several respects, including from the hypocrisy perspective.

Ottawa's recent arms deal scandals with Saudi Arabia and the Philippines underscore this point rather vividly.

However, the Swedish situation contains even deeper predicaments: Sell weapons to the likes of the Saudis, and you fail as a feminist. But stop those sales and you'll be a hypocrite again, this time for your status quo dealings with, for example, Iran.

The latter is precisely what happened in February 2017, when Sweden's minister of trade and her female colleagues were pictured wearing the hijab during a state visit to Tehran (days after Sweden's deputy minister and her female colleagues staged a photo-op maligning U.S. president Donald Trump's treatment of women).

How Can Arms Sales and Feminism Co-Exist?

Can arms exports, without which no contemporary arms industry can function, co-exist with a feminist foreign policy?

Government officials in Stockholm and Ottawa would answer in the affirmative, pointing to the rise of the "responsible" export regime centred on the United Nations Arms Trade Treaty. The UN agreement's main purpose is to diminish the risk of exported weapons being used for human rights violations, including all types of gender-based violence.

In addition, Swedish parliamentarians last year passed a bill that further tightens Sweden's export regulations, while their Canadian counterparts last month made amendments to Bill C-47, which is about Canada's long overdue accession to the UN treaty.

Yet these and other moves towards more "responsible" arms trade have elicited mixed feelings among human rights and arms control organizations.

While they can and do make it more difficult for governments to strike deals with countries like Saudi Arabia, the new regime is decidedly not being designed to abolish weapon flows as such. Worse, some think the UN Arms Trade Treaty "is full of holes, watered down after years of negotiations into a tool that will achieve little good, maybe even more bad"—more wars and more fighting, for example.

Responsible Arms Sales an Oxymoron?

Canada's situation could be worse still considering that Bill C-47, in its current form, is not actually binding Ottawa to a requirement of tracking and reporting exports to the United States, which buys the majority of Canada's arms and regularly transfers Canadian-made weapons to other countries.

Feminist activists and scholars have been even less sanguine.

Some contend that responsible arms trade is an oxymoron while also adding that feminist foreign policy is the latest tool for co-opting female emancipation in the service of imperial and white masculinity, also known as the rules-based international order.

Others accept the reforms, but only as the first step in a longer-term march towards a world without arms and without gender subordination.

Others still, albeit a small minority, might suggest that arms trade could in fact advance feminist foreign policy goals in some cases—the next time female Kurdish fighters in Syria appeal for feminist solidarity, why not send them some weapons?

But almost all feminists will agree that most forms of militarism and militarization are fundamentally anti-feminist.

That arms trade and feminist foreign policy are inherently at odds with each other is clear. Feminist governments have the power to either amplify or mitigate those tensions.

One way for the Trudeau government to do the latter is to go beyond Bill C-47 and come up with more ways to make Canada's arms export regime ever more responsible.

Print Citations

CMS: Vucetic, Srdjan. "The Uneasy Co-Existence of Arms Exports and Feminist Foreign Policy." In *The Reference Shelf: U.S. National Debate Topic 2019-2020 Arms Sales,* edited by Micah L. Issitt, 122-124. Amenia, NY: Grey House Publishing, 2019.

MLA: Vucetic, Srdjan. "The Uneasy Co-Existence of Arms Exports and Feminist Foreign Policy." *The Reference Shelf: U.S. National Debate Topic 2019-2020 Arms Sales,* edited by Micah L. Issitt, Grey House Publishing, 2019, pp. 122-124.

APA: Vucetic, S. (2019). The uneasy co-existence of arms exports and feminist foreign policy. In Micah L. Issitt (Ed.), *The reference shelf: U.S. national debate topic 2019-2020 arms sales* (pp. 122-124). Amenia, NY: Grey House Publishing.

4

The Wrong Hands: Arms Deals, War, and Terror

By The Blackbird (Jay Black), via Wikimedia.

Protest against U.S. involvement in the Saudi-Arabian-led intervention in Yemen, New York City. The Pentagon has lost track of $500 million worth of military equipment given to Yemen, and it is believed that it has been seized by Iranian-backed rebels or al-Qaeda.

The Wrong Hands

One of the key arguments against the international arms trade is that weapons traded between nations can be captured or resold to rogue states and other bad actors beyond the scope of original arms deals. Weapons traded by the United States have ended up in the hands of radical groups, have been used by unscrupulous governments to oppress citizens, and have fueled humanitarian crises. The question that legislators must contend with is whether the economic and foreign policy benefits of arms trading are worth the possibility of American weapons leading to unintentional violence and suffering.

Fueling War

One of the most controversial issues involving the U.S. arms trade is the civil war in Yemen, currently classified by some human rights organizations as the world's worst humanitarian crisis, overtaking the ongoing civil war in Sudan and in Syria. The civil war began in 2014 when a group of insurgents known as the Houthi, who are Shiite Muslims with links to Iran, captured Sana'a, the country's largest city, in protests against government fuel-price gouging and corruption. Since March 2015, a coalition of Arab states led by Saudi Arabia have been fighting Houthi insurgents, who are supported by Iran. In the midst of the chaos of the civil war, secessionists in Southern Yemen, supported by the United Arab Emirates (UAE), have launched attacks against the UN-recognized government, which is supported by the United States and Saudi Arabia.[1]

The United States is also militarily active in Yemen, conducting airstrikes against Al-Qaeda in the Arabian Peninsula (AQAP). Airstrikes in Yemen have intensified under the Trump administration; there were 35 strikes in 2016, and 130 in 2017. It has been estimated that one-third of the airstrikes conducted by the coalition in Yemen strike civilian targets. A 2018 report found that cases of cholera in children have increased by more than 170 percent in areas impacted by the Saudi Arabia-UAE-U.S. offensive in Yemen, linked to attacks on water supply infrastructure in the area. Damaged water supplies complicate the efforts to combat cholera.[2]

Since 2015, the war has resulted in more than 16,200 civilian casualties and has left more than 2 million displaced. The military forces of the UAE and Saudi Arabia are dependent on foreign weapons. Saudi Arabia is one of the most important arms client for the United States. U.S. involvement has been justified by the need to protect Saudi Arabian infrastructure, including the oil industry, which has been a prime target of Houthi rebels, and to stabilize the region.[3]

In August 2018, it was reported that the UAE and Saudi Arabia were collaborating with Al-Qaeda militants in Yemen, a group that is considered an enemy of the state in the United States and classified as a terrorist group. In February 2019, journalistic investigations revealed that U.S. weapons traded to Saudi Arabia have been used to arm Al-Qaeda radicals. According to CNN, the Saudi-led coalition was using U.S. weapons as "currency" to purchase the loyalty of Al-Qaeda-aligned militia members. However, it was also revealed that U.S. weapons have been captured or purchased by Houthi rebels in late 2017 when Houthi broadcasts showed militia members in possession of a Mine-Resistant Ambush Protected Vehicle (MRAP), made in the United States, as the Houthi crowds chanted "Death to America." This vehicle was found to be part of a $2.5 billion sale to the UAE in 2014. [4]

U.S. involvement in the Yemen civil war has been a controversial issue since 2015. Current administration policies on the issue have brought the issue to the forefront of the U.S. arms debate. Is the United States arms agreement with Saudi Arabia and the UAE actually helping to stabilize the conflict or exacerbating existing tensions by encouraging military, rather than diplomatic, solutions?

The Yemeni civil war is one of a number of conflicts in which American weapons have ended up in the hands of American enemies. After the Iranian Revolution of 1979, the revolutionary government of Iran acquired billions of dollars worth of fighter jets and other weapons sold to Iran by the United States, a situation that greatly contributed to American conflict with Iran in the 2010s. Further, the Somalian war of the early 1990s was fueled by weapons sold to Somalia by the United States and the Soviet Union during the Cold War. When the United States intervened in the Somalian conflict in the 1990s, U.S. soldiers were left fighting militants armed with American weapons. [5]

Fueling Terror and the Black Market

There are numerous cases in which U.S. arms have been either captured or purchased by armed militants classified by the United States as terrorists. In 2015, the radical group known as the Islamic State captured weapons from three Iraqi army divisions, including tanks, armored vehicles, and firearms, that were supplied by the United States as part of the state-building effort in Iraq. Reports indicated that more than $22 billion in arms had been captured by ISIS militants. In 2017, it was revealed that the Iraqi government gave U.S.-made weapons to Shiite paramilitary groups, known as the Popular Mobilization Units (PMU), consisting of some 40-50 militia groups that were established in 2014 to fight against the Syrian radical group ISIS. These organizations have been linked to kidnappings of young children, nonjudicial executions, and torture in violation of the Geneva Convention. [6]

Likewise, U.S. involvement in the ongoing civil war in Syria has resulted in numerous unintended consequences. The CIA funneled weapons to Syrian rebel groups fighting against both the regime of President Bashar al-Assad and the radical group ISIS. In 2016, a *Wall Street Journal* report indicated that Syrian rebels had been working with and providing American weapons and material support to radical rebel factions with close links to Al-Qaeda. [7] In providing weapons to rebels fighting the Assad regime, the United States has also fueled rebel groups involved in numerous documented attacks on civilians. Rebels armed by CIA weapons were also working with the radical organization Al-Nusra, which was again closely linked to Al-Qaeda.[8]

American-sold weapons fuel a black-market weapons trade that fuels criminal as well as extremist violence. In 2016, it was revealed that weapons shipped to Jordan through the CIA, intended to be used by Syrian rebels fighting the radical group ISIS, had been siphoned into the black market, after being stolen by Jordanian intelligence officials. These stolen weapons were used in a November 2015 shooting that killed two Americans and three Jordanians at a police training facility in Amman. Among the weapons stolen and sold in the black market deal were Kalashnikov assault rifles, mortars, rocket-propelled grenades, and other heavy weapons.[9]

Unintended Consequences and Ineffective Policies

While the ultimate benefits to the United States of the international arms trade is a matter of debate, it is clear that U.S. arms dealing has exacerbated the black market arms trade, helped arm radical groups linked to violence against civilians in various regions, and intensified regional violence and warfare. The latest news involving the unintended consequences of weapons dealing in the UAE and Saudi Arabia is one of numerous documented instances of this occurring, but has raised an uncommon level of concern in the U.S. In a 2018 report from the Cato Institute, A. Trevor Thrall and Caroline Dorminey explain:

> In the past two years, Congress has tried (and failed) twice to halt American arms sales to Saudi Arabia in response to the country's intervention in Yemen's civil war. This level of concern is historically unusual. Arms sales rarely spur much debate in Washington, where they are viewed as a critical tool of American policy. The traditional refrain holds that arms sales promise leverage over recipient countries, help the United States support allies and manage regional balances of power, and generate economic benefits to boot.

However, Dorminey and Thrall argue that the United States reaps little in the way of economic benefit from arms dealing and has been largely unable to utilize arms trades to either influence the behavior of recipient nations or to stabilize troubled regions. Given this, Thrall and Dorminey argue that the United States needs to adopt a new approach, beginning by changing the way that the approval process for arms transactions works:

> For the United States to make more responsible use of arms sales, the approval process needs to change. . . . There are often compelling reasons to consider providing weapons even (and sometimes especially) to risky clients, but the United States should account more carefully for both the benefits and the costs. The easiest place to start is cases of sales and transfers to nations engaged in conflict, fragile states, or states with poor human rights records, as well as in cases that do not directly enhance American national security. In these cases, the approval process should be more transparent, the bar for approval should be higher, and the government should do more to monitor weapons after they are sold to better understand unintended consequences that may blunt the benefits of arms sales and undermine U.S. security.[10]

Works Used:

Abi-Habib, Maria. "Syria Rebels Draw Closer to al Qaeda-Linked Group." *The Wall Street Journal*. Sep 29, 2016. Retrieved from https://www.wsj.com/articles/syria-rebels-draw-closer-to-al-qaeda-linked-group-1475197943.

DePetris, Daniel. "The US Sold Weapons That Ended Up in Terrorists' Hands, and Congress Shrugs." *Washington Examiner*. Feb 6, 2019. Retrieved from https://www.washingtonexaminer.com/opinion/the-us-sold-weapons-that-ended-up-in-terrorists-hands-and-congress-shrugs.

"Hodeidah 'Cholera Cases Triple after Saudi-UAE Offensive': Report." *Al Jazeera*. Oct 1, 2018. Retrieved from https://www.aljazeera.com/news/2018/10/hodeidah-cholera-cases-triple-saudi-uae-offensive-report-181001173828553.html.

Mazzetti, Mark and Ali Younes. "C.I.A. Arms for Syrian Rebels Supplied Black Market, Officials Say." *The New York Times*. Jun 26, 2016. Retrieved from https://www.nytimes.com/2016/06/27/world/middleeast/cia-arms-for-syrian-rebels-supplied-black-market-officials-say.html.

Salisbury, Peter. "Yemen's Southern Powder Keg." *Chatham House*. March 2018. Retrieved from https://www.chathamhouse.org/sites/default/files/publications/research/2018-03-27-yemen-southern-powder-keg-salisbury-final.pdf.

Sanger, David E. "Donald Trump Likely to End Aid for Rebels Fighting Syrian Government." *The New York Times*. Nov 11, 2016. Retrieved from https://www.nytimes.com/2016/11/12/world/middleeast/donald-trump-syria.html?_r=0.

"Saudi Arabia, UAE Gave US Arms to al-Qaeda-Linked Groups: Report." *Al Jazeera*. Feb 5, 2019. Retrieved from https://www.aljazeera.com/news/2019/02/saudi-arabia-uae-gave-weapons-al-qaeda-linked-groups-cnn-190205055102300.html.

Thrall, A. Trevor and Caroline Dorminey. "A New Framework for Assessing the Risks from U.S. Arms Sales." *Cato*. Cato Institute. Jun 13, 2018. Retrieved from https://www.cato.org/publications/commentary/new-framework-assessing-risks-us-arms-sales.

Uawo, Belet. "Somali Civil War Is Fueled by Huge Stockpiles of Weapons." *Christian Science Monitor*. Oct 14, 1992. Retrieved from https://www.csmonitor.com/1992/1014/14012.html.

"War in Yemen." *CFR*. Global Conflict Tracker. 2019. Retrieved from https://www.cfr.org/interactive/global-conflict-tracker/conflict/war-yemen.

Notes

1. Salisbury, "Yemen's Southern Powder Keg."
2. "Hodeidah 'Cholera Cases Triple after Saudi-UAE Offensive': Report," *Al Jazeera*.
3. "War in Yemen," *CFR*.
4. "Saudi Arabia, UAE Gave US Arms to al-Qaeda-Linked Groups: Report," *Al Jazeera*.
5. Uawo, "Somali Civil War Is Fueled by Huge Stockpiles of Weapons."
6. DePetris, "The US Sold Weapons That Ended Up in Terrorist' Hands, and Congress Shrugs."

7. Abi-Habib, "Syria Rebels Draw Closer to al Qaeda-Linked Group."
8. Sanger, "Donald Trump Likely to End Aid for Rebels Fighting Syrian Government."
9. Mazzetti and Younes, "C.I.A. Arms for Syrian Rebels Supplied Black Market, Officials Say."
10. Thrall and Dorminey, "A New Framework for Assessing the Risks from U.S. Arms Sales."

Sale of U.S. Arms Fuels the Wars of Arab States

By Mark Mazzetti and Helene Cooper
The New York Times, April 18, 2015

WASHINGTON—To wage war in Yemen, Saudi Arabia is using F-15 fighter jets bought from Boeing. Pilots from the United Arab Emirates are flying Lockheed Martin's F-16 to bomb both Yemen and Syria. Soon, the Emirates are expected to complete a deal with General Atomics for a fleet of Predator drones to run spying missions in their neighborhood.

As the Middle East descends into proxy wars, sectarian conflicts and battles against terrorist networks, countries in the region that have stockpiled American military hardware are now actually using it and wanting more. The result is a boom for American defense contractors looking for foreign business in an era of shrinking Pentagon budgets—but also the prospect of a dangerous new arms race in a region where the map of alliances has been sharply redrawn.

Last week, defense industry officials told Congress that they were expecting within days a request from Arab allies fighting the Islamic State—Saudi Arabia, the Emirates, Qatar, Bahrain, Jordan and Egypt—to buy thousands of American-made missiles, bombs and other weapons, replenishing an arsenal that has been depleted over the past year.

The United States has long put restrictions on the types of weapons that American defense firms can sell to Arab nations, meant to ensure that Israel keeps a military advantage against its traditional adversaries in the region. But because Israel and the Arab states are now in a de facto alliance against Iran, the Obama administration has been far more willing to allow the sale of advanced weapons in the Persian Gulf, with few public objections from Israel.

"When you look at it, Israel's strategic calculation is a simple one," said Anthony H. Cordesman of the Center for Strategic and International Studies. The Gulf countries "do not represent a meaningful threat" to Israel, he said. "They do represent a meaningful counterbalance to Iran."

Industry analysts and Middle East experts say that the region's turmoil, and the determination of the wealthy Sunni nations to battle Shiite Iran for regional supremacy, will lead to a surge in new orders for the defense industry's latest, most high-tech hardware.

The militaries of Gulf nations have been "a combination of something between symbols of deterrence and national flying clubs," said Richard L. Aboulafia, a defense analyst at the Teal Group. "Now they're suddenly being used."

Saudi Arabia spent more than $80 billion on weaponry last year—the most ever, and more than either France or Britain—and has become the world's fourth-largest defense market, according to figures released last week by the Stockholm International Peace Research Institute, which tracks global military spending. The Emirates spent nearly $23 billion last year, more than three times what they spent in 2006.

Qatar, another Gulf country with bulging coffers and a desire to assert its influence around the Middle East, is on a shopping spree. Last year, Qatar signed an $11 billion deal with the Pentagon to purchase Apache attack helicopters and Patriot and Javelin air-defense systems. Now the tiny nation is hoping to make a large purchase of Boeing F-15 fighters to replace its aging fleet of French Mirage jets. Qatari officials are expected to present the Obama administration with a wish list of advanced weapons before they come to Washington next month for meetings with other Gulf nations.

American defense firms are following the money. Boeing opened an office in Doha, Qatar, in 2011, and Lockheed Martin set up an office there this year. Lockheed created a division in 2013 devoted solely to foreign military sales, and the company's chief executive, Marillyn Hewson, has said that Lockheed

> **All sales to the Middle East are evaluated based on how they will affect Israeli military superiority.**

needs to increase foreign business—with a goal of global arms sales' becoming 25 percent to 30 percent of its revenue—in part to offset the shrinking of the Pentagon budget after the post-Sept. 11 boom.

American intelligence agencies believe that the proxy wars in the Middle East could last for years, which will make countries in the region even more eager for the F-35 fighter jet, considered to be the jewel of America's future arsenal of weapons. The plane, the world's most expensive weapons project, has stealth capabilities and has been marketed heavily to European and Asian allies. It has not yet been peddled to Arab allies because of concerns about preserving Israel's military edge.

But with the balance of power in the Middle East in flux, several defense analysts said that could change. Russia is a major arms supplier to Iran, and a decision by President Vladimir V. Putin to sell an advanced air defense system to Iran could increase demand for the F-35, which is likely to have the ability to penetrate Russian-made defenses.

"This could be the precipitating event: the emerging Sunni-Shia civil war coupled with the sale of advanced Russian air defense systems to Iran," Mr. Aboulafia said. "If anything is going to result in F-35 clearance to the Gulf states, this is the combination of events."

At the same time, giving the Gulf states the ability to strike Iran at a time of their choosing might be the last thing the United States wants. There are already questions about how judicious Washington's allies are in using American weaponry.

"A good number of the American arms that have been used in Yemen by the Saudis have been used against civilian populations," said Daryl Kimball, executive director of the Arms Control Association, an assertion that Saudi Arabia denies.

Mr. Kimball said he viewed the increase in arms sales to the region "with a great deal of trepidation, as it is leading to an escalation in the type and number and sophistication in the weaponry in these countries."

Congress enacted a law in 2008 requiring that arms sales allow Israel to maintain a "qualitative military edge" in the region. All sales to the Middle East are evaluated based on how they will affect Israeli military superiority. But the Obama administration has also viewed improving the militaries of select Arab nations—those that see Iran as a threat in the region—as critical to Israeli security.

"It is also important to note that our close relationships with countries in the region are critical to regional stability and Israel's security," Andrew J. Shapiro said in a speech in 2011, when he was an assistant secretary of state for political-military affairs. "Our relationships with Egypt, Jordan, Lebanon and many Gulf countries allow the United States to strongly advocate for peace and stability in the region."

There is an unquestionably sectarian character to the current conflicts in the Middle East, nowhere more so than in the Saudi-led air campaign in Yemen. The Saudis have assembled a group of Sunni nations to attack Houthi militia fighters who have taken over Yemen's capital, Sana, and ousted a government backed by Saudi Arabia and the United States. Saudi officials have said that the Houthis, a Shiite group, are being covertly backed by Iran. Other nations that have joined the coalition against the Houthis, like Morocco, have characterized their participation in blunt sectarian terms.

"It's a question of protecting the Sunnis," Mbarka Bouaida, Morocco's deputy foreign minister, said in an interview.

But Sunni nations have also shown a new determination to use military force against radical Sunni groups like the Islamic State. A number of Arab countries are using an air base in Jordan to launch attacks against Islamic State fighters in Syria. Separately, the Emirates and Egypt have carried out airstrikes in Libya against Sunni militias there.

Meanwhile, the deal to sell Predator drones to the Emirates is nearing final approval. The drones will be unarmed, but they will be equipped with lasers to allow them to better identify targets on the ground.

If the sale goes through, it will be the first time that the drones will go to an American ally outside of NATO.

Print Citations

CMS: Mazzetti, Mark, and Helene Cooper. "Sale of U.S. Arms Fuels the Wars of Arab States." In *The Reference Shelf: U.S. National Debate Topic 2019-2020 Arms Sales,* edited by Micah L. Issitt, 133-136. Amenia, NY: Grey House Publishing, 2019.

MLA: Mazzetti, Mark, and Helene Cooper. "Sale of U.S. Arms Fuels the Wars of Arab States." *The Reference Shelf: U.S. National Debate Topic 2019-2020 Arms Sales,* edited by Micah L. Issitt, Grey House Publishing, 2019, pp. 133-136.

APA: Mazzetti, M., & H. Cooper. (2019). Sale of U.S. arms fuels the wars of Arab states. In Micah L. Issitt (Ed.), *The reference shelf: U.S. national debate topic 2019-2020 arms sales* (pp. 133-136). Amenia, NY: Grey House Publishing.

Time to Rethink America's Vast Arms Deals

By Daniel R. DePetris

The National Interest, November 19, 2018

Selling weapons is big business for the United States. The State Department cleared $75.9 billion in arms deals in fiscal year 2017, a one-year record since the Defense Security Cooperation Agency started keeping tallies. President Donald Trump is a firm believer in selling American weapons, aircraft, missiles, anti-air systems, and military technology to overseas buyers, both to grow America's domestic defense manufacturing workforce and to increase U.S. foreign policy leverage over the countries choosing to buy American. The Cato Institute assessed that Washington has delivered a $197 billion worth of conventional weapons platforms, equipment, and related training services to 167 countries between 2002–2016.

What Trump sees as good business, however, many Europeans see as a contributor to insecurity in conflict zones. This week, the European Parliament passed a non-binding resolution all but condemning the United States for systemically violating end-user agreements and making the world a more dangerous place. While Brussels also denounced European countries like Bulgaria and Romania for skirting European Union arms export procedures, the bloc appeared to put most of the responsibility on Washington. In a particularly pointed provision, the parliament called for an EU-side embargo on defense transfers to the United States.

It's a stunning rebuke from Washington's European allies, but a nevertheless understandable one given the vast quantities of American military equipment that have been seized by terrorist organizations on the battlefields of Iraq and Syria. In fact, the Islamic State has been a prime benefactor of a loose U.S. arms export policy, one that is more reflexive—and based on short-term considerations—than strategic. Who can forget the iconic image of the black-clad, long-bearded Islamic State fighter doing doughnuts in a U.S.-manufactured humvee? Or pictures of ISIS militants posing in front of U.S.-made personnel carrier looted from the Iraqi army?

ISIS has gotten its hands on so much U.S. weaponry that Washington has been forced to bomb its own equipment to mitigate the damage. Former Iraqi Prime Minister Haider al-Abadi estimated the loss of 2,300 humvees from Iraqi government stocks during ISIS's 2014 blitz into Mosul. When Iraqi forces conducted a hasty retreat from Ramadi in 2015, ISIS overran army warehouses and bases, claiming what a Pentagon spokesman at the time said was one hundred heavy vehicles and "maybe a half-dozen tanks." The terrorist organization even converted "Made in the USA" humvees into nearly impenetrable suicide car bombs,

> **What Trump sees as good business, however, many Europeans see as a contributor to insecurity in conflict zones.**

a formidable foe to an Iraqi army suffering from demoralization, poor leadership and exhaustion.

In Syria, American arms destined for moderate opposition factions were forcibly seized by the very terrorist groups the weapons were meant to combat. A 2017 report from Conflict Armament Research found multiple instances of U.S.-purchased weapons from the Balkans being stolen, sold, or siphoned off to more radical groups. Anti-tank weapons made in Europe, sold to America, and transferred to Syrian opposition forces were later discovered in the custody of ISIS. According to the report, "Supplies of materiel into the Syrian conflict from foreign parties—notably the United States and Saudi Arabia—have indirectly allowed IS to obtain substantial quantities of anti-armour ammunition. These weapons include ATGWs and several varieties of rocket with tandem warheads, which are designed to defeat modern reactive armour."

The Europeans have had their own problems on this score. Balkan nations like Bulgaria, Croatia, and Montenegro—which previously sold Soviet-era small arms and ammunition to Saudi Arabia, Jordan, and Turkey—saw these same weapons being diverted into Syria and Yemen. In some cases, the arms would be wind up in the possession of Islamic extremist groups.

Recent history gives credence to the EU Parliament's concern on the increasingly influential arms industry. Blowback, whereby arms delivered to proxies can be acquired by adversarial groups and used against you, is a legitimate issue confirmed by the extensive field work of UN investigators and non-governmental arms researchers. End-user agreements, which require the buyer to seek permission from the supplier before selling the weapons to a third-party, are violated repeatedly and with hardly any consequence.

But EU politicians should get their own house in order before pointing the finger at the United States. As much as the EU may like to preach from a pedestal and lecture Washington about the moral hazards of defense sales, EU members are also to blame for the mountain of small arms in the Arab world's war zones and arms bazaars.

Print Citations

CMS: DePetris, Daniel R. "Time to Rethink America's Vast Arms Deals." In *The Reference Shelf: U.S. National Debate Topic 2019-2020 Arms Sales,* edited by Micah L. Issitt, 137-139. Amenia, NY: Grey House Publishing, 2019.

MLA: DePetris, Daniel R. "Time to Rethink America's Vast Arms Deals." *The Reference Shelf: U.S. National Debate Topic 2019-2020 Arms Sales,* edited by Micah L. Issitt, Grey House Publishing, 2019, pp. 137-139.

APA: DePetris, D.R. (2019). Time to rethink America's vast arms deals. In Micah L. Issitt (Ed.), *The reference shelf: U.S. national debate topic 2019-2020 arms sales* (pp. 137-139). Amenia, NY: Grey House Publishing.

Fired Up Over Firearms: How Do Export Controls Relate to 3-D Printing of Guns?

By Andrew Philip Hunter and Samantha Cohen

Center for Strategic & International Studies, August 2, 2018

In 2013 the first 3-D printed gun was shot and its echo continues to resonate to-day, especially after the recent Trump administration decision authorizing the non-profit, Defense Distributed, to publish its gun designs online. Defense Distributed, joined by a community of Second Amendment advocates, has been seeking this approval for several years. This summer, the Trump administration suddenly reversed the government's previous policy to withhold government approval. This shift raises a number of issues for the control and regulation of firearms, and potentially other kinds of weapons, not least of which are those related to the enforcement of export controls. The ability for anyone to download a blueprint of a gun, and subsequently fabricate it easily using 3-D printing, raises the inherent possibility that foreign actors (potentially including enemies of the United States) will access this technology which poses implications for national security.

3-D printing technology allows the manufacturing of metal-free guns that are nearly impossible to identify with metal-detection security measures such as those used by the U.S. Transportation Security Administration (TSA). Moreover, traditional security and tracking measures applied to the distribution and exports of U.S. firearms, such as serial numbers and other manufacturing markings, are not clearly required for firearms produced using these designs. This means that state and non-state actors could have easy, untraceable access to these weapons. Understanding how and why export controls have taken on such a central role in the debate over 3-D printing of guns is critical to understanding what the Trump administration's policy reversal means, and what its implications may be in the years ahead.

Q1: How are firearm exports regulated in the United States?

A1: There are a variety of laws and regulations in the United States that control the production, sale, export, delivery, possession, and transfer of firearms and weapons. For instance, the Federal Firearms Act, the National Firearms Act, the Gun Control Act, the Undetectable Firearms Act, the Brady Handgun Violence Protection Act, and the Arms Export Control Act are all firearms-related laws. Of these, the Arms Export Control Act (AECA) applies to the export of firearms. But AECA and the regulations which implement it—otherwise known as the International Trafficking in Arms Regulation (ITAR)—are concerned with more than simply the physical shipment of firearms overseas. They put restrictions on a range of activities including the storage and sharing of the underlying technical information required to produce and operate firearms, and the services necessary to train on and maintain these arms. Because the technical information related to exported items and the training on how to use them are often located in the United States, ITAR places numerous requirements on activities occurring within the United States, prior to, during, and after an actual export. Adding to this complexity, is the fact that information hosted on the internet may or may not be physically located in the United States and is instantly available to users anywhere in the world. In other words, information may be exported simply by the act of publishing it on the web.

Q2: How does ITAR apply to Defense Distributed's 3-D printing efforts?

A2: AECA is applicable to anything covered by the U.S. Munitions List (USML) and is enforced through the ITAR. If the material or information in question is covered by a category on the USML, then the access to and transfer of said material or information is subject to ITAR requirements and restrictions. Specifically, the AECA states that anyone in the United States who is engaged in the business of manufacturing, exporting, or importing "defense articles" must register themselves with the Directorate of Defense Trade Controls at the State Department and obtain a license to continue manufacturing, exporting, or importing their "defense articles." Under the law, this is applicable even if the manufacturer is not currently exporting or importing their "defense articles." Furthermore, ITAR requires firms to obtain an export license to provide software, technical data, or a related defense service for an item that is covered by the USML to foreign nationals in the United States or abroad.

The USML covers a wide range of weapons-related items such as ammunition, guns, missiles, bombs, and aircraft. These weapons-related items are sorted by category and cover physical products, services, and software or other technical data. While ITAR is applicable to all items on the USML, the State Department reviews license applications on a case-by-case basis and has the discretion to evaluate individual categories differently. In other words, a handgun might be treated differently than a fully-automatic assault rifle of a higher caliber in practice, however both weapons are currently covered under ITAR.

> **The ability for anyone to download a blueprint of a gun, and subsequently fabricate it easily using 3-D printing, raises the inherent possibility that foreign actors will access this technology which poses implications for national security.**

How ITAR applies to the Defense Distributed case is multifaceted as the printing of 3-D guns involves multiple weapons-related items on the USML that are controlled under ITAR. Defense Distributed is currently offering three kinds of products: 3-D printed weapon parts, computer-controlled machine tools, and the blueprints required for a 3-D printer or computer-controlled machine tool to create these weapons. First, the weapon parts and machine tools that Defense Distributed sells could require registration and licensing under ITAR as part of manufacturing a defense article but may not require such registration if Defense Distributed is simply reselling them, not directly producing them, and not involved in shipping them overseas. Second, the electronic blueprints holding the data required for the 3-D printer to manufacture a gun or gun parts that Defense Distributed allows anyone to download for free from the internet fall under the software and technical data controlled by ITAR. Third, if Defense Distributed helped a foreign national properly use or understand its published blueprints, that could qualify as an ITAR controlled defense service.

Q3: How did Defense Distributed get an ITAR exemption?

A3: Back in 2013 when Defense Distributed published its initial 3-D printed gun design online, the Obama administration's State Department intervened to require Defense Distributed to take down this technical data using its authority under ITAR. The State Department also required that Defense Distributed seek prepublication approval from the government prior to publishing (e.g., posting on its website) any future ITAR-controlled information. Defense Distributed subsequently submitted multiple sets of electronic blueprints to the government for publication approval but never received any approvals. Defense Distributed filed suit in 2015 in Federal court asserting that the U.S. government's requirement that they seek approval prior to publishing their design files violated their rights under the First Amendment right of free speech and the Second Amendment right to bear arms as well as the Fifth Amendment right to due process. Initial litigation in the case revolved around Defense Distributed's request for a preliminary injunction against the US government's prepublication requirement. This request was denied by the Federal District Court in Austin, Texas on August 4, 2015, and the district court's ruling was upheld by the 5thCircuit Court of Appeals on September 20, 2016. The Supreme Court in early 2018 refused to take up the case leaving the lower court rulings in place.

The initial stages of the litigation, however, did not determine the full merits of Defense Distributed's claims. Rather it dealt with the question of whether the government's action to limit Defense Distributed's right to publish its electronic blueprints was so harmful to Defense Distributed's constitutional rights and so clearly unsupported by the public interest that the government's action should be immediately enjoined. Even though Defense Distributed failed to meet the legal standard for a preliminary injunction, their underlying claims remained an active subject of litigation. It should be noted that the district court examined the merits of Defense Distributed's claims to evaluate whether to grant a preliminary injunction, but the higher court rulings did not.

After the Supreme Court refused to overturn the lower court rulings, the Trump administration initially moved to dismiss Defense Distributed's case, but then reversed course approximately three weeks later and entered into settlement negotiations with Defense Distributed and its co-plaintiff, the Second Amendment Foundation. The settlement was reached on June 29, 2018. Under the settlement, the specific electronic blueprints that Defense Distributed had previously sought government approval to publish were exempted from ITAR licensing under an exception for information approved for public release by a cognizant U.S. government agency. The U.S. Department of State published a temporary modification to the ITAR on July 27, 2018 excluding this technical data from ITAR licensing and is pursuing a final rule making this change permanent. The U.S. government also agreed to pay legal costs of $39,000 to the plaintiffs.

Q4: What are the implications of the Trump administration's decision to settle this case?

A4: The immediate implications of the Trump administration's decision to settle this case are that the electronic blueprints that Defense Distributed has sought to publish will not be controlled under ITAR once the settlement takes effect. The initial date for their publication was August 1, 2018; however, a coalition of state attorneys general successfully sued to temporarily block publication, and an August 10 hearing has been scheduled to review their claims. The electronic blueprints covered by the settlement include a variety of gun designs such as the blueprints needed to produce critical parts for the AR-15 rifle, the initial single shot plastic handgun developed by Defense Distributed in 2013, and several newer designs. Because these files were granted a narrow ITAR exception because they had been approved for release by a U.S. government agency, neither Defense Distributed nor other private actors are currently authorized to release any other design files not specifically included in the settlement. In this respect, the implications of the settlement are immediate but restricted to a small number of electronic blueprints.

Separately, the Trump administration has proposed to move jurisdiction for review of export controls on smaller caliber firearms (.50 caliber or less) from the U.S. Department of State to the U.S. Department of Commerce. By moving these items to the Commerce Control List, instead of the USML, the Trump administration has argued that the export controls for firearms will be clarified by focusing ITAR on systems primarily intended for military uses. Critics of this proposal have argued that moving these smaller-caliber firearms to the Commerce Control List will reduce the level of congressional awareness of these exports, increase the possibility that exports of these firearms could get diverted to unintended users, and allow for a broader range of exempted, unlicensed exports. If this proposed rule is finalized, it is possible that Defense Distributed and other like-minded organizations could utilize an exception for already published technical data that would exempt their electronic blueprints from Commerce's export controls.

The longer-term implications of the settlement are harder to predict. The fact that the government decided to settle the case with Defense Distributed, and to pay legal fees to the plaintiffs, suggests that the Trump administration was not eager to continue arguing against Defense Distributed's claims in federal court. Some may perceive this as a signal that future litigation against ITAR controls on firearms would likewise result in a favorable settlement, potentially expanding the scope of the exemption that Defense Distributed has obtained. It is highly likely that Defense Distributed and other like-minded organizations will submit requests for ITAR exemptions for approving additional electronic blueprints. Others may also bring litigation to fully test the legality of ITAR licensing requirements for firearms.

If a court in the future were to rule that the State Department's restrictions on publishing arms-related technical data violated constitutional rights under the first and second amendments, the implications would be wide-ranging and profound. Violations of ITAR and AECA carry substantial civil and criminal penalties. For this reason, many cases of industrial espionage are prosecuted primarily as ITAR violations. While espionage can be hard to prove, it is relatively easy to prove a failure to get an export license when information is transmitted overseas. A broad precedent establishing that publishing weapons-related technical data on the internet was not an ITAR violation could substantially affect U.S. government efforts to combat industrial espionage by removing AECA as an effective enforcement tool. And make no mistake, industrial espionage is a serious and growing problem. One highlighted, in fact, by the Trump administration itself as it has adopted a more aggressive trade posture toward China. This concern may help explain the Trump administration's decision to make a narrow settlement with Defense Distributed rather than risk an unexpected outcome in litigation. If this is the case, however, the timing is curious. At the time of the settlement, the government had yet to receive an unfavorable court ruling in the case.

Print Citations

CMS: Hunter, Andrew Philip, and Samantha Cohen. "Fired Up over Firearms: How Do Export Controls Relate to 3-D Printing of Guns?" In *The Reference Shelf: U.S. National Debate Topic 2019-2020 Arms Sales,* edited by Micah L. Issitt, 140-144. Amenia, NY: Grey House Publishing, 2019.

MLA: Hunter, Andrew Philip, and Samantha Cohen. "Fired Up over Firearms: How Do Export Controls Relate to 3-D Printing of Guns?" *The Reference Shelf: U.S. National Debate Topic 2019-2020 Arms Sales,* edited by Micah L. Issitt, Grey House Publishing, 2019, pp. 140-144.

APA: Hunter, A.P., & S. Cohen. (2019). Fired up over firearms: How do export controls relate to 3-D printing of guns? In Micah L. Issitt (Ed.), *The reference shelf: U.S. national debate topic 2019-2020 arms sales* (pp. 140-144). Amenia, NY: Grey House Publishing.

Pentagon Loses Track of $500 Million in Weapons, Equipment Given to Yemen

By Craig Whitlock
The Washington Post, March 17, 2015

The Pentagon is unable to account for more than $500 million in U.S. military aid given to Yemen, amid fears that the weaponry, aircraft and equipment is at risk of being seized by Iranian-backed rebels or al-Qaeda, according to U.S. officials.

With Yemen in turmoil and its government splintering, the Defense Department has lost its ability to monitor the whereabouts of small arms, ammunition, night-vision goggles, patrol boats, vehicles and other supplies donated by the United States. The situation has grown worse since the United States closed its embassy in Sanaa, the capital, last month and withdrew many of its military advisers.

In recent weeks, members of Congress have held closed-door meetings with U.S. military officials to press for an accounting of the arms and equipment. Pentagon officials have said that they have little information to go on and that there is little they can do at this point to prevent the weapons and gear from falling into the wrong hands.

"We have to assume it's completely compromised and gone," said a legislative aide on Capitol Hill who spoke on the condition of anonymity because of the sensitivity of the matter.

U.S. military officials declined to comment for the record. A defense official, speaking on the condition of anonymity under ground rules set by the Pentagon, said there was no hard evidence that U.S. arms or equipment had been looted or confiscated. But the official acknowledged that the Pentagon had lost track of the items.

"Even in the best-case scenario in an unstable country, we never have 100 percent accountability," the defense official said.

Yemen's government was toppled in January by Shiite Houthi rebels who receive support from Iran and have strongly criticized U.S. drone strikes in Yemen. The Houthis have taken over many Yemeni military bases in the northern part of the country, including some in Sanaa that were home to U.S.-trained counterterrorism units. Other bases have been overrun by fighters from al-Qaeda in the Arabian Peninsula.

As a result, the Defense Department has halted shipments to Yemen of about $125 million in military hardware that were scheduled for delivery this year, including unarmed ScanEagle drones, other types of aircraft and Jeeps. That equipment will be donated instead to other countries in the Middle East and Africa, the defense official said.

Although the loss of weapons and equipment already delivered to Yemen would be embarrassing, U.S. officials said it would be unlikely to alter the military balance of power there. Yemen is estimated to have the second-highest gun ownership rate in the world, ranking behind only the United States, and its bazaars are well stocked with heavy weaponry. Moreover, the U.S. government restricted its lethal aid to small firearms and ammunition, brushing aside Yemeni requests for fighter jets and tanks.

In Yemen and elsewhere, the Obama administration has pursued a strategy of training and equipping foreign militaries to quell insurgencies and defeat networks affiliated with al-Qaeda. That strategy has helped to avert the deployment of large numbers of U.S. forces, but it has also met with repeated challenges.

Washington spent $25 billion to re-create and arm Iraq's security forces after the 2003 U.S.-led invasion, only to see the Iraqi army easily defeated last year by a ragtag collection of Islamic State fighters who took control of large parts of the country. Just last year, President Obama touted Yemen as a successful example of his approach to combating terrorism.

"The administration really wanted to stick with this narrative that Yemen was different from Iraq, that we were going to do it with fewer people, that we were going to do it on the cheap," said Rep. Mac Thornberry (R-Tex.), chairman of the House Armed Services Committee. "They were trying to do with a minimalist approach because it needed to fit with this narrative … that we're not going to have a repeat of Iraq."

Washington has supplied more than $500 million in military aid to Yemen since 2007 under an array of Defense Department and State Department programs. The Pentagon and CIA have provided additional assistance through classified programs, making it difficult to know exactly how much Yemen has received in total.

> **Pentagon officials have said that they have little information to go on and that there is little they can do at this point to prevent the weapons and gear from falling into the wrong hands.**

U.S. government officials say al-Qaeda's branch in Yemen poses a more direct threat to the U.S. homeland than any other terrorist group. To counter it, the Obama administration has relied on a combination of proxy forces and drone strikes launched from bases outside the country.

As part of that strategy, the U.S. military has concentrated on building an elite Yemeni special-operations force within the Republican Guard, training counterterrorism units in the Interior Ministry and upgrading Yemen's rudimentary air force.

Making progress has been difficult. In 2011, the Obama administration suspended counterterrorism aid and withdrew its military advisers after then-President

Ali Abdullah Saleh cracked down against Arab Spring demonstrators. The program resumed the next year when Saleh was replaced by his vice president, Abed Rabbo Mansour Hadi, in a deal brokered by Washington.

In a 2013 report, the U.S. Government Accountability Office found that the primary unclassified counterterrorism program in Yemen lacked oversight and that the Pentagon had been unable to assess whether it was doing any good.

Among other problems, GAO auditors found that Humvees donated to the Yemeni Interior Ministry sat idle or broken because the Defense Ministry refused to share spare parts. The two ministries also squabbled over the use of Huey II helicopters supplied by Washington, according to the report.

A senior U.S. military official who has served extensively in Yemen said that local forces embraced their training and were proficient at using U.S. firearms and gear but that their commanders, for political reasons, were reluctant to order raids against al-Qaeda.

"They could fight with it and were fairly competent, but we couldn't get them engaged" in combat, the military official said, speaking on the condition of anonymity because he was not authorized to speak with a reporter.

All the U.S.-trained Yemeni units were commanded or overseen by close relatives of Saleh, the former president. Most were gradually removed or reassigned after Saleh was forced out in 2012. But U.S. officials acknowledged that some of the units have maintained their allegiance to Saleh and his family.

According to an investigative report released by a U.N. panel last month, the former president's son, Ahmed Ali Saleh, looted an arsenal of weapons from the Republican Guard after he was dismissed as commander of the elite unit two years ago. The weapons were transferred to a private military base outside Sanaa that is controlled by the Saleh family, the U.N. panel found.

It is unclear whether items donated by the U.S. government were stolen, although Yemeni documents cited by the U.N. investigators alleged that the stash included thousands of M-16 rifles, which are manufactured in the United States.

The list of pilfered equipment also included dozens of Humvees, Ford vehicles and Glock pistols, all of which have been supplied in the past to Yemen by the U.S. government. Ahmed Saleh denied the looting allegations during an August 2014 meeting with the U.N. panel, according to the report.

Many U.S. and Yemeni officials have accused the Salehs of conspiring with the Houthis to bring down the government in Sanaa. At Washington's urging, the United Nations imposed financial and travel sanctions in November against the former president, along with two Houthi leaders, as punishment for destabilizing Yemen.

Ali Abdullah Saleh has dismissed the accusations; last month, he told the *Washington Post* that he spends most of his time these days reading and recovering from wounds he suffered during a bombing attack on the presidential palace in 2011.

There are clear signals that Saleh and his family are angling for a formal return to power. On Friday, hundreds of people staged a rally in Sanaa to call for presidential elections and for Ahmed Saleh to run.

Although the U.S. Embassy in the capital closed last month, a handful of U.S. military advisers have remained in the southern part of the country at Yemeni bases controlled by commanders that are friendly to the United States.

Print Citations

CMS: Whitlock, Craig. "Pentagon Loses Track of $500 Million in Weapons, Equipment Given to Yemen." In *The Reference Shelf: U.S. National Debate Topic 2019-2020 Arms Sales,* edited by Micah L. Issitt, 145-148. Amenia, NY: Grey House Publishing, 2019.

MLA: Whitlock, Craig. "Pentagon Loses Track of $500 Million in Weapons, Equipment Given to Yemen." *The Reference Shelf: U.S. National Debate Topic 2019-2020 Arms Sales,* edited by Micah L. Issitt, Grey House Publishing, 2019, pp. 145-148.

APA: Whitlock, C. (2019). Pentagon loses track of $500 million in weapons, equipment given to Yemen. In Micah L. Issitt (Ed.), *The reference shelf: U.S. national debate topic 2019-2020 arms sales* (pp. 145-148). Amenia, NY: Grey House Publishing.

Can Selling Weapons to Oppressive and Violent States Ever Be Justified?

By James Christensen
The Conversation, **February 28, 2018**

Democratic governments regularly supply weapons to what are sometimes called "outlaw states"—oppressive regimes that violate the basic rights of their own citizens, or aggressive regimes that wrongfully threaten the security of outsiders. Sometimes democratic governments sell the weapons themselves; sometimes they issue export licenses to private arms firms within their jurisdiction.

Both practices are frequently condemned on moral grounds. But how might governments who help to arm outlaw states try to defend themselves? What arguments could they appeal to in an attempt to justify their actions?

Politicians sometimes claim that their acts make no difference to the degree of suffering inflicted by the regimes that they arm—that if they didn't sell weapons to the regimes in question, some other government would. For example, when it was revealed in 2014 that Hong Kong's riot police had used British-made tear gas against unarmed pro-democracy protesters, then foreign secretary Philip Hammond remarked: "CS gas is available from large numbers of sources around the world. To be frank, I think that is a rather immaterial point. They could buy CS gas from the US."

But as I argue in an article for the journal *Political Studies*, this kind of argument has multiple shortcomings. When a government permits its firms to compete for certain customers in the international arms market, it puts downward pressure on prices, and this could allow outlaw or oppressive states to purchase weapons in larger quantities. Some governments also offer certain kinds of weapons, or weapons of a particularly high quality, that recipients would not be able to acquire from elsewhere. By offering these weapons, governments increase the efficiency with which their trading partners can pursue their unjust ends.

In addition, the intentions of other suppliers should not be regarded as inalterable features of the world. After all, this is not generally how governments regard the intentions of their foreign counterparts. If it were, diplomacy would be dismissed as a waste of time and resources. When a government wants another to change its behaviour, it tries to persuade it to do so.

If the British government thought it would be better if the Hong Kong authorities lacked easy access to tear gas, it could have impressed its rationale upon its American allies, rather than simply taking the Americans' behaviour as a given and then trying to exploit that behaviour as a justification for its own.

> **Outlaw states may pass on weapons to third parties, or be unable to ensure the security of stockpiles.**

The Enemy's Enemy

As I've tried to demonstrate in recent work, while many of the arguments that governments employ to defend the sale of weapons to outlaw states are weak and self-serving there is one that, when applicable, has potentially greater force.

Sometimes, arms transfers to an oppressive regime can reasonably be expected to actually reduce the degree of oppression that is inflicted. Arms transfers can do this when they help a regime to repel an even more oppressive rival that threatens to overthrow it. Consider the US Lend-Lease programme, which sanctioned arms transfers to the Soviet Union during World War II. This policy could be defended on the plausible grounds that arms transfers enabled the Red Army to resist the greater oppression that would otherwise have been imposed by the Nazis.

Of course, situations like this don't arise often—and even when they do, arms transfers are not necessarily justifiable.

Evaluation of a proposed arms transfer to an outlaw state must take a comparative form. Whether the transfer can be justified depends on how it fares compared to other actions that could be taken instead. If the transfer is expected to produce worse outcomes than alternative available options, then it isn't morally acceptable.

Different kinds of intervention or assistance have to be evaluated on a case-by-case basis, but arms transfers always come with serious problems. Most obviously, they provide outlaw states with tools that can be used for oppressive and aggressive ends (in addition to any legitimate defensive ends): other types of support lack this feature. Then there's the problem of "leakage." Outlaw states may pass on weapons to third parties, or be unable to ensure the security of stockpiles. The risk of stockpiles being looted is especially high in times of crisis.

In short, supplying weapons to outlaw states is difficult to justify even under the most favourable circumstances. If democratic politicians care about the ethical status of their acts, and aspire to conduct themselves in a manner that can be justified to others, then they should take this fact seriously, and end their casual, callous promotion of trade with tyrants.

Print Citations

CMS: Christensen, James. "Can Selling Weapons to Oppressive and Violent States Ever Be Justified?" In *The Reference Shelf: U.S. National Debate Topic 2019-2020 Arms Sales*, edited by Micah L. Issitt, 149-150. Amenia, NY: Grey House Publishing, 2019.

MLA: Christensen, James. "Can Selling Weapons to Oppressive and Violent States Ever Be Justified?" *The Reference Shelf: U.S. National Debate Topic 2019-2020 Arms Sales*, edited by Micah L. Issitt, Grey House Publishing, 2019, pp. 149-150.

APA: Christensen, J. (2019). Can selling weapons to oppressive and violent states ever be justified? In Micah L. Issitt (Ed.), *The reference shelf: U.S. national debate topic 2019-2020 arms sales* (pp. 149-150). Amenia, NY: Grey House Publishing.

American Weapons in the Wrong Hands

By Jodi Vittori

Carnegie Endowment for International Peace, February 19, 2019

Earlier this month, a CNN investigation provided further evidence that U.S. military equipment has been transferred from Saudi Arabia and the United Arab Emirates (UAE) to a variety of militias, including some linked to al-Qaeda. Given the additional scrutiny of U.S.-Saudi relations since the murder of journalist Jamal Khashoggi, recent U.S. Senate and House resolutions on arms sales to Saudi Arabia, and ongoing Saudi and Emirati tensions with neighbor Qatar, now is the time for a full-scale review of U.S. arms sales to the Gulf region.

There are clear rules against arms transfers to third parties. There are also end-use monitoring requirements for U.S. arms exports, but these checks are hardly universal. Given that at least some of the equipment found in militia hands can be tied to U.S. arms sales, the Department of Defense, State Department, and Commerce Department are clearly not adequately monitoring sales. (Which U.S. agency is responsible for end-use checks depends on the type of sale conducted.)

The United States is the largest arms supplier to Saudi Arabia and the UAE, two lucrative customers of the U.S. defense industry. Saudi Arabia was the largest importer of U.S. arms, having purchased $112 billion in weapons from 2013 through 2017. The UAE was the second-largest importer of U.S. arms in the same time span. Since 2009, over $27 billion in weapons have been offered to the UAE in thirty-two separate deals under the Pentagon's Foreign Military Sales program.

These arms sales continue, despite both countries' history of diverting arms to favored militias. Saudi Arabia has been purchasing weapons from third parties to pass on to allied governments and groups at least since the 1970s, sometimes on behalf of the U.S. government. Transparency International's Government Defense Anti-Corruption Index ranks Saudi Arabia and the UAE in its high-risk category for corruption, with Saudi Arabia receiving a score of zero out of four (zero being the worst) and the UAE receiving a score of one for lacking a well-scrutinized process for arms export decisions that aligns with international protocols.

Examples of Gulf States Diverting U.S. Arms

- 1970s—Saudi Arabia financed U.S.-made hardware for the Afghan Mujahideen

- 1980s—Saudi Arabia was a conduit for U.S. weapons to Iraq and a financier of the Iran-Contra scandal

- More recently, Saudi Arabia purchased weapons from Croatia and Bulgaria for Syrian anti-government rebels—and some of these weapons ended up in the hands of the self-proclaimed Islamic State

- 2014—Saudi Arabia financed $2 billion in Russian arms for Egypt's military-backed government

- The UAE has been accused of shipping weapons to Libyan General Khalifa Haftar in violation of UN sanctions and to various Syrian rebel groups.

The CNN investigation comes as Congress ramps up its opposition to U.S. support for the Saudi-led coalition. Former U.S. president Barack Obama's administration only reluctantly agreed to support the Saudi-led coalition as it went on the offense in 2015, seeing it as an unwinnable proxy war against Iran. Obama had put restrictions on arms sales and intelligence cooperation with the coalition in 2016, but President Donald Trump's administration lifted those restrictions in March 2017, just prior to Trump's overseas visit to Saudi Arabia.

Saudi human rights abuses in Yemen using U.S. weapons, such as the airstrike on a school bus in August 2018 that killed forty children, and the murder of Khashoggi have shocked the U.S. public and Congress. In the National Defense Authorization Act for Fiscal Year 2018, Congress required the departments of Defense and State to certify that the Saudi-led coalition was doing all it could to prevent civilian casualties; the State Department failed to provide that justification when it was due earlier this month. In December, the Senate approved a measure to end arms shipments to Saudi Arabia, despite the Trump administration's strong opposition to the bill. The measure did not have enough votes to override a presidential veto, but senators have promised to introduce an even tougher bill in 2019. Last week, the House also passed a measure to end U.S. assistance to the Saudi-led coalition in Yemen, but again without enough votes to override an expected presidential veto.

The Trump administration continues to approve arms shipments to the Saudi coalition. In 2018 alone, the United States directly sold $4.4 billion in arms to Saudi Arabia, and the administration approved the latest sale of Patriot missile upgrades in December. Tens of billions of dollars in deals with Saudi Arabia remain in the pipeline as well, awaiting approvals as part of the controversial, alleged May 2017

> **Now is the time for a full-scale review of U.S. arms sales in the Gulf region. There are clear rules against arms transfers to third parties.**

$110 billion arms deal with Saudi Arabia. The Trump administration has shown little inclination to loosen its close ties with Saudi Arabia and the UAE despite the death of Khashoggi or the conduct of the war in Yemen.

The monarchs of Saudi Arabia and the UAE can conduct these proxy operations and divert equipment with no oversight and almost no input from their own citizens. Both countries are absolute monarchies, and their legislative bodies are advisory and contain only regime-approved members. Both countries also stamp out any free press and most independent civil society. Information on defense policies, including the war in Yemen, is kept secret by the monarchs and their inner circles.

Most available information on Saudi and Emirati coalition operations and weapons transfers comes from external parties, such as U.S. government weapons sales notifications, news organizations, and human rights organizations. Given the lack of effective Saudi and Emirati citizen or parliamentary oversight on the conduct of the war in Yemen and associated weapons transfers, it is crucial that the United States and other arms-exporting nations conduct additional due diligence and put controls on any exports to Saudi Arabia and the UAE. The CNN investigation demonstrates that the stringent due diligence and accountability that should be required for such sales has not been conducted. As the Trump administration continues to approve arms sales, an emboldened Congress inches ever closer—often across partisan lines—to cutting off those very same sales.

Print Citations

CMS: Vittori, Jodi. "American Weapons in the Wrong Hands." In *The Reference Shelf: U.S. National Debate Topic 2019-2020 Arms Sales,* edited by Micah L. Issitt, 151-153. Amenia, NY: Grey House Publishing, 2019.

MLA: Vittori, Jodi "American Weapons in the Wrong Hands." *The Reference Shelf: U.S. National Debate Topic 2019-2020 Arms Sales,* edited by Micah L. Issitt, Grey House Publishing, 2019, pp. 151-153.

APA: Vittori, J. (2019). American weapons in the wrong hands. In Micah L. Issitt (Ed.), *The reference shelf: U.S. national debate topic 2019-2020 arms sales* (pp. 151-153). Amenia, NY: Grey House Publishing.

5
The Human Cost

A U.S. Air Force unmanned MQ-9 Reaper flies a combat mission over southern Afghanistan. The Trump administration recently eased export controls on military drones, which are often linked to civilian casualties.

The Human Dimension: Arms Trades and Human Rights

The United States has been continuously engaged in some form of warfare, either directly or indirectly, since World War II. Throughout the Cold War, U.S. military forces struggled against the perceived threat of communism in Asia and the Middle East. In the twenty-first century, thousands of American soldiers have been sent to locations around the world to secure American interests in an era marked by the rise of radical movements. As the world's most prolific arms supplier, America indirectly supports warfare and other forms of violent conflict around the world. American weapons have fueled radical militant movements, have given technological power to oppressive governments, and have fueled the black-market trade in military-grade equipment and weaponry.

It is argued that all of America's military-industrial activities, and the nation's long-term direct and indirect support of international warfare, serves a constructive purpose. Supporters of America's role in arms trading argue that this activity ultimately increases American security by strengthening allies and providing America with more potent international influence. It is also argued that America's arms deals provide essential economic benefits and help to stabilize regions that might otherwise fall under the control of nefarious forces. However, war and violence are always a detriment to any society, resulting in the loss of life and posing a threat to welfare, even if and when the cause of a conflict might be seen by some as just or necessary. Debates about America's role in the arms trade therefore necessarily include questions about human rights and whether or not the United States has a responsibility to engage in arms dealing in such a way as to limit threats to human welfare that may be exacerbated by the presence of American weapons.

War and Welfare

Wars result in civilian casualties. In Yemen, where the United States, Saudi Arabia, and the United Arab Emirates (UAE) have been engaged in civil war with anti-government rebels since 2015, the United Nations has estimated an average of 123 civilian casualties per week, 33 percent of whom were women and children.[1] The Iraq War resulted in more than 180,000 civilian deaths between 2003 and 2018, through direct violence, and at least as many wounded. Further, the human welfare issue in Iraq is more severe than even the number of confirmed casualties shows, as hundreds of thousands of Iraqis have died because of damage to systems that provide food, health care, drinking water, and other basic needs. More than 6 million were forced from their homes by violence in Iraq over this same period.[2]

Conflicts in Yemen and Iraq are only two of the many with which the United States is connected. U.S. weapons and military equipment have also been transferred and sold in Afghanistan, Egypt, and Syria. Some U.S. weapons are sold to agents that utilize them in attacks that harm civilians and noncombatants; some are sold to countries in unstable regions and end up in "the wrong hands."A prominent case of the latter involves the Syrian radical group ISIS, which purchased illicit weapons through unauthorized dealers, and as much as 90 percent of their weapons were initially part of arms deals conducted by the United States, Saudi Arabia, and European Union nations.[3] The number of civilians killed in the ongoing Syrian civil war, in which the United States has played a leading role, is in the hundreds of thousands. In the U.S.-led effort to capture the city of Mosul, that began in October2016, for instance, at least 9,000-11,000 civilians are believed to have been killed.[4]

The statistics show how U.S. involvement in global conflict, both directly and indirectly, has led to hundreds of thousands of civilian deaths over the past 20 years. While it is difficult enough to estimate casualties, the impact of war and violent conflict extends far beyond casualties. In Syria, for instance, more than 6 million individuals and families have been displaced, and more than 13 million are in need of humanitarian aid in the form of food, water, medicine, or shelter. As the largest arms producer and exporter in the world, the United States creates equipment that is used in the many conflicts of the modern world. One of the biggest debates surrounding the arms trade is whether or not the United States is responsible for violence caused using U.S.-made weapons or for exacerbating global conflicts. Research shows that arms dealing does not cause conflict in situations where existing conditions are stable. However, when arms are sold in unstable regions, the result can be significant. As Oliver Pamp reported in a 2018 study published in the *Journal of Peace Research*:

> While arms imports are not a genuine cause of instrastate conflicts, they significantly increase the probability of an onset in countries where conditions are notoriously conducive to conflict. In such situations, arms are not an effective deterrent but rather spark conflict escalation.[5]

Supporters of America's role in the global arms trade often argue that the United States does not seek to increase warfare or violence, but simply utilizes weapons in an effort to stabilize other countries or to address conflicts in which human welfare is already at stake. Opponents to weapons trading argue that this is not the case, and that U.S. policy has been motivated more by economic considerations than by concern for human welfare. They go on to argue that the United States has willfully ignored the human rights implications of arms dealing and thus bears responsibility for the contributions of America's military and weapons to the world's violent conflicts.

Women's Rights and Children's Rights

It can be difficult, when assessing violent interstate or civil conflicts, to determine which actors or groups are responsible for the continuation of violence. Estimating "noncombatant" casualties and injuries is a difficult process and resulting calculations involve considerable uncertainty. When estimating the human rights impact of military activity, or the weapons trade specifically, it is often useful to see how specific aspects of human rights are intertwined with military industrial activities.

For instance, in terms of human rights abuses, it is widely agreed that children, those under the age of 18, are comparatively "innocent" victims of global conflict, both because they lack the emotional and intellectual maturity to assume responsibility for the roles they play in such conflicts and because, as agents with little direct power to impact the unfolding of political social evolution, they are victims of decisions and activities undertaken by adults in power.

When it comes to child welfare, research has shown that the trade in small arms has a direct correlation with child death in conflict-ridden regions and with the potential for state and non-state militants to utilize child soldiers in violent conflicts. The link between the small arms (firearms) trade and child soldiers is a practical one, as young soldiers are better able to engage in conflict if provided with small arms, such as AK-47 assault rifles. Thus, easy-to-use small weapons provide the tools for those who would conscript child soldiers to do so.[6]

Another interesting academic discussion surrounding the arms trade looks at how "feminist foreign policy" aligns (or fails to align) with prevailing attitudes about the arms trade. In 2014, the Scandinavian nation of Sweden adopted what it called "a feminist foreign policy," meaning that the nation's legislators agreed to make women's rights a centerpiece of the nation's diplomatic efforts. Sweden's feminist foreign policy was based on the "three laudable R's:

Rights—Fighting against gender-based violence and discrimination and promoting equal rights for women.

Representation—Supporting female involvement at all levels of decision making, in both the private and public sector, including the military.

Resources—Ensuring equitable distribution of resources regardless of gender barriers.[7]

Sweden's decision to adopt a feminist foreign policy was not based solely on the belief that gender equality was a subjective "good" for global society; rather it was the result of an increasingly robust body of research in Europe and North America showing that involving women in the "peace process" as a whole reduces conflict and increases stability. For instance, a study from the Belfer Center, International Interactions, and the World Bank found that higher levels of gender equality are associated with lowered potential for violent conflict; a study from the International Peace Institute found that when women participate in peace talks, the resulting agreements are 35 percent more likely to last for at least 15 years; and a study from International Interactions found that the participation of women and women's groups in a peace agreement makes the peace agreement 64 percent less likely to fail. However, peace agreements and diplomatic negotiations between nations rarely include discussions of women's rights or gender equality. Between 1990 and 2017, only 19 percent of all peace agreements contained any reference to women's rights, and only 5 percent make any mention of gender-based violence.

The Council on Foreign Relations said in 2018, "Continued failure to include women in peace processes ignores their demonstrated effectiveness and overlooks a potential strategy to respond effectively to security threats around the world."[8]

The feminist foreign policy adopted by Sweden, and also by Canada, raises interesting questions about arms trading. For instance, though the Swedish and Canadian governments have officially condemned Saudi Arabia for the nation's record on gender-based violence and lack of equality for women, both nations have continued to supply Saudi Arabia with arms. Likewise, the United States government has taken an ideological stance against the abuse and exploitation of women and yet this stance has not been reflected in the nation's foreign policies. For instance, Saudi Arabia, America's biggest weapons purchaser, maintains a society without gender equality or child welfare policies, and women and children within that nation suffer from abuses that would be classified as violations of human rights under international law as established by the United Nations.[9]

In a landmark speech delivered in 1995 in Beijing, China, at the United Nations Fourth World Conference on Women, Hillary Clinton stated, "If there is one message that echoes forth from this conference, let it be that human rights are women's rights and women's rights are human rights, once and for all."[10] Nations that share this ideal must therefore contend with the question of whether a nation should limit or suspend arms trades with nations that fail to adopt international standards with regard to the treatment of women, like Saudi Arabia or the UAE. As the studies indicate, utilizing influence to promote gender equality may itself be a key piece of the puzzle in encouraging stability, which is one of the goals that both supporters of the arms trade and opponents hope to achieve through America's foreign policy.

Like children, women in many parts of the world lack political agency and play a lesser role in determining political or social policies, including whether or not governmental or other groups engage in armed conflict. Women in much of the world suffer from abuse in part due to the ongoing effects of patriarchic attitudes regarding the roles of women, both in leadership and male-dominated institutions of power (church, state, family, etc.). One of the most pressing debates in the field of arms trading and sales is whether or not the United States should utilize arms deals to encourage international adherence to the principles of equality and child welfare that U.S. citizens claim to favor.

Works Used:

Goldenberg, Suzanne. "Carter Uses Peace Prize Speech to Condemn US Policy." *The Guardian*. Dec 11, 2002. Retrieved from https://www.theguardian.com/world/2002/dec/11/usa.suzannegoldenberg.

"Hillary Clinton Declares 'Women's Rights Are Human Rights'." *PBS*. Sep 8, 1995. Retrieved from https://www.pbs.org/weta/washingtonweek/web-video/hillary-clinton-declares-womens-rights-are-human-rights.

"Iraqi Civilians." *Watson Institute*. Brown University. Nov 2018. Retrieved from https://watson.brown.edu/costsofwar/costs/human/civilians/Iraqi.

Keyton, David and Rohan, Brian. "UN Says Civilian Casualties in Yemen Average 123 per Week." *AP*. Associated Press. Dec 7, 2018. Retrieved from https://www.apnews.com/3e5cff9378594c9aba2374644f3634d6.

Newman, Katelyn. "Report: ISIS Gets Its Weapons from Around the World—Including the U.S." *US News & World Report*. Dec 14, 2017. Retrieved from https://www.usnews.com/news/world/articles/2017-12-14/report-isis-gets-its-weapons-from-around-the-world-including-the-us.

Oakford, Samuel. "Counting the Dead in Mosul." *The Atlantic*. Apr 5, 2018. Retrieved from https://www.theatlantic.com/international/archive/2018/04/counting-the-dead-in-mosul/556466/.

Pamp, Oliver, Rudolph, Lukas, and Paul W. Thurner. "The Build-Up of Coercive Capacities: Arms Imports and the Outbreak of Violent Intrastate Conflicts." *Journal of Peace Research*. Jan 31, 2018. Retrieved from https://journals.sagepub.com/doi/10.1177/0022343317740417.

"Strong Link between Child Soldiers and Small Arms Trade, UN Experts Say." *UN News*. Jul 15, 2008. Retrieved from https://news.un.org/en/story/2008/07/266342-strong-link-between-child-soldiers-and-small-arms-trade-un-experts-say.

Vogenstein, Rachel and Alexandra Bro. "Sweden's Feminist Foreign Policy, Long May It Reign." *FP*. Foreign Policy. Jan 30, 2019.

Vucetic, Srdjan. "The Uneasy Co-Existence of Arms Exports and Feminist Foreign Policy." *The Conversation*. Apr 8, 2018. Retrieved from https://theconversation.com/the-uneasy-co-existence-of-arms-exports-and-feminist-foreign-policy-93930.

"Women's Participation in Peace Processes." *CFR*. Council on Foreign Relations. Jan 30, 2019. Retrieved from https://www.cfr.org/interactive/womens-participation-in-peace-processes.

Notes

1. Keyton and Rohan, "UN Says Civilian Casualties in Yemen Average 123 per Week."
2. "Iraqi Civilians," *Watson Institute*.
3. Newman, "Report: ISIS Gets Its Weapons from Around the World—Including the U.S."
4. Oakford, "Counting the Dead in Mosul."
5. Pamp, Rudolph, and Thurner, "The Build-Up of Coercive Capacities: Arms Imports and the Outbreak of Violent Intrastate Conflicts."
6. "Strong Links between Child Soldiers and Small Arms Trade, UN Experts Say," *UN News*.
7. Vogelstein and Bro, "Sweden's Feminist Foreign Policy, Long May It Reign."
8. "Women's Participation in Peace Processes," *CFR*.

9. Vucetic, "The Uneasy Co-Existence of Arms Exports and Feminist Foreign Policy."

10. "Hillary Clinton Declares 'Women's Rights are Human Rights'," *PBS*.

How U.S. Guns Sold to Mexico End Up with Security Forces Accused of Crime and Human Rights Abuses

By John Lindsay-Poland
The Intercept, April 26, 2018

In a room full of weapons industry representatives in Washington, D.C., in February, one by one, people stood to introduce themselves. They had come together as part of the Defense Trade Advisory Group, which advises the State Department about how to make it easier to export U.S. weapons around the world. On the docket for the day was a proposal for something called "batch filing," which would allow weapon companies to submit multiple applications for export licenses at a time.

Many of [the] companies present had a particularly large stake in Mexico: There were representatives from Lockheed Martin, which sends Black Hawk helicopters to Mexico, and from Textron, which owns Bell helicopters, also purchased by Mexico's military. There was someone from Nammo Talley, from which the Mexican military bought more than 2,000 weapons in 2016 for a little over $8.3 million.

So when the time came for public comment on the proposal, Antonio Tizapa stood. Tizapa's son Jorge Antonio was one of 43 students from a teachers college in Ayotzinapa in the Mexican state of Guerrero, who were attacked and forcibly disappeared in 2014. The local police implicated in the students' disappearance were armed with U.S.-produced Colt assault rifles.

The chair, Bill Wade of the Pentagon contractor L3 Technologies, clearly did not want Tizapa to say anything. "We're really pressed for time, unless you have a question," Wade said. Tizapa had planned to speak in Spanish through an interpreter, but, faced with the chair's hostility, he spoke directly in English.

"My name is Antonio, I am the father of one of the 43 disappeared students in Mexico," he said. "Because the police used weapons, my son disappeared 40 months ago. He is my son. Please, don't send more weapons to Mexico. I am looking for my son. There are not just 43, it's more."

After Tizapa spoke, Wade moved on to the next comment without missing a beat or acknowledging his appeal in any way.

The Trump administration is set to make it easier for guns to flow to forces like those that disappeared Tizapa's son. As part of an "Arms Transfer Initiative" aimed at boosting all U.S. weapons sales, the administration will likely soon announce policies that would ease the rules by which the United States sends guns and munitions abroad. Under the new regime, oversight of export licenses is expected to move from the State Department to the Commerce Department, and many fear there will be less scrutiny with regards to human rights and national security concerns.

Mexico has already been a major beneficiary of easy U.S. arms exports. Since 2007, Mexico and the United States have undertaken a joint security strategy aimed at battling cartels and controlling narcotrafficking and other illicit activities. That strategy has coincided with an enormous increase in firearms sales from the U.S. to Mexico.

Recent Mexican and U.S. government data analyzed by the *Intercept* shows that legal U.S. gun and explosives exports to Mexico are higher than ever, and that the guns are flowing to all levels of the Mexican security and police apparatus. Legal U.S. firearm and ammunition exports to Mexico between 2015 and 2017 amounted to almost $123 million, according to U.S. Census Bureau trade records—more than a dozen times what they were between 2002 and 2004. Last year, four times such exports went to Mexico than to any other Latin American nation. But if the aim of firearms sales to Mexico is to abate criminal violence, it has failed dramatically. Homicide victims in 2017 in Mexico surpassed 29,000, the highest on record.

> **Legal U.S. firearm and ammunition exports to Mexico between 2015 and 2017 amounted to almost $123 million.**

The exponential growth in sales to Mexico has not been accompanied by controls to track where the guns go or to ensure that they do not land in the hands of police or military units that are credibly alleged to have committed gross human rights abuses or colluded with criminal groups—the very groups that security forces are being armed to combat. Legally exported U.S. firearms have been used in massacres, disappearances, and by security forces that collude with criminal groups in Mexico on a broad scale.

How Guns Flow from the Military to Local and State Police

The Mexican military is the only legal importer of firearms into Mexico. In turn, the Mexican army is the only legal distributor of guns within the country; personal possession of firearms is highly restricted, with a single military-run retail store for gun sales in Mexico City. Aside from the weapons that the military acquires for its own forces, most legally imported guns in Mexico are sold to state and local police forces. More than half of the 305,086 guns sold by the Mexican Secretariat of National Defense—which includes the army and air force and is known by its Spanish acronym SEDENA—from 2010 through 2016 were sold to police, according to documents released by SEDENA in response to a public records request.

Since criminal organizations arm themselves with U.S. assault weapons illegally trafficked from the U.S. retail market, legal exports to police and the military are part of a deadly arms race with these organizations. More than 20,000 firearms obtained by Mexican state and federal police went missing or were stolen from 2006 to 2017, according to SEDENA data. More than 7,000 of the weapons went missing from police in Mexico City and Mexico state. In the state of Guerrero, the number of guns gone missing or stolen between 2010 and 2016 amounts to nearly one-fifth of the firearms police acquired in the state during the same period.

There is also evidence that firearms legally imported from the United States have been used in some of the worst human rights violations in Mexico in recent years. The local police who attacked the 43 Ayotzinapa students were armed with AR6530 rifles, a model variant of the AR-15, legally supplied through licensed shipments from Colt, according to documents in the judicial record.

An investigation by Mexico's National Human Rights Commission found that Federal Police, who carried out the massacre of 22 persons in Tanhuato, Michoacán, in 2015, killed five of them with Dillon Aero guns mounted on Black Hawk helicopters. The Dillon guns fire some 125 rounds per second, and Mexico obtained 16 of them for the army in 2013, for just over $1 million, and then another 12 in 2015, according to Mexico's most recent Arms Trade Treaty report.

These are unusual cases, in that we know which weapons were involved. Most homicides in Mexico—including those carried out by state forces—are never investigated, so there is no judicial record identifying the firearms that were used. But the volume of U.S. firearms going to Mexico, combined with the well-established record of police and military forces colluding with organized crime and committing gross human rights violations, means that U.S. guns are certainly at the scene of many more crimes.

The example of U.S. gun producer Sig Sauer is instructive as to how guns move from the military to police. In April 2015, the U.S. State Department issued a $266 million license to Sig Sauer: $265 million for gun sales, and $1 million for other equipment and technical support to the Mexican navy, defense ministry, interior ministry, and federal and state police forces. That year, Mexico imported 3,060 rifles, 3,819 pistols, and 505 machines guns produced by Sig Sauer's New Hampshire production facilities. The license also permits the Mexican navy to assemble Sig Sauer MPX submachine guns, capable of firing 850 rounds a minute, from "kits" made of parts produced by the company. All told, as of January, $29.3 million in guns and gun parts had been exported from Sig Sauer and other New Hampshire manufacturers to Mexico since April 2015, according to Census Bureau trade records—meaning that Sig Sauer has at least $235 million left in sales to make before its license expires in 2024.

On its end, since 2014, the Mexican military has sold 1,400 U.S.-produced Sig Sauer firearms to police in 18 Mexican states, including states where there is an extensive record of collusion with organized crime, such as Tamaulipas, Michoacán, and Chihuahua, SEDENA records show. State authorities also distribute these weapons to local police; in the state of Mexico, for example, Sig Sauer weapons were sold to police in five municipalities, while Colt weapons went to three other municipalities, as well as state police, according to a state police document.

According to data recently released by the Mexican military, other U.S. gun producers that have exported thousands of firearms each to Mexico for use by the police or private individuals include: Colt, Bushmaster, Mossberg, Smith & Wesson, DS Arms, Remington, and Browning. The Mexican military has also purchased military weapons from U.S. producers Nammo Talley, Barrett Firearms, and Knight Armament Company since 2014. In Veracruz, the police responsible for at least 15 death squad murders purchased, since 2013, at least 674 firearms exported by three U.S. arms companies: Colt, Bushmaster, and Combined Systems, according to the Veracruz public security secretariat. Local police in Veracruz also obtained weapons from Sig Sauer and Connecticut-based Mossberg.

Beyond guns, U.S. Census Bureau trade data show that just over $8.3 million in military explosives were delivered to Mexico from Arizona in September and October 2017, more than in any year in the last decade for all states combined. (In all of 2016, military explosives exported from the entire United States to Mexico amounted to less than $800,000.) The Census records do not indicate which company exported the explosives. In addition, Milkor USA, based in Tucson, sold M32A1 grenade launchers used by the Mexican military special forces. In 2017, more than $5 million worth of grenade launchers were exported to Mexico from Texas alone.

The permissive U.S. attitude toward gun exports has prompted several gun producers based in the European Union to beef up production in the United States, thus evading EU restrictions on arms sales to countries with widespread violence or human rights violations. Sig Sauer, for instance, whose parent company is in Germany, more than quadrupled global exports from the United States between 2009 and 2016, according to data from the Bureau of Alcohol, Tobacco and Firearms. (Germany stopped approving licenses for gun exports to Mexico after 2010.) Beretta (Italy) and Glock (Austria) produce guns in Tennessee and Georgia, respectively, and are the two brands that Mexico has imported in the largest numbers since 2007, per SEDENA records. The State Department in February 2016 issued a license to Glock to export more than 11,000 9mm and .45 caliber pistols from its Smyrna, Georgia, facility for re-sale to Mexican police.

More Guns, Less Tracking

The State Department is supposed to track end users of U.S. arms exports, to ensure that they don't go missing or end up in the hands of criminal elements—exactly as is feared is the case in Mexico. But the methods for tracking gun shipments have systemic problems, State Department officials admit behind the scenes. And with the Trump administration's proposed changes, the process could be undermined even further.

Officials in the State Department's Directorate of Defense Trade Controls, speaking on background during a meeting last summer, told me that U.S. and Mexican systems for identifying firearm shipments from the United States to Mexico are incompatible and incapable of talking with each other, making it impossible to track firearm shipments without physical inspections, which happen only occasionally.

In addition, when the State Department Bureau of Human Rights, Democracy and Labor, or DRL, receives firearms exports license applications to review for human rights concerns, approximately 80 percent of the applications show the end user as the military in Mexico City, according to a DRL official in December, who also spoke on background. That's entirely inconsistent with SEDENA's data, which shows that most of more than 305,000 firearms it distributed between 2010 and 2016 went to police and private users outside Mexico City. (Although the U.S. government compiles and releases some records on gun exports, Mexican public records requests have resulted in this more granular look at the end users in Mexico of U.S. guns. But Mexico recently passed an "Internal Security Law," which classifies more military information and may make it harder for the public to access those records.)

When the applications did identify units that would receive the firearms, according to a State Department official who spoke on background in May 2017, DRL did not crosscheck those units with a human rights database known as INVEST, which is designed for screening military and police units nominated for U.S. assistance. A State Department spokesperson said that commercial arms sales are subject to a different process from assistance, "which still takes into account reports of human rights violations, including by foreign security units," but neglecting the INVEST database may help explain how many end users with tarred records received U.S. gun exports.

For its part, the Trump administration is poised to make the gun export licensing system favor the arms industry even more, with a planned transfer of export licensing from the State Department to the Commerce Department.

The arms industry has long pushed for this change—and won significant changes from the Obama administration easing export restrictions on many types of military equipment. Despite soaring arms sales under Obama, human rights controls remained nominally a priority, but many are concerned that the Trump administration's overhaul will jettison them. In announcing the Arms Trade Initiative last week, the White House included human rights among the things to be taken into consideration, but it remains to be seen how vetting will actually be applied. A move to Commerce would remove congressional oversight of the licenses, which has in the past led to the cancellation of gun export deals to the Philippines—where armed forces have allegedly carried out thousands of extrajudicial killings—and to Turkey's presidential guard, after guard members beat up demonstrators in Washington, D.C.

Worried by Trump's proposal, three U.S. senators wrote last September that firearms exports "should be subject to more—not less—rigorous controls and oversight."

Given the record under today's controls, it seems certain that loosening them further will mean that Antonio Tizapa and the tens of thousands of other Mexicans who have lost family members to gun violence will be joined by new victims of U.S.-sourced weaponry.

Print Citations

CMS: Lindsay-Poland, John. "How U.S. Guns Sold to Mexico End Up with Security Forces Accused of Crime and Human Rights Abuses." In *The Reference Shelf: U.S. National Debate Topic 2019-2020 Arms Sales,* edited by Micah L. Issitt, 163-168. Amenia, NY: Grey House Publishing, 2019.

MLA: Lindsay-Poland, John. "How U.S. Guns Sold to Mexico End Up with Security Forces Accused of Crime and Human Rights Abuses." *The Reference Shelf: U.S. National Debate Topic 2019-2020 Arms Sales,* edited by Micah L. Issitt, Grey House Publishing, 2019, pp. 163-168.

APA: Lindsay-Poland, J. (2019). How U.S. guns sold to Mexico end up with security forces accused of crime and human rights abuses. In Micah L. Issitt (Ed.), *The reference shelf: U.S. national debate topic 2019-2020 arms sales* (pp. 163-168). Amenia, NY: Grey House Publishing.

Ukraine: US Arms Sales Making Big Business Money While Ordinary People Pay the Price

By Liana Semchuk

The Conversation, March 27, 2019

Selling lethal weapons to Ukraine is the equivalent of pouring kerosene onto a flame. But ongoing hostilities between Ukraine and Russia—including the Kerch strait crisis, which began late last year when Russia intercepted three Ukrainian vessels and took 24 crew members captive—are also a major business opportunity for the world's largest defence contractors. Despite the risk of serious escalation, these companies continue to provide Ukraine with lethal aid so it can defend itself against Russia—for a price, of course.

The US special representative for Ukraine negotiations, Kurt Volker, stated recently that Washington remains committed to providing support to Ukraine and its military, including anti-tank systems. He even hinted that the US is considering expanding the types of lethal aid that it could begin selling to Ukraine, saying: "We also need to be looking at things like air defence and coastal defence."

This is a troubling prospect. In March, US army general Curtis Scaparrotti said that the US could also bolster the Ukrainian military's sniper capabilities. Speaking to the Senate Armed Services Committee, he said:

> There are other systems, sniper systems, ammunition and, perhaps looking at the Kerch Strait, perhaps consideration for naval systems, as well, here in the future as we move forward.

This comment has been widely underreported and has not received nearly as much attention as it deserves considering the potential consequences.

At worst, more lethal aid could escalate the conflict further. At best, it will continue to keep alive a conflict that has already claimed more than 10,000 lives. Finding a straightforward policy alternative is difficult, but sending more lethal aid to achieve the unattainable goal of Ukraine defeating Russia is certainly no solution.

Impact

Despite attempts by Volker and Scaparrotti to market the proposition as a way to help Ukraine defend itself against Russia, the immediate benefits seem clearer to

America's weapons manufacturing sector than to Ukrainian civilians, who will undoubtedly get caught in the crossfire.

The Stockholm International Peace Research Institute reported that the US is home to five of the world's ten largest defence contractors. Lockheed Martin, by far the largest in the field, in 2017 had an estimated US$44.9 billion in arms contracts globally.

The company was also contracted (with Raytheon) in 2018 to provide Ukraine with Javelin anti-tank missiles.

The US Pentagon said: "The Javelin system will help Ukraine build its long-term defense capacity to defend its sovereignty and territorial integrity in order to meet its national defense requirements."

But Lockheed Martin likely profited handsomely from the deal. Meanwhile, the company's financial reports showed fourth quarter 2018 net sales of US$14.4 billion, compared to US$13.8 billion in the fourth quarter of 2017. This year, the company is expecting sales to grow by

The West should not abandon its rhetoric of support for Ukraine's territorial integrity.

as much as 6%. This is unlikely to be the case if the number of conflicts around the world declines.

It's clear why Washington wants to sell more weapons to Ukraine. But whether Ukraine remains receptive and willing to continue buying them may hinge on the outcome of the upcoming presidential election, which is scheduled for March 31.

Presidential candidate Volodymyr Zelensky, who is currently leading in the polls, seems to offer hope that Ukraine may change its current strategy. This is reflected in a statement Zelensky made in March in which he emphasised the need to negotiate with Russia in order to "save people's lives".

Is There a Solution?

As well as better diplomacy, Zelensky also sees direct democracy as a way to resolve the crisis. Rather than pursuing the same ineffective policy, which has achieved absolutely nothing except for a greater death toll and growing human misery, he proposed a referendum on the outcome of his negotiations with Russia on the conflict in eastern Ukraine. This approach might not lead to a quick fix or immediately restore peace in the region—but it is more likely to succeed than simply supplying more weapons with which to prolong the fighting.

The West should not abandon its rhetoric of support for Ukraine's territorial integrity. But policymakers and society more broadly should be careful not to assume that simply selling more weapons to Ukraine will yield a definitive victory over Russia and its separatist allies.

While the ongoing war in the eastern Donbas region and the recent Kerch incident offer an opportunity for big businesses to make a profit, it's ordinary people who will pay the price. The current approach to deescalating the conflict needs to be dramatically reevaluated—and lethal weapons must be taken off the negotiating table.

Print Citations

CMS: Semchuk, Liana. "Ukraine: US Arms Sales Making Big Business Money While Ordinary People Pay the Price." In *The Reference Shelf: U.S. National Debate Topic 2019-2020 Arms Sales,* edited by Micah L. Issitt, 169-171. Amenia, NY: Grey House Publishing, 2019.

MLA: Semchuk, Liana. "Ukraine: US Arms Sales Making Big Business Money While Ordinary People Pay the Price." *The Reference Shelf: U.S. National Debate Topic 2019-2020 Arms Sales,* edited by Micah L. Issitt, Grey House Publishing, 2019, pp. 169-171.

APA: Semchuk, L. (2019). Ukraine: US arms sales making big business money while ordinary people pay the price. In Micah L. Issitt (Ed.), *The reference shelf: U.S. national debate topic 2019-2020 arms sales* (pp. 169-171). Amenia, NY: Grey House Publishing.

U.S. Points Finger, and Arms Exports, at Human Rights Abusers

By Zach Toombs and Jeffrey Smith
The Center for Public Integrity, May 19, 2014

Every May and June, different branches of the State Department paint contrasting portraits of how Washington views dozens of strategically significant countries around the world, in seemingly rivalrous reports by its Human Rights and Political-Military Affairs bureaus.

The former routinely criticizes other nations for a lack of fealty to democratic principles, citing abuses of the right to expression, assembly, speech and political choice. The latter tallies the government's latest successes in the export of American weaponry, often to the same countries criticized by the former.

This year was no different. The State Department's Military Assistance Report on June 8 stated that it approved $44.28 billion in arms shipments to 173 nations in the last fiscal year, including some that struggled with human rights problems. These nations include the United Arab Emirates, Qatar, Israel, Djibouti, Honduras, Saudi Arabia, Kuwait, and Bahrain.

Three nations with records of suppressing democratic dissent in the last year—Algeria, Egypt, and Peru—are listed in the report as recently receiving U.S. firearms, armored vehicles, and items from a category that includes chemical and riot control agents like tear gas. The State Department confirmed that U.S. tear gas was delivered to Egypt up to the end of November, but has declined to confirm it was also sent to Algeria and Peru.

The export of American arms to countries around the world—what the State Department calls a tangible expression of American "partnership" —is in fact booming. The commercial arms sales reviewed by the State Department reached $44.28 billion in fiscal year 2011, a $10 billion sales increase since 2010. Next year should see another increase of 70 percent, the department says.

Those sales—plus the government-to-government arms exports overseen by the Pentagon—make the United States the world's top provider of major conventional weapons, according to the Stockholm International Peace Research Institute. Russia, France, and China followed behind. Much of the recent U.S. increase came from vastly expanded sales to Saudi Arabia, Brazil and India.

"Obviously, we're going to continue to press and advocate for U.S. arms sales," said Assistant Secretary for the Bureau of Political-Military Affairs Andrew Shapiro in a June 14 news conference addressing arms exports. "We are hopeful that arms sales to India will increase. We've made tremendous progress in this relationship over the last decade."

Shapiro explained that by "progress" he meant that U.S. arms sales to India went from "nearly zero" to around $8 billion in that period.

Here's what the May 24 report issued by State's Bureau of Democracy, Human Rights and Labor said about India: "The most significant human rights problems were police and security force abuses, including extrajudicial killings, torture, and rape; widespread corruption at all levels of government; and separatist, insurgent, and societal violence. Other human rights problems included disappearances, poor prison conditions that were frequently life threatening, arbitrary arrest and detention, and lengthy pretrial detention."

India is not alone in getting U.S. arms sales pitches at the same time Washington points at rights abuses. Commercial arms sales totaling $2.4 billion were approved to the United Arab Emirates, which the State Department said had abridged key political freedoms; sales totalling $1.7 billion were approved to Qatar, which lacks independent media and restricts freedom of assembly; and sales totalling $1.39 billion were approved to Djibouti, which State said had harassed, abused and detained government critics. (A top 10 country list appears at the end of this article.)

"When we deem that cooperating with an ally or partner in the security sector will advance our national security, we advocate tirelessly on behalf of U.S. [arms manufacturing] companies," Shapiro said.

No law requires that U.S. arms be exported only to countries that the State Department—in its annual human rights assessments—determines are treating their citizens well. Instead, a more narrow restriction known as the so-called "Leahy Law," named for author Sen. Patrick Leahy (D-VT.) and passed in 1997, prohibits U.S. assistance to specific military and police units deemed responsible for human rights abuses.

Moreover, as Leahy spokesman David Carle pointed out in an interview, the law only covers direct government-to-government transfers overseen by the Defense Department, a stream of exports separate from the commercial sales reviewed and approved by the State Department. So, although the Defense Department's $34.8 billion in direct government-to-government sales are covered by the Leahy Law, the $44.28 billion in sales authorized by State are not.

Adotei Akwei, the managing director of Amnesty International's government relations efforts, said that "In all of these countries, there's a need for a much more rigorous process for looking at where these weapons are going and how they're being used. Even though the State Department identifies problems, we still see these sales taking place over and over again. There's a much-exemplified disconnect between the identifying of abuse and the sales."

Shapiro, at the press conference, said his Bureau of Political-Military Affairs ensures any military assistance to foreign militaries and companies "is fully in line with U.S. foreign policy." Officials vet governments as well as the companies on both sides of the sale, he said. "We only allow a sale after we carefully examine issues like human rights, regional security, and nonproliferation concerns."

The State Department emphasizes that many items shipped to foreign militaries are used only for external defense, not for internal suppression. In the case of the United Arab Emirates, for example, a $29.4 billion sale authorized in January for fiscal year 2012 consisted mostly of the purchase of 84 F-15 fighter aircraft. But State also authorized billions of dollars in sales of small arms, ammunition and toxicological agents to various countries, including $3,091,166 of firearms to Peru and $1,153,617 to Honduras.

Although State's public export declaration lists such broad categories of exported weaponry, determining exactly what the shipments contained is still a challenge. Spokesman David McKeeby declined to discuss whether Peru and Algeria got riot control agents, for example, despite the department's confirmation that Egypt did. Asked why, he said "Egypt was a very unique case. Unfortunately, I can't tell you any more details about these countries, or these licenses."

McKeeby added that "what I can tell you in Bahrain and Algeria's case, for example, is that a lot of these licenses predate the Arab Spring period, and that's something that's being considered for licenses for the next fiscal year. But the information you want falls under ITAR. That's how these reports are written, and that's what we leave it at." ITAR stands for State's International Traffic in Arms Regulations, which say that details of the arms exports "may generally not be disclosed to the public."

Representatives of several companies linked in public accounts to shipments of tear gas canisters to Middle Eastern nations declined to comment. Jose Corbera, a spokesman for the Peruvian embassy's Commercial Office did not return a request for comment, and officials at Algeria's embassy also declined to provide data on imports of U.S. munitions.

State spokeswoman Beth Gosselin did note that some of the weapons exports listed in the State Department's report were meant for use by U.S. forces abroad, not by foreign militaries. In Bahrain, for example, $266.7 million of the $280.3 million worth of military arms and equipment were items for the Navy's "Fifth Fleet" station on the island nation, she said. Gosselin declined to provide similar data for other countries.

Matt Schroeder, director of the Arms Sales Monitoring Project at the Federation of American Scientists, said the U.S. vetting process for militaries and governments receiving arms is better than that of many nations, but that information on which weapons go to U.S. forces and which weapons go to other users is rarely accessible. "It's difficult to take the dollar value of arms shipped to a country and extrapolate which section of these items may be vulnerable to misuse," Schroeder said. "It's tough to make that call."

A provision written by Leahy and passed by Congress in 2011 requires legislative approval for the sale of crowd-control material to Middle Eastern governments facing democratic unrest. That provision forced an initial halt to weapons transfers to Bahrain, which has seen protests dating back to last year's Arab Spring. But in May, the U.S. ended the months-long freeze for some items, renewing the export of arms meant to be used for external defense, such as harbor security boats and engines for jet planes.

The issue of arms exports to countries engaged in repression of their own populaces has been debated recently by top U.S. and Russian officials. Secretary of State Hillary Clinton on June 12 accused Russia of shipping attack helicopters to Syrian President Bashar al-Assad's regime, charging that those weapons were being turned against Syria's own people. In a retort, Russian Foreign Minister Sergey Lavrov said, "We are not supplying to Syria or anywhere else things that are used in fighting with peaceful demonstrators, in contrast to the United States, which is regularly sending such special means to countries in the region."

Lavrov did not mention any nation by name, but Shapiro took the comment as a critique of U.S. exports to Bahrain and called the Russian criticism "totally specious …We have made clear that we're not selling equipment to Bahrain now that can be used for internal security purposes until there is improvement on human rights, and … as Secretary Clinton pointed out, the sales to Syria are directly implicated in attacking innocent people, innocent civilians. So we believe that that comparison does not hold water."

Next month, the United Nations is scheduled to discuss a global treaty that would require annual reports from all nations detailing the value and type of weapons they exported. Although President George W. Bush's administration opposed the U.N. Arms Trade Treaty in favor of handling weapons tracking on a national level, Clinton reversed that position in a statement in October 2009, saying, "The United States is prepared to work hard for a strong international standard."

U.S. officials have said the treaty, expected to be approved by the end of July, would effectively force other nations to make declarations comparable to what the State Department already does in its annual military assistance report. Akwei expressed hope that the result will be a more concrete system for tracking international arms shipments and ensuring they're not used in cases of human rights abuse.

"The treaty finally focuses an international lens on this huge trade where the oversight is scarce and haphazard," Akwei said. "It will be largely dependent on cooperation of countries like China and Russia, but it will give NGOs in those countries, and worldwide, the ability to see records and ask questions about arms trade."

What follows is a list of the top 10 national recipients in fiscal 2011 of commercially sold U.S. weapons that were cited by the State Department for human rights shortcomings in calendar 2011:

United Arab Emirates
Commercial arms authorized:

Total:	$2,465,144,471 (4th highest value out of 173 nations)
Types of weapons:	Missiles / rockets / torpedoes, firearms, toxicological agents (may have included tear gas and riot control agents)
Types of equipment:	Aircraft and equipment, ammunition

Human rights problems

"Three core human rights issues continue to be of concern: citizens' inability to change their government; limitations on citizens' civil liberties (including the freedoms of speech, press, assembly, and association); and lack of judicial independence ... political parties are not permitted. The government continued to interfere with privacy and to restrict civil liberties, including usage of the Internet."

"Political organizations, political parties, and trade unions are illegal."

The government does not provide equal rights for women and foreign workers. UAE courts reserve the option of imposing flogging as punishment for adultery, prostitution, consensual premarital sex, pregnancy outside marriage, defamation of character, and drug or alcohol abuse.

Qatar
Commercial arms authorized:

Total:	$1,792,415,581 (8th)
Types of weapons:	Explosives, missiles / rockets / torpedoes
Types of equipment:	Military electronics, aircraft and equipment, ammunition

Human rights problems

"The constitution provides for, but strictly regulates, freedom of assembly. Organizers must meet a number of restrictions and conditions to acquire a permit for a public meeting. For example, the Director General of Public Security at the Ministry of Interior must give permission for a meeting, a decision which is subject to appeal to the minister of interior, who has the final decision."

"The constitution provides for freedom of speech and press in accordance with the law, but the government limited these rights in practice ... The law provides for restrictive procedures on the establishment of newspapers, closure, and confiscation of assets of a publication. It also criminalizes libel and slander, including injury to dignity. All print media were owned by members of the ruling family or proprietors who enjoyed close ties

to government officials. There were no independent broadcast media, and state-owned television and radio reflected government views ... In at least one case, the authorities contacted a reporter with a warning after the reporter published an article critical of the government." There is no law criminalizing domestic violence or spousal rape.

Israel
Commercial arms authorized:

Total:	$1,462,319,370 (10th)
Types of weapons:	Firearms, toxicological agents (may have included tear gas and riot control agents), missiles / rockets / torpedoes
Types of equipment:	Armored vehicles, aircraft and equipment, ammunition

Human rights problems

"The most significant human rights issues during the year were terrorist attacks against civilians; institutional and societal discrimination against Arab citizens—in particular issues of access to housing and employment opportunities; and societal discrimination and domestic violence against women."

"NGOs continued to criticize ... detention practices they termed abusive, including isolation, sleep deprivation, and psychological abuse, such as threats to interrogate family members or demolish family homes."

Djibouti
Commercial arms authorized:

Total:	$1,396,999,702 (12th)
Types of weapons:	Heavy guns / armament, missiles / rockets / torpedoes
Types of equipment:	Military electronics, cameras / auxiliary equipment, ammunition

Human rights problems

"The most serious human rights problem in the country was the government's abridgement of the right of citizens to change or significantly influence their government; it did so by harassing, abusing, and detaining government critics and by its unwillingness to permit the population access to independent sources of information within the country."

"Numerous persons were detained for political reasons during the months leading up to the election and released afterwards. For example, the government charged eight men—including human rights activist Jean Paul Noel Abdi—with conspiring against

the state. The prisoners were permitted legal representation and were allowed to meet with their attorneys before trial. Noel Abdi was released two weeks later. The remaining prisoners were detained for two months and released shortly after the election."

"Although the constitution provides for freedom of assembly, the government severely restricted this right. The Interior Ministry requires permits for peaceful assemblies and denied such permits to opposition groups during the election campaign."

Honduras
Commercial arms authorized:

Total:	$1,390,675,958 (13th)
Types of weapons:	Firearms
Types of equipment:	Aircraft and equipment, fire-control systems, guided missile tracking equipment

Human rights problems

"Among the most serious human rights problems were corruption within the national police force, institutional weakness of the judiciary, and discrimination and violence against vulnerable populations. Police and government agents committed unlawful killings. Vigilantes and former members of the security forces carried out arbitrary and summary killings ... Although the constitution and law prohibit such practices, there were instances in which the police and military employed them, including police beatings and other abuse of detainees."

"On December 7, unknown gunmen on a motorcycle shot and killed former senior government adviser for security Alfredo Landaverde. In the weeks preceding his death, Landaverde had publicly called for cleaning up the National Police and alleged that its leadership was linked to organized crime. An investigation into his death continued at year's end."

"During the year confrontations over a long-standing land dispute between owners of African palm plantations and rural field workers in the Aguan Valley, Colon Department, resulted in the deaths of or injuries to approximately 55 persons, including field hands, private security guards, security force members, one judge, and bystanders. At year's end responsibility for all but two of these deaths had not been established. Human rights groups alleged that police, soldiers, and private security guards used disproportionate force against the protesting workers."

Saudi Arabia

Commercial arms authorized:

Total:	$877,678,790 (16th)
Types of weapons:	Firearms, toxicological agents (may have included tear gas and riot control agents), heavy guns / armament, explosives, missiles / rockets / torpedoes
Types of equipment:	Armored vehicles, aircraft and equipment, guided missile systems

Human rights problems

"The most important human rights problems reported included citizens' lack of the right and legal means to change their government; pervasive restrictions on universal rights such as freedom of expression, including on the Internet, and freedom of assembly, association, movement, and religion; and a lack of equal rights for women and children, as well as for workers."

"… on July 27, security officials reportedly took a prominent human rights activist, Mekhlef bin Daham al-Shammary, from his prison cell at the Damman General Prison to a room where there were no surveillance cameras and severely beat him. A guard then allegedly poured an antiseptic cleaning liquid down al-Shammary's throat, resulting in his being taken to a hospital."

"There were reports that at least two of a group of 16 men found guilty of security-related offenses were tortured in the period between their arrest in 2007 and their conviction on November 22. Among them, according to the nongovernmental organization (NGO) Amnesty International (AI), was Suliman al-Reshoudi, a 73-year-old former judge, who was subjected in prison to "severe physical and psychological tortures," including more than three years of solitary confinement. One of the detainees was allegedly beaten on at least seven occasions with metal sticks and received electric shocks. Saud al-Hashimi was reportedly abused by being placed for five hours in a severely cold cell and forced to confess, among other acts, to contacting Al-Jazeera television station and to collecting money without the permission of the ruler."

> **No law requires that U.S. arms be exported only to countries that the State Department—in its annual human rights assessment—determines are treating their citizens well.**

Kuwait
Commercial arms authorized:

Total:	$693,691,173 (19th)
Types of weapons:	Firearms, toxicological agents (may have included tear gas and riot control agents), heavy guns / armament, missiles / rockets / torpedoes
Types of equipment:	Armored vehicles, aircraft and equipment

Human rights problems

"... there were reports that some police and members of the security forces abused detainees during the year. Police and security forces were more likely to inflict such abuse on noncitizens, particularly non-Gulf Arabs and Asians. Security forces reportedly detained, harassed, and sexually abused transgender persons."

"The government restricted freedom of speech, particularly in instances purportedly related to national security. The law also specifically prohibits material insulting Islam, the emir, the constitution, or the neutrality of the courts or Public Prosecutor's Office. The law mandates jail terms for anyone who "defames religion," and any Muslim citizen may file criminal charges against a person the citizen believes has defamed Islam, the ruling family, or public morals."

"In December 2010 authorities shut the local offices of the Al Jazeera television network and withdrew its accreditation after it broadcast footage of police using force to break up an unauthorized gathering of oppositionists and subsequently gave airtime to opposition parliamentarians who strongly criticized the government for the police actions."

Algeria
Commercial arms authorized:

Total:	$406,056,112 (20th)
Types of weapons:	Firearms, heavy guns / armament, explosives, toxicological agents (may have included tear gas and riot control agents)
Types of equipment:	Armored vehicles, aircraft and equipment

Human rights problems

"There were reports of dozens of individuals detained for political reasons, including peaceful assembly in Algiers. In virtually all of the instances, police detained activists participating in protests or marches and held them either in the backs of riot trucks on site or transported them to nearby police precincts. Police released the activists without

charges once the protests had subsided … Other human rights concerns were reports of unlawful killings, overuse of pretrial detention, poor prison conditions, abuse of prisoners, and lack of judicial independence."

"Every Saturday from February 12 to late April, government security forces prevented protesters with the political opposition group National Coordination for Change and Democracy (CNCD) from staging a march in Algiers. On several occasions, CNCD organizers submitted paperwork to local officials requesting permission to march, but the requests were denied on security grounds. In some cases police arrested protesters and injured some of them as a result of participation in unsanctioned protests."

"Between 3,000 and 5,000 university students on April 12 staged the first successful public march in Algiers since 2001, despite police efforts to prevent it. Students were largely nonviolent, but there were approximately 100 injuries."

"Radio and television were government-owned and frequently broadcasted coverage favorable to the government. Sources maintained that broadcast media did not grant sufficient access to opposition parties and critical NGOs. During nonelection periods opposition parties and spokesmen regularly were denied access to public radio or television."

Peru

Commercial arms authorized:

Total:	$404,325,333 (21st)
Types of weapons:	Firearms, heavy guns / armament, toxicological agents (may have included tear gas and riot control agents)
Types of equipment:	Armored vehicles, aircraft and equipment

Human rights problems

"The following human rights problems …were reported: killings by security forces of protesters during demonstrations, harsh prison conditions, abuse of detainees and inmates by prison security forces, lengthy pretrial detention and inordinate trial delays, intimidation of the media, incomplete registration of internally displaced persons, and discrimination against women."

"Allegations of abuse most often arose immediately following an arrest, when families were prohibited from visiting suspects and when attorneys had limited access to detainees. In some cases police and security forces threatened or harassed victims, relatives, and witnesses to prevent them from filing charges of human rights violations."

Bahrain
Commercial arms authorized:

Total:	$280,373,829 (28th)
Types of weapons:	Firearms, heavy guns / armament
Types of equipment:	Ammunition, aircraft and equipment, military electronics

Human rights problems

"On several occasions government forces used unnecessary and disproportionate force to disperse protesters … the government used excessive force on February 17 when it used tear gas, shotguns, batons, sound bombs, and rubber bullets to disperse protesters from the GCC/Pearl Roundabout. Approximately 1,000 MOI [Ministry of Interior] personnel entered the GCC/Pearl Roundabout at 3 a.m. to disperse camping protesters. Personnel from the BNSA, CID, and BDF Intelligence were also on site. Security forces fired numerous rounds of tear gas to disperse protesters and engaged protesters directly. The MOI indicated that a number of protesters assaulted police officers with rocks, sticks, metal rods, swords, knives, and other sharp objects. As a result, more than 40 officers sustained injuries, including severe cuts to limbs. The clearing operation and subsequent clashes between security personnel and protesters led to the deaths of four individuals from shotgun wounds and injuries to 50 protesters. Soon after the police crackdown, BDF tanks occupied the GCC/Pearl Roundabout to stop demonstrators from occupying the area. On February 19, security forces withdrew from the GCC/Pearl Roundabout, allowing demonstrators to retake control of the area."

"[In prisons] Many reports followed a similar pattern of abuse: arbitrary arrest, beating without interrogation, beating with interrogation, harassment and intimidation without further physical abuse, and then release of the detainee after any visible wounds or signs of mistreatment had healed."

Print Citations

CMS: Toombs, Zach, and Jeffrey Smith. "U.S. Points Finger, and Arms Exports, at Human Rights Abuses." In *The Reference Shelf: U.S. National Debate Topic 2019-2020 Arms Sales,* edited by Micah L. Issitt, 172-182. Amenia, NY: Grey House Publishing, 2019.

MLA: Toombs, Zach, and Jeffrey Smith. "U.S. Points Finger, and Arms Exports, at Human Rights Abuses." *The Reference Shelf: U.S. National Debate Topic 2019-2020 Arms Sales,* edited by Micah L. Issitt, Grey House Publishing, 2019, pp. 172-182.

APA: Toombs, Z., & J. Smith. (2019). U.S. points finger, and arms exports, at human rights abuses. In Micah L. Issitt (Ed.), *The reference shelf: U.S. national debate topic 2019-2020 arms sales* (pp. 172-182). Amenia, NY: Grey House Publishing.

Want to Punish Saudi Arabia? Cut Off Its Weapons Supply

By Jonathan D. Caverley
The New York Times, October 12, 2018

More than a week after Jamal Khashoggi, a Saudi Arabian journalist, commentator and intellectual disappeared inside the Saudi consulate in Istanbul, the United States is starting to realize it may be time to hold the government in Riyadh accountable for its reckless behavior and its violations of human rights.

On Oct. 10, Bob Corker and Bob Menendez, the top Republican and Democrat in the Senate Foreign Relations Committee, triggered the Global Magnitsky Act, a bipartisan bill to punish human rights violators, to force the Trump administration to investigate and consider sanctions against Saudi Arabia. The crisis over Mr. Khashoggi's disappearance piles on to growing—if belated—concern over Saudi Arabia's disastrous war in Yemen, which has produced little geopolitical gain and much human suffering.

If American officials really want to encourage a change in Saudi policy, they should begin by looking at Saudi Arabia's largest imports from the United States: weaponry. Cutting off the flow of American arms to Saudi Arabia would be an effective way to put pressure on Riyadh with little cost to the American economy or national security.

President Trump, however, is skeptical. "I don't like stopping massive amounts of money that's being poured into our country," he said on Thursday. "They are spending $110 billion on military equipment and on things that create jobs for this country." This figure is vastly inflated, but there's a reason Mr. Trump is inclined to believe it. While the amount of new deals approved under President Trump is closer to $20 billion, the Saudi government has visibly linked itself as the foremost client of the administration's export push.

Peter Navarro, the White House's director of trade and industrial policy, has argued that increased arms sales "will be an important catalyst for strengthening American industry; the stewardship of our national security; and the strengthening of our international partnerships." But the truth is that in the case of Saudi Arabia, the benefits on all three fronts are slight.

Despite recent increases, Saudi arms orders remain a manageably small part of the United States' exports. According to the Defense Security Cooperation Agency, in 2017, a near-record year for annual purchases, the United States delivered

$5.5 billion worth of arms, 20 percent of all foreign military sales. That may sound like a lot, but the United States exports only 25 to 30 percent of its defense industry production, so exports to Saudi Arabia clearly remain a relatively small slice of the enormous defense industrial pie.

Cutting off the flow of American arms to Saudi Arabia would be an effective way to put pressure on Riyadh with little cost to the American economy or national security.

And contrary to President Trump's statement, exports to Saudi Arabia create relatively few American jobs. Based on Commerce Department figures, releasing the billion dollars of munitions currently on hold in the Senate would "create or sustain" fewer than 4,000 jobs. Here's a more specific example: Publicizing a recent $6 billion helicopter deal with Saudi Arabia, Lockheed Martin predicted that it would "support" 450 American jobs.

To date these sales have not "stewarded our national security." Beyond its tragic war in Yemen, Saudi Arabia has blockaded Qatar, an ally that hosts the Middle East's largest American military base. And Saudi Arabia provides little help when it comes to Washington's real regional priorities, such as fighting the Islamic State and stabilizing Iraq. The Pentagon's National Defense Strategy specifically de-emphasizes the war on terror to focus on competition with China and Russia.

Perhaps selling weapons "strengthens international partnerships," as Mr. Navarro put it, or at least discourages Saudi Arabia from finding different ones. Mr. Trump on Thursday cited "four or five alternatives" to American weapons, and the need to avoid "letting Russia have that money and letting China have that money." This, however, is unlikely even in the long term.

Saudi Arabia is in the middle of a major war, and more than 60 percent of its arms deliveries over the past five years came from the United States. The Saudi military relies not just on American tanks, planes and missiles but for a daily supply of maintenance, training and support, such as intelligence and refueling. In the longer term, almost all of Saudi Arabia's remaining exports come from Europe. To truly squeeze Saudi Arabia, a coordinated embargo—much like the one now in place against Russia—would be necessary but relatively easy. European governments already feel strong domestic political pressure not to export to regimes like Saudi Arabia.

Transforming the Saudi military to employ Russian, much less Chinese, weapons would cost a fortune even by Gulf standards, would require years of retraining and would greatly reduce its military power for a generation. Russia cannot produce next-generation fighter aircraft, tanks and infantry fighting vehicles for its own armed forces, much less for the export market. China has not produced, never mind exported, the sophisticated aircraft and missile defense systems Saudi Arabia wants.

Last month, Secretary of State Mike Pompeo certified that Saudi Arabia was minimizing civilian casualties in the Yemen air campaign apparently to avoid jeopardizing $2 billion in weapons sales. That small number does not show how powerful the Saudis are so much as how cheaply the United States can be bought. Given these sales' low domestic economic impact and the enormous costs of going elsewhere for Saudi Arabia, the United States has the preponderance of influence in this arms trade relationship. It should act accordingly.

Print Citations

CMS: Caverley, Jonathan D. "Want to Punish Saudi Arabia? Cut Off Its Weapons Supply." In *The Reference Shelf: U.S. National Debate Topic 2019-2020 Arms Sales,* edited by Micah L. Issitt, 183-185. Amenia, NY: Grey House Publishing, 2019.

MLA: Caverley, Jonathan D. "Want to Punish Saudi Arabia? Cut Off Its Weapons Supply." *The Reference Shelf: U.S. National Debate Topic 2019-2020 Arms Sales,* edited by Micah L. Issitt, Grey House Publishing, 2019, pp. 183-185.

APA: Caverley, J.D. (2019). Want to punish Saudia Arabia? Cut off its weapons supply. In Micah L. Issitt (Ed.), *The reference shelf: U.S. national debate topic 2019-2020 arms sales* (pp. 183-185). Amenia, NY: Grey House Publishing.

Trump Will Fuel War across World by Increasing U.S. Global Arms Sales

By John Haltiwanger
Newsweek, September 30, 2017

President Donald Trump is reportedly planning to roll back restrictions on U.S. arms sales abroad, despite the fact he's already selling record numbers of weapons to other countries. Trump is planning to make these changes via an executive order or memorandum at some point this fall, *Politico* reports. In doing so, experts worry the Trump administration will both intensify existing conflicts and spark new ones across the globe.

"The transfer of arms and the process of arms racing has been a long-standing reason that conflicts begin, spread, and escalate," Dr. Brandon Valeriano, Donald Bren Chair of Armed Politics at Marine Corps University, tells *Newsweek*.

"New weapons give states the confidence they might not otherwise have to launch or exacerbate ongoing antagonisms and hatreds. This new expansion of our effort to promote the transfer of arms will have devastating effects on the international community and will be the root of the evil that will spread throughout the system," Valeriano adds.

But the Trump administration is seemingly more concerned with the economic benefits of increasing arms sales than the overall impact it might have on the wider world.

"The presence of weapons almost always exacerbates conflict, particularly in places of existing conflict or rising tension... The Trump administration is sending a clear signal that profit, not people, is what matters most to this government," says Allison Pytlak, a program manager in the disarmament program of the Women's International League for Peace and Freedom. "The implications will be felt by the people living in countries and cities that are already drowning in weapons."

The National Security Council confirmed to *Politico* Trump has "undertaken a review of our policy on arms sales and wherever possible is working to remove unreasonable constraints on the ability of our companies to compete."

Generally, the president wants to make it easier for American arms manufacturers to sell to international buyers and is also looking at revamping export regulations on drone technology. On the latter point, some experts say Trump might be onto something.

"An increased willingness by the United States to export drones to responsible countries can help advance U.S. security goals of building the capacity of allies and partners, and in a way that enhances interoperability with the United States military,"

> The Trump administration is seemingly more concerned with the economic benefits of increasing arms sales than the overall impact it might have on the wider world.

says Dr. Michael C. Horowitz, professor of political science at the University of Pennsylvania. "U.S. exports also make it more likely that countries will use their drones in a way that complies with the law of war, due to the training and support that goes along with U.S. drone exports."

Thus, there is arguably at least some merit in increasing drone exports. From a broader standpoint, however, reducing restrictions on arms exports overseas is a slippery slope.

The U.S. has long been the world's number one exporter of arms and Trump has built on this precedent in a massive way since entering the White House.

The Obama administration was hardly reserved when it came to international arms deals, but Trump is poised to outsell his predecessor on a historic scale, according to recent data on weapons sales. In the first eight months of 2017, Trump almost doubled the total value of U.S. arms sales (to $48 billion) than under Obama during the same period in 2016.

Moreover, Trump could be complicit in war crimes due to some of the arms sales he's already made. In Yemen, for example, it was recently discovered a U.S.-made bomb was used by the Saudi-led coalition in a strike last month that killed civilians, including children. It's possible this bomb was sold via deals made under Obama, but the larger point is Trump's apparent determination to sell more and more arms arguably increases the probability he'll be linked to atrocities committed by other countries.

"In the context of horrific human rights abuses in the Middle East region, we're very concerned about the possibility of easing restrictions on U.S. weapons sales overseas," Raed Jarrar, Amnesty International's advocacy director for the Middle East and North Africa, tells *Newsweek.* "There is damning evidence that many recipients of U.S. weapons in the Middle East—such as Saudi Arabia, Egypt and Israel—are already involved in serious violations of human rights and international law.

A decision to reduce restrictions on global arms sales by the U.S. will be "perceived by foreign governments as a green light to continue, if not increase, their disregard to human rights," Jarrar adds.

This is precisely why there are restrictions on arms sales in the first place—to avoid inflaming conflicts, limit the potential for human rights violations and keep weapons out of the hands of dictators.

"Arms should only be given to those states that are responsible, careful, and judicious in their use of weapons. Are we convinced that we can trust those that will receive these weapons to be as precise and careful?" says Valeriano.

In the past, arms the U.S. has sold to foreign governments have also ended up in the hands of terrorists—including ISIS—because America didn't have stricter regulations and safeguards in place. In this sense, rolling back restrictions is arguably very dangerous.

Print Citations

CMS: Haltiwanger, John. "Trump Will Fuel War across World by Increasing U.S. Global Arms Sales." In *The Reference Shelf: U.S. National Debate Topic 2019-2020 Arms Sales,* edited by Micah L. Issitt, 186-188. Amenia, NY: Grey House Publishing, 2019.

MLA: Haltiwanger, John. "Trump Will Fuel War across World by Increasing U.S. Global Arms Sales." *The Reference Shelf: U.S. National Debate Topic 2019-2020 Arms Sales,* edited by Micah L. Issitt, Grey House Publishing, 2019, pp. 186-188.

APA: Haltiwanger, J. (2019). Trump will fuel war across world by increasing U.S. global arms sales. In Micah L. Issitt (Ed.), *The reference shelf: U.S. national debate topic 2019-2020 arms sales* (pp. 186-188). Amenia, NY: Grey House Publishing.

Arms Sales to Saudi "Illicit" Due to Civilian Deaths in Yemen: Campaigners

By Stephanie Nebehay
Reuters, August 22, 2016

GENEVA (Reuters)—A group that campaigns for stricter arms sales controls said on Monday that Western powers were breaking international law by selling vast amounts of weapons to Saudi Arabia that are being used to hit civilians in Yemen. The Control Arms Coalition said Britain, France and the United States were flouting the 2014 Arms Trade Treaty (ATT), which bans exports of conventional weapons that fuel human rights violations or war crimes.

"It is extremely concerning that many transfers are still continuing, in particular the governments of the United States, the UK and France have authorized and are continuing to export very large quantities of weapons, including explosive weapons, bombs which are being used daily against civilians in Yemen," said Anna MacDonald, director of the Control Arms Coalition.

She was speaking to a news briefing as week-long U.N. negotiations began in Geneva aimed at putting teeth into the ATT which lacks a mandatory public reporting system for the $100 billion global arms trade.

France authorized arms licenses worth $18 billion to Saudi Arabia last year, followed by the United States at $5.9 billion and Britain's $4 billion, the group said in its latest study.

Nigeria's ambassador Emmanuel Imohe, who chairs the conference, said: "The allegation is quite grave and it should be of concern to everyone including the ATT secretariat itself."

Medecins Sans Frontieres (MSF) said last week it was evacuating its staff from six hospitals in northern Yemen after a Saudi-led coalition air strike hit one of its hospitals, killing 18 people.

No Blank Check

The coalition says it does not target civilians and accuses the Houthi group that it is battling in Yemen of placing military targets in civilian areas. A body that the coalition set up to look into civilian casualties is investigating the MSF incident, among others.

The war has killed more than 6,500 people since it began 16 months ago and raised the prospect of famine in the Arab world's poorest country.

Outcry over civilian casualties has led some members of the U.S. Congress to push for restrictions on arms transfers. The Obama administration this month approved a potential $1.15 billion arms package for Saudi Arabia.

In a statement on Friday, the Pentagon cautioned that its support for Saudi Arabia in its campaign was not "a blank check," however, and said it has pressed the coalition on the need to minimize civilian casualties.

Campaigners said arms exports also drove fighting in South Sudan last month that killed hundreds, prompting fears of a return to civil war.

> **The Pentagon cautioned that its support for Saudi Arabia in its campaign was not a "blank check."**

"We think that governments of other countries have fueled this violence by repeatedly authorizing arms transfers to South Sudan," said Geoffrey Duke, head of South Sudan Action Network on Small Arms. He named China, Ukraine and South Africa as the main suppliers to the Juba government.

To date, 87 countries have ratified the ATT, while another 46—including the United States—have signed it, leaving important gaps, Imohe said.

"For example, in the Arab world only Mauritania is listed amongst states parties, while Asia Pacific has only three states parties," he said, referring to Japan, Samoa and Tuvalu.

Amnesty International said: "Big arms traders Russia and China have not joined the ATT and have supplied gross violators of human rights."

Print Citations

CMS: Nebehay, Stephanie. "Arms Sales to Saudi 'Illicit' Due to Civilian Deaths in Yemen: Campaigners." In *The Reference Shelf: U.S. National Debate Topic 2019-2020 Arms Sales*, edited by Micah L. Issitt, 189-190. Amenia, NY: Grey House Publishing, 2019.

MLA: Nebehay, Stephanie. "Arms Sales to Saudi 'Illicit' Due to Civilian Deaths in Yemen: Campaigners." *The Reference Shelf: U.S. National Debate Topic 2019-2020 Arms Sales*, edited by Micah L. Issitt, Grey House Publishing, 2019, pp. 189-190.

APA: Nebehay, S. (2019). Arms sales to Saudi "illicit" due to civilian deaths in Yemen: Campaigners. In Micah L. Issitt (Ed.), *The reference shelf: U.S. national debate topic 2019-2020 arms sales* (pp. 189-190). Amenia, NY: Grey House Publishing.

Trump's Arms Exports Rules Will Undermine US Security and Risk Human Rights Abuses

By William D. Hartung
The Hill, July 15, 2018

This was the last week for public comments on the Trump administration's plan to reduce restrictions on the export of firearms from the United States. There was much to criticize. A number of arms control, human rights, and firearms safety groups have submitted detailed critiques of the proposed firearms export rule.

As Reps. Sander Levin (D-Mich.), Eliot Engel (D-N.Y.), James McGovern (D-Mass.), Norma Torres (D-Calif.) and Jamie Raskin (D-Md.) noted in a recent letter to Secretary of State Mike Pompeo and Secretary of Commerce Wilbur Ross it would be a mistake to move regulation of dangerous firearms from the State Department to the less restrictive Department of Commerce. The lawmakers warned the Trump plan as proposed would make it more likely that weapons of U.S. origin "will end up in the hands of traffickers, terrorists, and cartels." The new rule may be good news for the firearms industry, but it is bad news for anyone who is concerned about human rights and global security.

One major flaw in the new plan is that it would eliminate notifications to Congress of exports of firearms and related equipment worth $1 million or more. Statistics gathered by the Security Assistance Monitor have documented that the State Department approved $662 million worth of firearms exports to 15 countries in 2017, including to places like Mexico, Honduras, El Salvador, the Philippines, the United Arab Emirates and Turkey where there is a risk that

> **The Trump administration's firearms deregulation would lead to additional unnecessary deaths, bolster repressive regimes, and make it easier for terrorists and criminal gangs to inflict violence on innocent individuals.**

these weapons will be used to abuse human rights, fall into the hands of criminal gangs, or fuel devastating conflicts like the Saudi/UAE-led intervention in Yemen.

Absent notification, Congress and the public would have little ability to debate, much less block, any of these problematic exports.

The administration rule has tried to obscure the true danger of its approach by suggesting that the bulk of the guns that are being removed from State Department oversight and licensing are commercially available. For many of the firearms being deregulated, this claim is dubious.

More importantly, many of the guns involved are military-grade, including sniper rifles. Others, like the AR-15, have been used in tragic incidents of gun violence such as the Parkland, Florida school shootings. Finally, in some cases, as with sniper rifles, these weapons could end up being used against U.S. troops involved in overseas operations. The Violence Policy Center has compiled a lengthy list of military firearms and other especially dangerous weapons that would be subjected to far looser restrictions under the proposed administration plan.

The firearms slated for deregulation are the primary tools in many of the world's most deadly conflicts, and have rightly been described as "slow motion weapons of mass destruction." They should be subjected to more rigorous scrutiny, not less.

In addition, the proposed rule would make it easier for private military contractors like the firm formerly known as Blackwater to train foreign security forces without a license, even for destinations like Libya and China that raise significant security concerns.

In another particularly unwise change, many companies that engage in firearms manufacturing would no longer have to register with the State Department, which will make it much harder to track their activities and prevent illegal sales or exports to security forces or non-state groups that will use the weapons they make to do grievous harm to civilians.

This relaxation of the monitoring of manufacturing activities will apparently extend to open source 3-D printing, meaning that anyone could post non-proprietary instructions for to use this process to produce untraceable hand guns and semi-automatic firearms without have to register with State or seek an export license from Commerce.

This will be an invitation to arms proliferation on a scale not yet seen. Congress should address the 3-D printing issue alongside efforts to block the Trump administration's proposed changes in firearms export regulations.

The proposal would also lift the obligation of U.S. arms exporting firms to report political contributions to foreign officials and fees paid to marketing agents in potential recipient countries. This would seriously hinder U.S. law enforcement agencies' ability to root out corruption and illegal transfers, which have long plagued the global trade in small arms and light weapons.

Last but certainly not least, taking dangerous firearms off of the U.S. Munitions List, as the new proposal would do, would mean that they are no longer described as "defense articles." As a result, they would likely fall outside the jurisdiction of a web of carefully constructed laws that impose specific human rights criteria on the export of such weapons.

The concerns outlined here underscore the risks inherent in the Trump administration's firearms deregulation scheme. The bottom line is that implementing these rules as written would lead to additional unnecessary deaths, bolster repressive regimes, and make it easier for terrorists and criminal gangs to inflict violence on innocent individuals. For all of these reasons, the new rule should be rejected.

At a minimum, Congress should move to restore the most important elements of the current regulatory scheme, including notification of major firearms exports and limits on the deregulation of military-grade firearms and guns most likely to be used in mass killings.

Print Citations

CMS: Hartung, William D. "Trump's Arms Exports Will Undermine US Security and Risk Human Rights Abuses." In *The Reference Shelf: U.S. National Debate Topic 2019-2020 Arms Sales,* edited by Micah L. Issitt, 191-193. Amenia, NY: Grey House Publishing, 2019.

MLA: Hartung, William D. "Trump's Arms Exports Will Undermine US Security and Risk Human Rights Abuses." *The Reference Shelf: U.S. National Debate Topic 2019-2020 Arms Sales,* edited by Micah L. Issitt, Grey House Publishing, 2019, pp. 191-193.

APA: Hartung, W. (2019). Trump's arms exports will undermine US security and risk human rights abuses. In Micah L. Issitt (Ed.), *The reference shelf: U.S. national debate topic 2019-2020 arms sales* (pp. 191-193). Amenia, NY: Grey House Publishing.

Bibliography

Abi-Habib, Maria. "Syria Rebels Draw Closer to al Qaeda-Linked Group." *The Wall Street Journal*. Sep 29, 2016. Retrieved from https://www.wsj.com/articles/syria-rebels-draw-closer-to-al-qaeda-linked-group-1475197943.

"American Civil War viewpoints: It Was British Arms That Sustained the Confederacy." *Military History*. Mar 3, 2011. *Military History*. Retrieved from https://www.military-history.org/blog/it-was-british-arms-that-sustained-the-confederacy-during-the-american-civil-war-peter-tsouras.htm.

Beck, Michael D., Cupitt, Richard T. Gahlaut, Seema, and Jones, Scott A. *To Supply or to Deny*. New York: Kluwer Law International, 2003.

Bove, Vincenzo, Deiana, Claudio, and Roberto Nisticò. "Global Arms Trade and Oil Dependence." *The Journal of Law, Economics, and Organization*. Vol. 34, No. 2, May 2018, 277-99.

Bowler, Tim. "Which Country Dominates the Global Arms Trade." *BBC News*. May 10, 2018. Retrieved from https://www.bbc.com/news/business-43873518.

DePetris, Daniel. "The US Sold Weapons That Ended Up in Terrorists' Hands, and Congress Shrugs." *Washington Examiner*. Feb 6, 2019. Retrieved from https://www.washingtonexaminer.com/opinion/the-us-sold-weapons-that-ended-up-in-terrorists-hands-and-congress-shrugs.

Erickson, Jennifer. *Dangerous Trade: Arms Exports, Human Rights, and International Reputation*. New York: Columbia University Press, 2015.

Fleurant, Aude, Kuimova, Alexandra, Tian, Nan, Wezeman, Pieter D., and Siemon T. Wezeman. "The SIPRI Top 100 Arms-Producing and Military Services Companies, 2017." *SIPRI*. Sipri Fact Sheet. Dec 2018. Retrieved from https://www.sipri.org/sites/default/files/2018-12/fs_arms_industry_2017_0.pdf.

Gold, David. "Costs of Arms Sales Undermine Economic Gains." *EPUSA*. 1998. Retrieved from http://www.epsusa.org/publications/newsletter/dec1998/gold.pdf.

Goldenberg, Suzanne. "Carter Uses Peace Prize Speech to Condemn US Policy." *The Guardian*. Dec 11, 2002. Retrieved from https://www.theguardian.com/world/2002/dec/11/usa.suzannegoldenberg.

Harris, Shane, and Matthew M. Aid. "Exclusive: CIA Files Prove America Helped Saddam as He Gassed Iran." *Foreign Policy*. Aug 26, 2013. Retrieved from https://foreignpolicy.com/2013/08/26/exclusive-cia-files-prove-america-helped-saddam-as-he-gassed-iran/.

Hartung, William D. "Arms Sales Decisions Shouldn't Be About Jobs." *Defense One*. Mar 26, 2018. Retrieved from https://www.defenseone.com/ideas/2018/03/arms-sales-decisions-shouldnt-be-about-jobs/146939/.

"Hillary Clinton Declares 'Women's Rights Are Human Rights'." *PBS*. Sep 8, 1995. Retrieved from https://www.pbs.org/weta/washingtonweek/web-video/hillary-clinton-declares-womens-rights-are-human-rights.

"Hodeidah 'Cholera Cases Triple after Saudi-UAE Offensive': Report." *Al Jazeera*. Oct 1, 2018. Retrieved from https://www.aljazeera.com/news/2018/10/hodeidah-cholera-cases-triple-saudi-uae-offensive-report-181001173828553.html.

Hyde, Charles K. *Arsenal of Democracy: The American Automobile Industry in World War II*. Detroit: Wayne State University Press, 1945.

Ingraham, Christopher. "The Entire Coal Industry Employs Fewer People Than Arby's." *The Washington Post*. Mar 31, 2017. Retrieved from https://www.washingtonpost.com/news/wonk/wp/2017/03/31/8-surprisingly-small-industries-that-employ-more-people-than-coal/?utm_term=.6a80be7f446b.

"The Iran-Contra Affair—1986-1987." *The Washington Post*. 1998. Retrieved from https://www.washingtonpost.com/wp-srv/politics/special/clinton/frenzy/iran.htm.

"Iraqi Civilians." *Watson Institute*. Brown University. Nov 2018. Retrieved from https://watson.brown.edu/costsofwar/costs/human/civilians/iraqi.

Joselow, Gabe. "ISIS Weapons Arsenal Included Some Purchased by U.S. Government." *NBC News*. Dec 14, 2017. Retrieved from https://www.nbcnews.com/news/world/isis-weapons-arsenal-included-some-purchased-u-s-government-n829201.

Kapstein, Ethan B. "America's Arms-Trade Monopoly." *Foreign Affairs*. May/June 1994. Retrieved from https://www.foreignaffairs.com/articles/1994-05-01/americas-arms-trade-monopoly.

Karlin, Mara. "Why Military Assistance Programs Disappoint." *Brookings*. Nov/Dec 2017. Retrieved from https://www.brookings.edu/articles/why-military-assistance-programs-disappoint/.

Kelly, Joe. "How British Businesses Helped the Confederacy Fight the American Civil War." *The Conversation*. The Conversation US. Mar 7, 2016. Retrieved from http://theconversation.com/how-british-businesses-helped-the-confederacy-fight-the-american-civil-war-52517.

Keyton, David, and Rohan, Brian. "UN Says Civilian Casualties in Yemen Average 123 per Week." *AP*. Associated Press. Dec 7, 2018. Retrieved from https://www.apnews.com/3e5cff9378594c9aba2374644f3634d6.

"Lend-Lease and Military Aid to the Allies in the Early Years of World War II." *U.S. Department of State*. U.S. Department of State. Milestones: 1937-1945. 2016. Retrieved from https://history.state.gov/milestones/1937-1945/lend-lease.

"Lockheed Martin." *Fortune*. Fortune 500. 2018. Retrieved from http://fortune.com/fortune500/lockheed-martin/.

Mazzetti, Mark, and Ali Younes. "C.I.A. Arms for Syrian Rebels Supplied Black Market, Officials Say." *The New York Times*. Jun 26, 2016. Retrieved from https://www.nytimes.com/2016/06/27/world/middleeast/cia-arms-for-syrian-rebels-supplied-black-market-officials-say.html.

Meshal, Sheikh, and Hamad Al-Thani. "The United Arab Emirates and Saudi Arabia Are Aiding Terrorists in Yemen." *The Washington Post*. Aug 29, 2018. Retrieved from https://www.washingtonpost.com/news/global-opinions/wp/2018/08/29/the-united-arab-emirates-and-saudi-arabia-are-aiding-terrorists-in-yemen/?utm_term=.7119c03534ab.

Newman, Katelyn. "Report: ISIS Gets Its Weapons from Around the World—Including the U.S." *US News & World Report*. Dec 14, 2017. Retrieved from https://www.usnews.com/news/world/articles/2017-12-14/report-isis-gets-its-weapons-from-around-the-world-including-the-us.

"Number of Employees at Defense Technology Supplier Lockheed Martin 2000-2018." *Statista*. 2018. Retrieved from https://www.statista.com/statistics/268924/number-of-employees-at-defense-supplier-lockheed-martin/.

Oakford, Samuel. "Counting the Dead in Mosul." *The Atlantic*. Apr 5, 2018. Retrieved from https://www.theatlantic.com/international/archive/2018/04/counting-the-dead-in-mosul/556466/.

Pamp, Oliver, Rudolph, Lukas, and Paul W. Thurner. "The Build-Up of Coercive Capacities: Arms Imports and the Outbreak of Violent Intrastate Conflicts." *Journal of Peace Research*. Jan 31, 2018. Retrieved from https://journals.sagepub.com/doi/10.1177/0022343317740417.

Salisbury, Peter. "Yemen's Southern Powder Keg." *Chatham House*. March 2018. Retrieved from https://www.chathamhouse.org/sites/default/files/publications/research/2018-03-27-yemen-southern-powder-keg-salisbury-final.pdf.

Sanchez, Casey. "When Native Americans Were Arms Dealers: A History Revealed in *Thundersticks*." *Los Angeles Times*. Dec 23, 2016. Retrieved from https://www.latimes.com/books/la-ca-jc-thundersticks-20161223-story.html.

Sanger, David E. "Donald Trump Likely to End Aid for Rebels Fighting Syrian Government." *The New York Times*. Nov 11, 2016. Retrieved from https://www.nytimes.com/2016/11/12/world/middleeast/donald-trump-syria.html?_r=0.

"Saudi Arabia, UAE Gave US Arms to al-Qaeda-Linked Groups: Report." *Al Jazeera*. Feb 5, 2019. Retrieved from https://www.aljazeera.com/news/2019/02/saudi-arabia-uae-gave-weapons-al-qaeda-linked-groups-cnn-190205055102300.html.

Savage, Jesse Dillon, and Jonathan D. Caverley. "When Human Capital Threatens the Capitol: Foreign Aid in the Form of Military Training and Coups." *Journal of Peace Research*. Jul 13, 2017. Retrieved from https://journals.sagepub.com/doi/abs/10.1177/0022343317713557.

Stohl, Rachel. "Trump Administration's New Weapons Export Policies Stress Benefit to U.S. Economy." *Just Security*. Apr 30, 2018. Retrieved from https://www.justsecurity.org/55496/trump-administrations-weapons-export-policies-stress-benefit-u-s-economy/.

"Strong Link between Child Soldiers and Small Arms Trade, UN Experts Say." *UN News*. Jul 15, 2008. Retrieved from https://news.un.org/en/story/2008/07/266342-strong-link-between-child-soldiers-and-small-arms-trade-un-experts-say.

Timmons, "US Defense Giants Show How American Capitalism Fails Taxpayers." *QZ*. Quartz. Feb 4, 2019. Retrieved from https://qz.com/1537885/defense-companies-like-lockheed-martin-dont-share-tax-benefits-equally/.

Thrall, A. Trevor, and Caroline Dorminey. "A New Framework for Assessing the Risks from U.S. Arms Sales." *Cato*. Cato Institute. Jun 13, 2018. Retrieved from https://www.cato.org/publications/commentary/new-framework-assessing-risks-us-arms-sales.

Thrall, A. Trevor, and Caroline Dorminey. "Risky Business: The Role of Arms Sales in U.S. Foreign Policy." *Cato*. Cato Institute. Policy Analysis No. 836. Mar 13, 2018. Retrieved from https://www.cato.org/publications/policy-analysis/risky-business-role-arms-sales-us-foreign-policy.

Uawo, Belet. "Somali Civil War Is Fueled by Huge Stockpiles of Weapons." *Christian Science Monitor*. Oct 14, 1992. Retrieved from https://www.csmonitor.com/1992/1014/14012.html.

Uchitelle, Louis. "The U.S. Still Leans on the Military-Industrial Complex." *The New York Times*. Sep 22, 2017. Retrieved from https://www.nytimes.com/2017/09/22/business/economy/military-industrial-complex.html.

"U.S. Arms Sales and Defense Trade." *U.S. Department of State*. Feb 4, 2019. Retrieved from https://www.state.gov/t/pm/rls/fs/2019/288737.htm.

"U.S.-Saudi Arabia Relations." *CFR*. Council on Foreign Relations. Dec 7, 2018. Retrieved from https://www.cfr.org/backgrounder/us-saudi-arabia-relations.

Vogenstein, Rachel, and Alexandra Bro. "Sweden's Feminist Foreign Policy, Long May It Reign." *FP*. Foreign Policy. Jan 30, 2019.

Vucetic, Srdjan. "The Uneasy Co-Existence of Arms Exports and Feminist Foreign Policy." *The Conversation*. Apr 8, 2018. Retrieved from https://theconversation.com/the-uneasy-co-existence-of-arms-exports-and-feminist-foreign-policy-93930.

"War in Yemen." *CFR*. Global Conflict Tracker. 2019. Retrieved from https://www.cfr.org/interactive/global-conflict-tracker/conflict/war-yemen.

Wezeman, Pieter D., Fleurant, Aude, Kuimova, Alexandra, Tian, Nan, and Siemon T. Wezeman. "Trends in International Arms Transfers, 2017." *Sipri*. Stockhold International Peace Research Institute. March 2018 Retrieved from https://www.sipri.org/sites/default/files/2018-03/fssipri_at2017_0.pdf.

Whiteside, Eric. "Top 5 Shareholders of Lockheed Martin (LMT)." *Investopedia*. Mar 5, 2018. Retrieved from https://www.investopedia.com/articles/personal-finance/081416/top-5-shareholders-lockheed-martin-lmt.asp.

"Women's Participation in Peace Processes." *CFR*. Council on Foreign Relations. Jan 30, 2019. Retrieved from https://www.cfr.org/interactive/womens-participation-in-peace-processes.

Wright, Lawrence. "The Twenty-Eight Pages." *The New Yorker*. Sep 9, 2014. Retrieved from https://www.newyorker.com/news/daily-comment/twenty-eight-pages.

Websites

Amnesty International
www.amnesty.org

Amnesty International is a human rights activist organization, started in 1961, and active around the world. Amnesty International provides data on the arms trade and its links to human rights abuses, warfare, regional instability, and other threats to international security.

Brookings Institution
www.brookings.edu

The Brookings Institution is a nonprofit public policy think tank located in Washington DC. Brookings scholars have researched and written about housing, economic inequality, and a variety of other issues. Brookings scholars have published a variety of articles on the arms trade, including evaluations of President Trump's Saudi arms deals, investigations of arms dealing in India, China, and Russia, and other issues.

Center for Nonproliferation Studies (CNS)
www.nonproliferation.org

The Center for Nonproliferation studies is a national research organization, led by the Middlebury Institute of International Studies, and dedicated to producing research on nuclear nonproliferation and the global arms industry. The CNS supports student research, works on policy proposals for U.S. legislators, and produces analysis of global arms treaties and policies.

RAND Corporation
www.rand.org

The RAND Corporation is a research institution that supports private and public research into issues relating to national and international security. RAND researchers have published numerous research studies on arms trading, arms policies, disarmament, and economic competition in the global arms industry.

Small Arms Survey (SAS)
www.smallarmssurvey.org

The Small Arms Survey is a research organization providing information, to policy makers, researchers, journalists, and the public, on issues involving small arms and the small arms trade. Headquartered in Switzerland, the SAS collects data on violent deaths, firearms holdings, small arms trade and transparency, and disarmament. Research from the SAS has been used by numerous U.S. publications researching small arms as a facet of the global arms trade.

Stockholm International Peace Research Institute (SIPRI)
www.sipri.org

SIPRI is an independent, international scholarly organization, established in 1966, that specializes in producing research on international conflict, arms control, and nuclear disarmament. SIPRI researchers provide policy proposals to European and North American governments, provide data for researchers and journalists, and fund and support original research into a variety of subjects surrounding conflict and the international arms and military industries.

United Nations Office for Disarmament Affairs (UNODA)
www.un.org/disarmament

The United Nations Office for Disarmament Affairs is the branch of the United Nations that supports research and international policy proposals on arms and disarmament. UNODA is active in the international debate over nuclear weapons as well as in debates over commercial and state arms deals and transfers and their relationship to global security and human rights. The UNODA website provides information on international arms treaties and law.

U.S. Department of State
www.state.gov

The U.S. Department of State is the department within the Executive Branch of the U.S. government in charge of establishing executive policy relating to arms dealing and U.S. policy on corporate arms deals. Specifically, the Bureau of Political-Military Affairs (PM) is the branch of the State Department charged with overseeing both government-to-government arms trades and establishing policies for commercial transactions. The U.S. Department of State website provides publications and information on a variety of related subjects, including relevant U.S. legislation on the issue, such as the Foreign Assistance Act of 1961 and the Conventional Arms Transfer Policy.

Index